TANK TURRET FORTIFICATIONS

TANK TURRET FORTIFICATIONS

NEIL SHORT

THE CROWOOD PRESS

First published in 2006 by
The Crowood Press Ltd
Ramsbury, Marlborough
Wiltshire SN8 2HR

www.crowood.com

British Library Cataloguing-in-Publication Data
A catalogue record for this book is available from the British Library.

ISBN 1 86126 687 1
EAN 978 1 86126 687 3

Dedication
This book is dedicated to my beautiful little daughter, Amy Elizabeth,
who entered this world on 17 May 2004. I hope Daddy doesn't embarrass
you too much with his strange interest!

Typeset by Textype, Cambridge

Printed and bound in Great Britain by The Cromwell Press

Contents

Preface

In many ways the writing of a book is very similar to undertaking a long journey. You start out inspired and full of energy, but the going is often tough and the end seems so far away. Nevertheless, it is invariably fulfilling and it has been no different for me on this occasion, which is due in no small part to the many people who have helped me along the way.

For me the introduction to tank turrets, or *panzerstellung*,* and the start of my journey, came many years ago when reading a copy of *AFV News*, a small, privately run magazine for armour enthusiasts. Included in this edition was a short item about Panther tank turrets used as fixed fortifications. I soon traced the author of this article and a previous piece on the same subject and entered into a lengthy communication with Dottore Nicola Pignato, the renowned tank expert, and Denis Seguin. Over the years they have helped me immensely with my research, as has the founder of *AFV News*, George Bradford. Without their help I would not have embarked on this odyssey.

In the following weeks and months my research continued, largely confined to the Panther turret, with visits to the Bundesarchiv, Freiburg and to London in order to access the records held by the Imperial Museum and the Public Record Office (now the National Archive). The staff in these institutions provided invaluable help, especially so in Germany where Herr Loos and Frau Brüninghaus identified pertinent material on this most unusual subject. Subsequently, I entered into communication with David Fletcher, the librarian at the Tank Museum, Bovington, Krzysztof Barbarski at The Polish Institute and staff at both the Canadian and United States National Archives, all of whose efforts were very much appreciated.

My research on the Panther turret gradually broadened to encompass not just the technical specification of the weapon, but also its fighting record. This involved contacting many veterans of the

Royal Armoured Corps who more than fifty years after the event were able to vividly recollect their experiences in Italy. Former members of 51st Royal Tank Regiment deserve particular mention and more especially G. Birdsall, G. Bradley, D. Featherstone and E. Hollands. I additionally tried to trace New Zealand veterans of the Italian campaign and although unsuccessful I did contact Jeff Plowman, a leading expert on New Zealand armour, who provided me with important details and photographs. While in the Antipodes, I would also like to thank J. Hornabrook, who scoured the New Zealand archives on my behalf, and the staff of the Alexander Turnbull Library and the Queen Elizabeth II Army Memorial Museum.

Aside from the major archives and museums, my research also brought me into contact with a number of other individuals who shared my interest in the use of Panther turrets. For their continued support I should like to thank Maciej Sledzinski, and Daniele Guglielmi.

This passing interest had turned into a vocation and I now began to research the origins of the idea of using tank turrets as fixed fortifications. I was given invaluable assistance in this quest by A. van Geeteruyen (Belgium) and staff at the ASBL Tank Museum, Brussels. E. Hitriak and I. Volkov, through their research on the Stalin and Molotov Lines, filled a huge void in my knowledge of the use of tank turrets in the Soviet border defences, and their evidence was supplemented by material from V. Kaminski and P. Lenfeld. I would also like to thank J-L. Burtscher and R. Klein for directing me to pertinent sources of information on the use of this type of fortification in the Maginot Line and for permission to use material from their respective Internet sites.

---

*The German word *panzerstellung* seems to best encompass the description of emplaced tank turrets and is used as a generic term throughout this book.

At the same time, the scope of my research grew to include all the tank turrets used in this way in the Second World War. This brought me into contact with a number of subject matter experts whose contribution to the finished article was inestimable. I would like to thank in particular: M. Airila (Finland); L. Bertelsen (Denmark); W. Brzoskwinia (Poland); M. Ginns (CIOS Jersey); A. Johansen (Denmark); D. Mouritzen (Denmark) E. Ritterbach (Germany), and O. Tønnesen (Denmark). A number of museums also provided valuable information: Dr Kunz at the Militärhistorisches Museum Der Bundeswehr (Germany) and the Sotamuseo (Finland).

Later still I broadened the scope of my research further to consider the use of tank turrets in the post-war period. Once again this involved me seeking help from numerous institutions and museums including the Coast Artillery Museum (Norway) and the Heeresgeschichtliches Museum (Austria). In addition, I was able to rely on knowledgeable and importantly, generous, authorities on this period. They included: O. Filip (Czechoslovakia); T. Gannon (Israel); R. Gils (The Netherlands); P. C. van Kerkum, Brig Gen, retired (The Netherlands); B. Lowry (UK); S. Netrebenko (Russia); D. O'Hara (Indo-China); and T. Tsiplakos (Greece).

A number of individuals deserve special thanks for their help throughout my voyage of discovery. In particular I would like to thank Margaret Pinsent (of the Fortress Study Group) and Herbert Jäger who not only replied to my various questions but also actively sought information on my behalf. A special mention should also go to Joe Kaufmann (the creator of Site O – an Internet site dedicated to fortifications) who put me in touch with many of the individuals above and who also answered many questions himself. I would also like to thank Svein Wiiger Olsen whose encyclopaedic knowledge of fortifications provided me with much valuable information, particularly about tank turrets in Scandinavia. Latterly, Caspar Vermeulen provided me with a number of useful leads in my research into the modern use of this form of defence and Steve Zaloga, an authority on armoured fighting vehicles, provided a number of rare photographs of tank turrets and kindly answered my many and varied questions.

Along the way I contacted many other people who helped me in often small but significant ways. It would be impossible to name them all, but your help was very much appreciated.

As the reader will have gathered by now, my journey eventually took me to the four corners of the globe and in so doing I amassed a wealth of material. Most of this, not surprisingly, was written in languages with which I was not always familiar and had to be translated into English. This was achieved largely through the good offices of the Institute of Linguistics and in particular the following translators:

J. Calderbank (French to English); A. George (Dutch to English); Z. Fec (Russian to English); M. Jepps (Italian to English); I. Knill (Czech to English); A. Ladd (German to English); C. Leach (Italian to English); I. Pursiainen (Finnish to English); B. Snell (German to English); and M. Stanley (French/German to English). I would like to thank in particular Gill Hunwicks for her painstaking work in translating the sheaf of highly technical and sometimes incomplete papers that I brought back from my initial visit to the Bundesarchiv.

I also owe an enormous debt of gratitude to Tomasz Idzikowski who completed the detailed drawings that adorn this book.

Of course in any journey it is important to have a good start and this was provided by mother, father and sister. It is also vital to have a supportive travelling companion – a Passerpartout – and my wife, Nikki, has ably filled this role. She has been with me through the majority of my research for this book and it is no exaggeration to say that without her this book would not have been completed.

Introduction

In the immediate aftermath of the Great War there was an overwhelming desire for peace. Never again would Europe be plunged into a bloody war of attrition that would turn factory and field alike into a wasteland and lead to the death of millions more innocent men, women and children. To that end the Central Powers were forced to accept a punitive peace settlement. Germany, deemed by the victors to be the guilty of starting the war, was particularly harshly dealt with. Her armed forces were emasculated; an army of occupation was posted and huge reparations imposed. More positively, a League of Nations was created to resolve differences between countries, and there was a move towards universal disarmament, not least because the size of the standing armies after the war was crippling the economies of the victorious powers.

The initial burst of optimism engendered by these measures was soon replaced by gloom and despondency as economic crisis and weak leadership saw Europe fall into the grip of political extremists. Countries increasingly questioned the effectiveness of politics and the League of Nations to maintain peace and began to build bunkers and blockhouses rather than bridges. These fortifications, the like and scale of which had never and will never, be seen again, stretched from France in the west to the Soviet Union in the east and from Greece in the south to Finland in the north.

In the development of these defences many countries drew heavily on their experiences in the First World War. The thinking of the French High Command was strongly influenced by the bloody battle of Verdun and in particular the crucial role played by the forts around which the gallant defence of *la patrie* had been organized. Not surprisingly then, when work began on France's border defences in 1929, later christened the Maginot Line,* their shape owed much to the perceived strengths of the forts at Verdun. As such a thin, but immensely strong line of defences was constructed along France's north-eastern frontier and along the border with Italy.

The German High Command drew very different conclusions from the fighting of the First World War. Despite the fact that the *Siegfriedstellung* (or Hindenburg Line as it was known by the Allies) had been breached, the senior staff believed that the idea of defence in depth was sound and Germany began to construct a chain of fortifications along her western border that utilized many of the principles developed in the war. A series of small reinforced concrete shelters, protected by a curtain of anti-tank obstacles, covering almost the whole length of the western border and built in considerable depth were constructed.

The First World War not only provided valuable lessons for future defensive strategies, it was also the proving ground for new ways and means of fighting. The devastating effect of high explosive and shrapnel shells and machine guns made it impossible for soldiers to survive in the open. Gradually the war of movement degenerated into stalemate as both sides 'dug-in' for the long haul. Trenches soon stretched from Switzerland to the North Sea and, as the war dragged on, they gradually became deeper, were built in greater depth and also became increasingly elaborate. Deep dugouts, often reinforced with concrete, protected the infantry from the enemy barrage enabling the defenders to emerge largely unscathed to meet the inevitable infantry assault. Later still the Germans developed reinforced concrete 'pillboxes' which were difficult to hit and were largely impervious to all but the heaviest shellfire. The idea was later copied by the Allies and after the war was widely used by engineers of many nations.

For every innovation there is inevitably an attempt to develop a viable counter measure and this was true

---

*Named after the new Minister for War, André Maginot.

One of the many German concrete pillboxes that were used to strengthen the trenches on the western front in the First World War. This example now sits at the heart of the British Cemetery at Tyne Cot, Belgium. (Author)

of the labyrinth of trenches that stretched across northern France and Belgium. The respective high commands desperately sought ways of overcoming the bloody stalemate of trench warfare and returning to a war of movement that had been anticipated prior to the outbreak of hostilities. The success of poison gas briefly offered the prospect of some success but the opportunity was lost and soon simple gas masks had been developed to neutralize the effects. More significant was the development of the tank, which had first been introduced by the British in battle of the Somme in 1916. At the outset the tanks were heavy, slow and unreliable and were equipped with fixed guns. However, in 1918 the French FT17 tank was introduced. This was a quick, light tank that had one very important difference to its British and German (and larger French) cousins – it had a traversable turret. This small tank, the brainchild of Gen Jean-Baptiste Estienne, was to revolutionize tank design and thereafter all tanks were fitted with turrets.

By the end of the First World War the two key elements for the development of the *panzerstellung* were in place; the revolving tank turret and the concrete pillbox. The catalyst for their combination came during the increasing tensions prior to the outbreak of the Second World War.

The interwar period saw the pace of tank

development quicken with new, faster and more powerfully armed tanks being produced. This presented something of a problem for the military since it left large numbers of outmoded tanks to be disposed of. In the Soviet Union, where industrialization was still in its infancy, the scrapping of perfectly serviceable turrets was deemed wasteful* and in 1931 the idea of using tank turrets as fixed fortifications was advanced. In the west France developed the *tourelle démontable*. This was a rotating armoured hood with an aperture for a machine gun that provided the crew with valuable protection against shrapnel and small arms fire. From 1935 these turrets were installed in fixed and temporary positions along the Maginot Line. At the same time the idea of using obsolete tank turrets was considered. During the 1930s the Renault FT17, for so long the backbone of the French cavalry, was gradually replaced by the Renault R35, Somua S35 and Hotchkiss models. Some FT17s were still in service when the Germans invaded in 1940, but a large number had been mothballed and a number were dug in to bolster the already impressive defences of the Maginot Line. France's neighbour and ally Belgium also adopted this idea. In 1936 the Belgian army had taken delivery of a batch of French tank turrets and instead of using them for their original purpose they were mounted on concrete bunkers along the border with Germany and on the coast.

As it transpired, the French and Belgian defences, including the emplaced tank turrets, did little to stem

One of the tourelle démontable armoured hoods that were used in the Maginot Line. This example was installed in the Alpine section to a cover a bridge over the river Isère near Bourg St Maurice. (Author)

---

*And this philosophy continued well into the Cold War when obsolete tanks were mothballed or their turrets removed and used in fixed positions.

the German advance in May 1940 and in only six weeks the rump of Continental Europe was under Nazi rule. The impressive defences that for so long had provided security, and on which rested the hopes for peace of the western democracies, were now subjected to a series of destructive tests to assess their effectiveness. Although spared this fate, German engineers made a detailed study of the various fortifications mounting tank turrets. However, with plans for the invasion of Britain still being finalized, this idea was simply noted and filed for future reference.

In 1941, Operation *Seelöwe* (Operation *Sea Lion*) – the invasion of Britain – was postponed indefinitely; Hitler turned his attention east and in June invaded the Soviet Union. Once again the *Wehrmacht* was confronted by a line of fortifications studded with emplaced tank turrets and once again these defences did little to slow the German advance; although this was largely the result of Stalin's decision to concentrate his efforts on the Molotov Line* at the expense of the more advanced defences of the line that bore his name.

As they had in the west, German engineers made a detailed study of the Soviet defences,[1] but by the time these reports were complete the dominant position of the Third Reich had begun to deteriorate. Already in 1942, in the seesaw battles in the Western Desert, the turrets of captured British Matilda turrets had been removed and incorporated in the German defences of the Halfaya Pass. More significantly, following a

series of raids on the French coast – the most significant being the Dieppe landings of August 1942 – a decision was taken to fortify the coast of Continental Europe against any future raids or even a full-scale invasion and plans to utilize captured French tank turrets were considered.

By 1942 the French tanks captured in the spring of 1940 were deemed unsuitable for frontline action. Though heavily armoured they were poorly armed and were very slow, designed, as they were, to move at the infantry's pace.[†] Accordingly, many of these tanks were consigned to second-line units guarding key military installations such as airfields, or were used in anti-partisan duties. Some were simply loaded onto armoured trains to provide added protection.[‡] Others had their turrets removed and a new superstructure constructed on the tank chassis to mount more powerful anti-tank guns and artillery pieces, while others were simply used as ammunition tractors or as driver instruction vehicles.[2] As a result the Germans were left with a large stockpile of seemingly useless tank turrets complete with their main armament. Rather than waste this valuable resource it was decided that they should be utilized in much the same way as France, Belgium and the Soviet Union had used them earlier in the war. Thus the French turrets were mounted on specially designed bunkers which were positioned all long the Atlantic Wall, but principally on the French coast.[¶]

The number of turrets available for use in this role grew dramatically following the arrival on the battlefield of the superior Russian T34. Almost overnight this rendered obsolete the mainstay of the *Panzer* divisions (*Panzer* I and II and Czech 35(t) and 38(t) tanks) that had swept all before them during the invasion of Poland, France, the Low Countries and

A Soviet emplaced tank turret, or Tankovaya Ognievaya Totshka. This T18 turret was installed in the Stalin Line and was captured by the advancing German forces in 1941. (J. Magnuski courtesy of S. Zaloga)

---

*Constructed further west after the partition of Poland.
[†] The Renault, Hotchkiss and Somua models mounted only 37mm guns and the Char B1 *bis* a 37mm gun in the turret and a fixed 75mm in the hull. In 1941 the Soviets introduced the T34 mounting a 76mm gun and in 1942 the Tiger entered German service with its 88mm main armament.
[‡] This is covered in more detail in Chapter 3.
[¶] Already in 1941 the idea of using a detachable turret had been considered by the Germans. However, the turret of the 'Heuschrecke 10', as it was known, mounted a light field howitzer and was primarily designed for indirect rather than direct fire support.

One of the many French tank turrets captured by the Germans in 1940. This FT 17 was used to strengthen the defences of Utah Beach at Sainte Marie du Mont. The turret is of a riveted design and sits on a non-standard bunker near the Musée du Débarquement. (Author)

One of the specially designed Panther turrets developed by the Germans for use as fixed fortifications. This example was positioned in the Gothic Line in Italy to cover a bend in the road leading to the strategically important Futa Pass. (Imperial War Museum)

Scandinavia. These tanks were now either relegated to second line duties, or experienced the same fate as those tanks captured in France: the chassis used as improvised anti-tank or self-propelled gun platforms and the turrets employed as makeshift pillboxes. These tank turrets, however, were used more extensively than the captured turrets – perhaps reflecting the greater numbers available, or the relative ease with which ammunition could be supplied – and were installed all over occupied Europe.*

By 1943 then the idea of using tank turrets in this way was accepted practice. However, because the guns mounted were small by the standards of the day, these turrets posed little threat to Allied tanks and often acted as little more than armoured observation posts. That was all to change in that same year, when the Germans took a new and far more radical step in the use of tank turrets. Up to that point only obsolete turrets had been used, but now a decision was taken to use Panther turrets in this role. These turrets, some specifically designed for the task, were mounted on concrete, steel and later wooden shelters and saw action in Italy, on the eastern front and as part of the reconstructed West Wall defences.

These positions took a heavy toll on Allied armour, but they were not able to stop the inexorable Allied advance and as the Germans retreated, positions earmarked for emplaced turrets were often overrun before they had been installed. As things became increasingly desperate the Germans were forced to use damaged tanks as improvised pillboxes and at the very end of the war guns from tanks were mounted on simple frameworks and installed in open pits.

With the defeat of Italy, Germany and Japan the peoples of the world looked forward to a period of sustained peace. Instead the world was plunged into a Cold War as communism battled capitalism for supremacy. On occasion this war of ideologies escalated into localized conflicts, but in Europe it developed into an uneasy stand off, as the countries of NATO and the Warsaw pact stood toe-to-toe and prepared for the ultimate showdown.

Post-war economic hardship, which resulted from years of war, meant that for most countries large armies were no longer sustainable and more cost effective security solutions had to be found. At the same time Europe in particular was awash with large numbers of tanks which, although serviceable, had often been rendered obsolete by the pace of military advances. These factors neatly dovetailed and saw the emergence of a new generation of fortifications that used tank turrets. This improvisation was seen not

*Nor did the Germans stop there. Armoured trains complete with tank turrets were also used for security and anti-partisan operations.

only as an effective way of defending a country's borders and its key installations, but was also cheap. As such this type of fortification was widely used after the war. Of the western powers Italy, Greece, the Netherlands and Norway adopted this idea, while on the other side of the divide the Soviet Union and a number of her satellite states, including Finland, Bulgaria and Czechoslovakia did likewise. Other states aligned with the Soviet Union, like Cuba, also used static tanks for defence against her nemesis the USA.

Squeezed between these great power blocs, the neutral nations also adopted this expedient. Switzerland, literally and metaphorically stuck between the two camps, turned the country into an impregnable fortress and employed tank turrets along its borders. Austria, when free from military restrictions imposed on her after the war, also used the idea, as did Sweden, which used tank turrets to defend her airfields and coastline.

The concept also spread to the Far East where European powers like France used them to protect key installations in its colonies as pro-independence revolutionaries fought to throw off the imperialist yoke. In the Middle East, Israel used tank turrets to protect its newly won territories while Jerusalem's hostile neighbours, like Syria, used dug-in tanks.

Although few of these turrets saw action, they signalled a country's intent to defend itself with whatever means were at its disposal and in that respect they were successful. However, with weapons becoming increasingly sophisticated the value of

Greece also made use of this expedient. This Sherman turret was installed at Evzoni on the border with the former Yugoslavia. Many of the turrets were remodelled with the 75mm gun being replaced with an aperture to take a machine gun. (Courtesy of T. Tsiplakos)

emplaced tank turrets diminished. Moreover, with the changing threat to national security, away from a traditional invasion to a more oblique and arguably more worrying threat of terrorism, traditional security measures have been reappraised and most fortifications have been mothballed or demolished, and this is also true of emplaced tank turrets. Most turrets, save for those in museums, have now been removed and the installation filled in or destroyed; a sad but understandable end to a fortification that belongs to a bygone age. This book will hopefully help to ensure that the use of tank turrets as fixed fortifications, although gone, is not quickly forgotten.

After the Second World War the Soviets made extensive use of emplaced tank turrets. This IS2 turret was installed on border with China. In the foreground it is just possible to see the steel rods that were used to reinforce the concrete. (Sergei Netrebenko)

1 The First World War

Even before the First World War tremendous strides had been made in the development of armoured turrets. The British navy had initially developed the idea as early as 1855 in order to protect guns and their crews from enemy fire and by the 1870s the concept had been adopted by all the major navies of the day. The potential for using this idea on land was soon recognized and despite initial concerns about the robustness of the structure, a decision was taken to mount a two-gun turret at Dover. This, like the turrets mounted on board ship, was little more than a covered circular box with ports for the guns.

On the continent, the Grüson company of Magdeburg, Germany in the 1860s had developed a technique for producing cast iron curved sections which could be 'welded' together to form a complete cupola which rotated on a turntable of rollers. One such turret, mounting two 16in guns weighing 120 tons, was used by Krupp to protect the Italian naval base at La Spezia.[1] And it was not long before the wider possibilities of using such turrets were recognized. The Belgian General Brialmont was a keen advocate of the idea and proposed using both fixed and retractable turrets and in 1865 he installed an armoured turret in the reduit of Fort III protecting Antwerp. A little later, Maximilian Schumann, a Prussian army engineer and subsequently chief turret designer for Grüson, designed a series of increasingly sophisticated armoured turrets to improve the protection for the gun and its firing ability, his work culminating in the design for a retractable turret.

In France, Mougin, designer for the St Chamond gun-making company, also developed a number of armoured turrets, one of the best known being the cast iron turret mounting twin 155mm long-range *de Bange* guns. Twenty-five of these were built as part of the Séré de Rivière fortifications; a series of fortifications that stretched from the English Channel to the border with Italy.* [2]

Thus, by the end of the nineteenth century a number of companies were producing and selling armoured turrets. However, despite the fact the German company Grüson was one of the leading

During the First World War the Germans installed old naval guns along the coast. 'Lange Max' or 'Long Max' was located at Moere, about 8 miles from Ostend. The 38cm gun was used to shell Dunkirk. (Author)

---

*One of Mougin's fixed turrets armed with twin 155mm guns was installed at Fort Barbonnet in 1887. It was still effective in the Second World War when it was instrumental in inflicting heavy casualties on the Italian attackers.

manufacturers of this technology, there was disagreement in the Imperial Army about how best to use armoured turrets in fortifications. What was clear though was that with the advent of the explosive shell open gun positions were no longer practical and some sort of protection had to be provided. In 1892 the first fort was built using armoured turrets. This included fixed and retractable turrets and additional firepower was also provided by the Grüson turret, or *Fahrpanzer*. This weapon is of particular interest because it was the precursor of the French *tourelle démontable* which formed part of the Maginot Line defences (and which is covered in more detail in the Interwar section of this book) and as such was arguably a forerunner of the *Panzerstellung*.[3]

The main body of the *Fahrpanzer* consisted of a cast-iron cylindrical base topped with a cupola that housed the main armament. It was 1,655mm (65in) high and 1,540mm (60in) round with 40mm (1½in) thick armour that provided the crew with adequate protection against shrapnel and small arms fire. A door at the rear gave the crew access to the fighting compartment.

The main body of the structure was set on four rollers some 60cms (24in) apart, which enabled the turret to be moved on tracks into a pre-prepared semi-circular concrete niche to augment the main armament of the fortification. When not in use it could be rolled back into a covered position for protection. These rollers also enabled the turret to be moved onto a specially designed carriage that allowed it to be moved more easily around the battlefield. This had four wheels – two larger wheels at the rear that bore the weight of the turret and weapon and two smaller wheels at the front on a pivot point to enable the carriage to be turned.* The wheels were somewhat unusual in that they were made of wood with a steel tyre, whereas the rest of the structure was constructed from iron. This arrangement may have been developed to smooth the ride, since the carriage had no suspension.

A seat at the front of the vehicle accommodated the driver who drove the three horses, which were attached to the carriage by a limber. A hand-operated

The Fahrpanzer was arguably an early forerunner of the panzerstellung. This example was captured by the Greeks in the First World War and is now housed at the Greek War Museum in Athens. The cast-iron cylindrical base and the domed turret that housed the main armament are both clearly shown.
(Author)

The Fahrpanzer could be mounted on a specially designed carriage. The access hatch to the turret is visible behind the driver's seat. Just below the hatch it is possible to see one of the rollers that enabled the turret to run on tracks.
(Author)

---

*Railway wheels were also developed which meant the turret could be moved short distances on purpose built tracks or transported longer distances along the mainline.

wheel under the driver's seat applied a brake to the larger wheels at the rear when the carriage was stationary.

Inside the turret a pedestal was located centrally with three branches rising from the centre to support the cupola. This sat on the main body of the structure on a series of small wheels and was rotated using a large hand wheel that permitted a full rotation of the turret in 15 seconds. A simple mechanism enabled the turret to be locked in position so that it did not deviate when fired. Around the inside of the turret was a band marked in degrees, which enabled the crew to accurately rotate the cupola. Two simple seats were provided for the gunner and loader/commander, which were attached to the pedestal. The ammunition (*circa* 130 rounds) for the weapon was stored vertically in racks at the base of the structure.

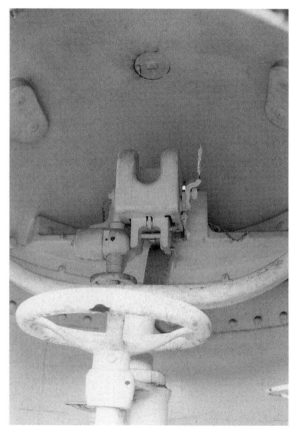

An inside view of the Fahrpanzer turret that clearly shows the gun breech and elevating gear. The central pedestal is also visible as is the small vent at the top. (Author)

The main armament was mounted in the cupola above a shelf. The gun trunions were secured to the shelf and there was no recoil mechanism. The gun was fitted with a simple falling type breech with the breech handle on the right and the elevation mechanism on the left. This consisted of a vertically mounted screw thread affixed to the breechblock and the shelf of the turret. By rotating a hand wheel the gun could be elevated and depressed +10 to –5 degrees. This set-up allowed for some very fine adjustments to be made, but it was not suited to quick changes in the angle of depression or elevation when in combat.

The 53mm *Schnelladekanone* could fire either high explosive or case shot. Its maximum range with HE shells was 3,200m (10,000ft) and 400m (1,300ft) with the shot. The simple breech mechanism and the one-piece ammunition enabled the weapon to be fired very rapidly; the crew of two were capable of firing the weapon at 25–30 shots a minute. An opening in the top of the turret was fitted to vent the fumes, but when using rapid fire it is likely that this would have been insufficient and the doors would have to be opened to prevent the asphyxiation of the crew.

The turret was not fitted with an optical sight. A small hole in the dome with aiming point above and to the right of the gun and a sight fitted outside on the barrel enabled the crew to aim the weapon. Additionally a number of vision slits were provided to give the crew greater visibility. These could be covered with armoured plates when not in use. A small rain guard above the weapon prevented any precipitation entering the turret.

Production of the *Fahrpanzer* began in 1889 and in total some 200 were produced (although other sources state 322). The turrets were exported to a number of countries and were employed by the Central Powers in the First World War.*[4]

By the turn of the century armoured turrets had been sufficiently refined that they were capable of being fitted to armoured cars. The Austrians installed a turret on the Austro-Daimler armoured car of 1904 (and the modified 1905 version) and the French

---

*The Greeks captured two Bulgarian turrets. These were manufactured by Krupp at the Grüsonwerk, Magdeburg-Buckau in 1894 and are now on display at the Greek War Museum in Athens.

Charron car from roughly the same period also had a turret. During the war all of the major belligerents used armoured cars with turrets. The Italian Lancia armoured car of 1915 was even fitted with a smaller turret atop the main turret. In that same year the Canadian Russell armoured car entered service. This was the first vehicle to have a turret basket that rotated with the turret.[5]

By the outbreak of the war the technology behind armoured turrets was well established. However, the first tanks that were developed were all fitted with fixed guns. For some time before the war experiments had been conducted to assess the effectiveness of caterpillar tracks. These peacetime trials led to the development of simple farm tractors. But with the outbreak of war these experiments were given added urgency as the British actively pursued this idea as a possible solution to the stalemate on the Western Front. An armoured vehicle fitted with tracks, it was hoped, would be able to advance across the broken terrain and engage enemy positions that had survived the preparatory bombardment and together with supporting infantry might offer the prospect of the thus far elusive breakthrough.

In Britain, somewhat unusually, the research was

A First World War British tank knocked out at Langemarck. The initial British and French designs were not fitted with turrets.
(Author)

undertaken by the Royal Navy with the full support of the First Lord of the Admiralty, Winston Churchill. The first prototypes of the 'tank'* were tested in September 1915 and were introduced on the Western Front in the latter stages of the Battle of the Somme in September 1916. In the spring of the following year the French fielded some 130 so-called 'assault cannons' in the action at Chemin des Dames.

The results were disappointing. There were too few tanks available to be decisive, they were unreliable and despite their armour, they were vulnerable to artillery fire and as such they were unable to deliver the hoped for strategic surprise. The abject failure of tanks on the Somme and in later battles convinced the German High Command that such armoured vehicles had little merit. Only in November 1917 was their first prototype ready for tests. The A7V, as it was known, was a lumbering monster of a machine armed with one front mounted 57mm gun and six machine guns. It was not particularly effective and continuing disputes about the value of the weapon meant only twenty were ever completed.

Unperturbed by the disappointing results, the British and the French pushed ahead with the development of their respective tank programmes. In France, Gen Jean-Baptiste Estienne, who had already been instrumental in the development of French armour, pressed for the introduction of a light tank, and Renault developed the FT17, which had the distinction of being the first tank to include a fully revolving turret. The turret could be fitted with either a short 37mm gun or a machine gun. It revolved on a ball race and could be rotated by hand with little difficulty. If necessary it could be locked in place with a hand brake. Several thousand of these tanks were produced before the end of the war and would no doubt have had a key role to play in the operations envisaged for 1919, but the armistice was announced in November 1918 and the plans were shelved.[†]

Of course for the majority of people the most memorable feature of the First World War is not the introduction of the tank, but the trenches. All too often these have been referred to in general terms,

---

*So named to deceive the enemy and because it was not dissimilar to a large water tank.
† The Germans also developed the LKI Light Tank with a revolving turret but few were produced.

ignoring the major strides that were taken in the development of fieldworks and reinforced concrete blockhouses or pillboxes. The so-called 'race to the sea' which saw the opposing armies trying to outflank the enemy and achieve a decisive breakthrough eventually resulted in the creation of a line of trenches on a scale never before seen, extending from the North Sea to the border with Switzerland. As the respective high commands struggled to find a solution to this bloody stalemate, the trench system was expanded. The main trench, or 'fire trench' that faced the enemy, was made deep and wide with a fire step and loopholes. Like all the trenches it was dug in a zigzag pattern to lessen the impact of shells and prevent a clear line of fire should the enemy occupy the position. Some 100m (110yd) to the rear a support trench was dug where the reserves were held and later a third trench line was added – 'the bombing trench'. This was between the fire and support trench and was used when the line was under attack by the enemy. In this eventuality soldiers particularly competent in the use of grenades, which were stockpiled in the trench, would occupy this intermediate position and throw the bombs into the forward trench to repulse any foray. Linking all the lines of trenches together were communication trenches that led to the rear.

As the war progressed the individual trenches also became increasingly elaborate and included dugouts that provided shelter for the infantry or could be used as makeshift command posts and first aid stations. But as the trenches and dugouts became deeper the military engineers were confronted with the age-old problem of water. This was particularly the case in and around Passchendaele where the water table meant that it was difficult to dig trenches. The German solution was to build concrete pillboxes.*† These miniature forts not only solved the problem of flooding but also provided more effective protection against the heavy barrage that preceded British and French attacks. The pillboxes did not adhere to any formal design because they were often built by troops in the field, albeit under the supervision of military engineers. Nevertheless they generally measured circa 9m (30ft) along the front and were about 3m (10ft) wide.

Concrete pillboxes were extensively used by the Germans in the *Siegfriedstellung* or the Hindenburg Line, as it was know to the Allies. This was begun in

One of the many concrete blockhouses built by the Germans all along the western front. This example was located at Lomme, near Armentieres and was destroyed by a mine. (Author)

September 1916 and was originally envisaged as a relatively narrow band of defences. The ability of these defences to defeat the anticipated Allied offensive concerned the Chief of Staff of the German First Army, Col Fritz von Lossberg. He planned to construct a defensive system that would consist of numerous zones each stronger than the last, which would gradually slow and ultimately stop the enemy attack. By building the defences in depth, the attacking infantry would soon outreach its supporting artillery making further progress all but impossible. Moreover, the attackers would become increasingly isolated from their own forces and thus vulnerable to counter-attack by reserves held in the rear, safe from the preliminary bombardment, and earmarked for the purpose.

---

*The term 'pillbox' was used by the British soldiers because the reinforced concrete construction was the same shape as the boxes in which chemists supplied tablets during the war.
† Interestingly, the British built very few pillboxes. The official reason was that 'such works were not worth the labour or the cost', but the real reason was more likely that the High Command feared that if the troops had such solid defences they would be less offensively minded.

The practical application of von Lossberg's ideas saw the construction of a series of defences in front of the main position. Forward of the first trench was the outpost zone which was designed to slow the enemy attack. If the enemy pierced this first line of defence it would enter the battle zone that was chequered with concrete blockhouses. These positions were all mutually supporting, providing fire for their own defence and cover for the flanks and rear of the adjacent units in the so-called 'Hedgehog' (*Igel*) pattern of defence. Behind this zone were further trenches (and more defensive lines further to the rear were also contemplated) so that the defensive system was some 6–8,000m (19–26,000ft) in depth.

By the end of the First World War the value of reinforced concrete shelters had been established as had the importance of armoured turrets in protecting their crew against explosive shells, small arms fire and shrapnel. In the interwar period these technologies were combined and lead to the development of some of the most elaborate fortifications ever constructed with huge casemates mounting armoured turrets. At the same time, but on a less grand scale, the first steps were taken in the development of what the Germans were to later christen the *panzerstellung*, with tank turrets mounted on concrete shelters for the first time.

As well as pillboxes, the Germans also developed armoured cupolas. This steel observation post with concrete apron was installed on the Western Front. (Imperial War Museum)

2 Interwar

The First World War cast a huge shadow over the interwar period. In the immediate aftermath, there was a determination to prevent a repeat of the death and destruction that for four long years had held the countries of Europe in its thrall. Initially this found its expression in a desire for peace founded on disarmament; swords would be beaten into ploughshares if only to save the economies of Europe from financial meltdown. Preliminary negotiations were instigated and conferences convened, but economic crisis and the rise of political extremism, particularly in Germany, meant that the discussions foundered and many countries, disillusioned by the lack of progress, steadily began to rearm. This rearmament was principally defensive in nature and was aimed at deterring an attack from the country still deemed to pose the greatest threat to European peace – Germany. Although the fledgling democracy had shown no aggressive intent, it was clear that it had taken the first tentative steps towards rearmament. The pace and scale of this build up quickened after Hitler's accession to power and Germany's neighbours reacted in kind.

In 1929 France began work on the Maginot Line and over the next seven years a thin line of powerful forts was constructed along France's north-eastern frontier. At much the same time and often with the aid of French expertise, her allies: Belgium, the Netherlands, Czechoslovakia and Poland did likewise, so completing Germany's encirclement.* Further east, the Soviet Union fortified her western frontier against her traditional enemies: Poland and Germany.

Paradoxically, the construction of these defensive lines was paralleled by the development of a weapon that was to demonstrate its awesome offensive potential in the Second World War – the tank. The lumbering behemoths of the Somme and Cambrai had been replaced with much quicker, more agile and above all turreted models that were to transform the face of the battlefield. The pace of change was such that many countries were left with a number of obsolete tanks that would have to be scrapped, stored or consigned to museums. Instead three countries: Belgium, France and the Soviet Union, used these tanks as improvised fixed fortifications. France used this expedient to supplement the defences of the Maginot Line and Belgium used them to bolster her border defences and protect her exposed coastline, while the Soviet Union used tank turrets to strengthen both the Stalin and later the Molotov lines, which protected her western border.

The use of tank turrets in this way was undoubtedly a valuable addition to the main fortifications providing extra firepower while at the same time protecting the crew from enemy fire. But although Belgium, France and the Soviet Union clearly recognized the benefits of using turrets in this way it is unclear whether they developed the idea independently – certainly the different designs developed by each country bear little resemblance to each other – or whether there was an exchange of information (either voluntarily or through espionage). What is clear is that by the outbreak of the Second World War, significant numbers of turrets had been installed and were encountered by German forces in 1940 and 1941.

SOVIET UNION

The first country to adopt the idea of using tank turrets as an extemporized fixed fortification was the

---

*Italy also fortified her northern border against the threat posed by the 'Greater Germany' following the German *Anschluss* with Austria in March 1938.

Soviet Union. Following the November revolution of 1917 the Bolsheviks under Lenin seized control of Russia. However, their effective sphere of influence stretched little further than the two great cities of St Petersburg (Leningrad) and Moscow. Elsewhere, control lay with anti-Bolsheviks, or 'White Russians' who quickly formed armies with a view to overthrowing the new revolutionary government. They were supported in this aim by Russia's former allies (principally Britain and France) who were not only keen to prevent a 'world revolution' but more importantly they wanted Russia to remain in the war not least to ensure that Russia repaid her debts.

In December 1917 the Bolsheviks agreed an armistice with Austria and Germany and although they initially balked at the peace terms on the table they eventually relented and in March 1918 signed the Treaty of Brest Litovsk. Lenin could now concentrate his efforts on the disparate forces ranged against him. Under the leadership of Trotsky, the Red Army, taking advantage of the good communications around its power base and the failure of the counter revolutionary forces to coordinate their attacks, managed to gain the ascendancy and by 1920 the Bolsheviks hold on power had been secured. Although still viewed with suspicion by the international community (and certainly the Western democracies) the new Bolshevik state was under no immediate threat of invasion and the government set about introducing wide-ranging reforms. Principal among these was defence, and soon the Soviet Union began to develop its own tanks and started to build border fortifications.

Fortifications

During the Civil War, 'The Workers' and Peasants' Red Army (*Robochiy Krestyanskaya Krasnaya Armiya* – RKKA)' or simply the Red Army, in its desperate attempts to safeguard the new revolutionary government, created a series of fortified areas, or *ukreplinnyje rajony* (UR), which were to be used not only for defence but were also to act as jumping off points for offensive operations. With little in the way of raw materials and no industrial base to build permanent fortifications, these positions were generally little more than field works and were built using the one resource they did have – manpower.

As the threat from the foreign backed 'White Russians' diminished and eventually disappeared, plans were drawn up to build a major set of fortifications along the western border. Almost immediately work began at the Engineering Research and Development Institute of the Military Engineering Academy in Moscow to develop a series of reinforced concrete pillboxes. But to construct such shelters all along the border would require huge amounts of material, which the weak Soviet economy could not sustain. When work began in 1926 it was therefore decided to concentrate the defences in the Polotsk and Karelian URs* (north and north-west fronts) where the greatest threat of attack was deemed to lie.

Agricultural and industrial reform saw the Soviet economy strengthen and grow and this gathered pace after the introduction of the first Five Year Plan in 1928. This coincided with a decision to extend the defences to include a further eleven fortified regions: Kingisep UR, Pskov UR, Minsk UR, Mozyr UR, Korosten UR, Novograd-Volynski (Zwiahel) UR, Leitchev UR, Mogilov-Yampolsky UR, Rybnitsk UR and Tiraspol UR. One further UR was built around Kiev. In 1938 work on a further eight new URs was begun. The main part of this work was concentrated in the Ukraine with the creation of the Shepetovka, Staro Konstantinov, Ostropol and Kaments-Podolski URs. Three further URs were created to plug perceived gaps in the line. The Ostrov and Sebezh URs closed the gap between the Pskov and Polotsk URs while the Slutsk UR extended the line from the old UR of Minsk to the Pripet Marshes.

In all, the front stretched over 2,000km (1,242 miles) from the Baltic to the Black Sea and consisted of more than 3,000 positions. These included larger forts, sometimes with subterranean facilities, machine gun and anti-tank positions, artillery blocks, and observation and command positions. These tended to be concentrated at key points with field works used to fill the gaps. These more traditional fortifications were supplemented by the addition of emplaced tank turrets or *Tankovaya Ognievaya Totshka* (TOT). Obsolete T18 and T24 tanks were buried in the ground so that just the turret was visible and old T26

*The latter built specifically to defend Leningrad against a possible Finnish attack.

In the interwar period the Soviets used tank turrets, or Tankovaya Ognievaya Totshka, in the Stalin and Molotov Lines. This T26 armed with a 45mm gun was installed in Minsk Fortified Region (Byelorussian Military District). It clearly shows the concrete shelter that it was mounted on. (Vladimir Kaminski)

turrets were mounted on specially prepared bunkers and used in the same way.

The actual work on the defences was coordinated by the Military Labour Directorate which oversaw separate labour directorates, each responsible for a single UR. They assigned engineers and supervised the construction. But despite the highly centralized organization of the work, the results were less than satisfactory. Workers were poorly paid and had to contend with difficult conditions and although Soviet propaganda tried to portray otherwise, the workers were not inspired by the revolutionary zeal of their leaders. More critically, military engineers, many of whom had been the victims of Stalin's purges, were in short supply, leaving unqualified civilian engineers to oversee the work.

By the time of the outbreak of the Second World War, the defences of the Stalin Line, as it became known, were largely complete. However, after the Soviet occupation of eastern Poland in October 1939 and the signing of the Nazi-Soviet pact the threat in the west had seemingly disappeared. The defences were also now too far behind the new Soviet border to be of any use as a potential springboard for an offensive. As a consequence the positions of the Stalin Line were mothballed. Stalin, however, was cautious and took steps to create a new defensive line inside Poland to ensure the integrity of the new Soviet border against any possible volte-face by Hitler.

The new border defences, which came to be known by the name of the Soviet Foreign Minister, Molotov, were to be built in much greater depth than the Stalin Line – up to 10km (7 miles) in places and were to have a much greater preponderance of anti-tank guns. Equipment was stripped from the Stalin Line and engineers and labourers who had previously worked on the defences were sent west. Winter prevented any serious work beginning before the summer of 1940 and only 25 per cent of the positions had been completed by the time of the German invasion in June 1941 but this did include a number of emplaced T18 turrets.

Tanks

Having defeated the counter-revolutionary forces and foreign armies in the civil war, the Red Army was demobilized and the make-up of the country's armed forces reappraised. The tank arm had consisted of little more than captured enemy vehicles and a few indigenous examples that were simply copies of foreign vehicles, principally the French Renault FT.

T18 (or MS1 – Malyi Soprovozhdieniya or Small Infantry Support Tank)
With the end of the fighting, attempts were made to design and build a Soviet tank but this proved unsuccessful and in 1924 a Tank Bureau was created to coordinate these efforts. The Bureau proposed the development of a 3-ton (later a 5-ton) tank armed with a 37mm gun. In common with many nations at this time, the design was based on the French Renault FT and was designated the T16. A number of improvements were made to the design and in 1928 the T18 was put into production. The first batch of tanks was delivered to the army in the following year. Production continued on and off until 1931 when the last of the 960 T18s rolled off the production line. In 1938 some 200 vehicles had their main armament replaced with a larger 45mm gun and was renamed the T18M.

The T18 was plagued by engine and transmission failures, which meant that increasing numbers of tanks could not be used. In 1934 in the Leningrad military district some of these tanks were transferred to the Karelian UR to be used as improvised fixed fortifications. In March 1938 the *Narkomat* (Peoples

Commissariat of Defence) ordered that all T18 tanks were to be transferred to the URs. Those tanks that were serviceable were to be employed in their original role and used to defend the fortified regions.* A further 450 machines which were not considered battle worthy were prepared for use as strong points.† Some retained their main armament, others had their main gun removed and replaced with twin Degtarov machine guns. The turret-mounted machine gun was also removed and the hole sealed with an armoured plate. A number of turrets had their armament removed completely and were used as observation positions. This simple idea had a number of obvious benefits; it provided the crew with protection from enemy fire, it was difficult to hit being so low to the ground and, by comparison with permanent fortifications, was very quick to construct.

Three separate and increasingly complex designs were developed. The first design involved digging a large hole and burying the T18, minus its running gear, so that just the turret protruded. Timber beams and stone/gravel were then used to provide the hull with greater protection. The spoil was then replaced and turfs used to camouflage the structure. A major shortcoming of this design was that the only means of entering the turret was through the top hatch, which in

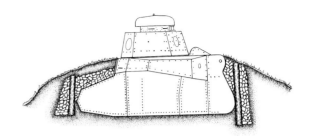

T18 observation post – original shelter configuration.

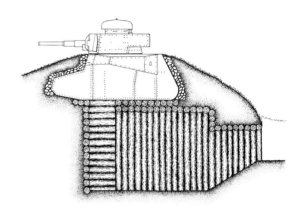

T18 with 45mm gun – revised shelter configuration.

combat made access extremely difficult. As a result a new design was developed. The position was constructed in much the same way as the original, but now an access hole was cut into the base of the hull. This was linked to a revetted tunnel that led to the rear. Finally, an even more elaborate construction was designed. Again the position was constructed in much the same way as the two previous designs, but now the hole in the base of the hull was linked by a vertical ladder to a shelter beneath the tank that acted as a storeroom for the ammunition. A revetted tunnel linked this room to the rear.

Few details can be found on the exact locations of any T18 turrets, not least because most were removed after the war. However, according to a report of

A number of T18 turrets had their weapons removed and were simply used as armoured observation posts. (Taken from Denkschrift uber die Russische Landesbefestigungen, *courtesy of E. Hitriak)*

---

*Some estimates predict that as many as 400 tanks were available for use when the Germans invaded the Soviet Union in June 1941.
† In the period from 1939 to 1941, 200 or so T-18 tanks were emplaced. B. Perzyk, 'Karelski Rejon Umocniony – fortyfikacje nieznane', *Nowa Technika Wojskowa* (May 2002), pp.27–33.

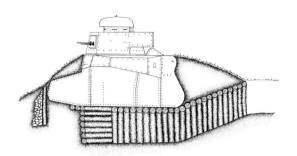

T18 with twin Degtarov machine guns – final shelter configuration.

A T18 tank in the process of being buried in the ground so that just the turret is visible. The turret is armed with twin DT machine guns. (Taken from Denkschrift uber die Russische Landesbefestigungen*, courtesy of E. Hitriak)*

March 1941, thirty-six tank turrets (including T18 turrets) were installed in the Osovetz UR (part of the Molotov Line). Another report of 22nd June 1941 stated that a further five turrets were supplied to the Vladimir-Volynsk UR (also part of the Molotov Line) for installation around the railway station at Ustilug. In the spring of 1941, forward positions of the Karelian UR were beefed up by the installation of approximately twenty-four tank turrets which it is believed were taken from obsolete T18s.*

T18 turrets were used in the Minsk UR, part of the Stalin Line, to protect bridges and ferry crossings. One such turret mounting a 45mm gun was located at Belynichi covering the River Drut. On 23 June 1941, the crew of this turret (Sgt Gvozdev and Pte Lyupov) engaged the enemy for some four hours and together

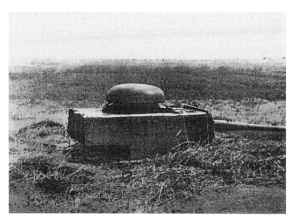

Some 200 T18 tanks were fitted with 45mm guns. Even so the design was not considered a success and many were used in the Stalin Line to provide extra anti-tank fire. (Russian State Archive, courtesy of E. Hitriak)

with troops guarding the bridge managed to destroy three German tanks, one half-track, a number of trucks and killed or injured a number of German infantrymen. For their gallantry the crew was awarded the *Boyevoe Krasnoye Znamya* (Fighting Red Banner).

T18 turrets mounted on specially prepared bunkers were also seemingly used in the Far East to protect the border between Mongolia and Manchuria where the Soviet Union had been involved in skirmishes with the Japanese since 1934.

T18

Turret statistics:
Armour (thickness/angle):

Gun mantlet	Front	Side	Rear	Roof
–	16mm	–	–	–

Weapon statistics:

Armament:	T18:	1 × 37mm PS 1 (originally fitted with the Hotchkiss Model 1916 37mm)
	T18M	1 × 45mm 1 × 7.62mm Fiodorov or Degtarov MG.
Traverse:		360°

*T18 turrets were also probably used in other parts of the Leningrad Military District – the Kingisep UR and Pskov UR.

T24

The T24 was the first Soviet medium tank and was somewhat unusual in having a smaller turret mounted on the main turret. The first prototype was completed in 1931 and permission granted for a pre-production run of twenty-four (with plans ultimately to build 300). These did not prove to be particularly reliable and the tank was relegated to training duties. In 1938, twenty-two T24s (the remainder had already been scrapped) were sent to the fortified regions. No records survive of where these turrets were used, nor are there seemingly any photographs. What is known is that for some reason many of the turrets (and those from T18s) sat in warehouses in the various fortified regions until the German invasion in 1941 by which time it was too late to install them.

T24	
Weapon statistics:	
Armament:	1 × 45mm Model 32
	2 × MG
Traverse:	360°

T26

Although treated as a pariah state in the immediate aftermath of the Civil War, the Soviet Union was gradually accepted, albeit grudgingly, into the wider international community. The country's reintegration was graphically demonstrated when a number of the major world powers entered into negotiations with Stalin's government about the possible sale of military equipment, especially tanks.

Fifteen British Vickers-Armstrongs 6-ton E tanks were purchased by the Soviets, the first of which was delivered in 1930. This design was to provide the basis for the T26 Light Infantry Tank. Numerous models were built, but the most widely produced was the T26 Model 1933, which was fitted with the 45mm 20K gun. Some 5,500 vehicles were produced prior to the closure of the line in 1936. During its production life several modifications were made including the addition of two extra machine guns and a more fundamental change in the way the turret was constructed. In 1934/35 the Soviet Army was engaged in fighting with the Japanese on the border between Mongolia and Manchuria. Engagements

between the Soviet T26 and enemy tanks highlighted an alarming weakness in the riveted construction of the turret. When hit by enemy fire, the rivets had a tendency to ricochet around inside with catastrophic results. As a consequence a new welded turret was introduced and in 1937 the T26 underwent a further redesign with the addition of sloping armour that offered greater protection. The improved vehicle was designated the T26S Model 1937.

The obsolete turrets from the old T26 tanks were used as fixed fortifications. As with the T18 and T24 shelters only the turret was visible above the ground and could be manually rotated through 360 degrees. No major modifications were made to the turret in its new role. Ammunition stowage, for example, was unchanged. Seven shells could be stored on either side of the turret with a further forty shells stored in the turret ammunition bin. Six magazines of ammunition for the machine gun were located on the right wall of the turret. The spent cartridge bag was linked to an extractor fan by a flexible rubber hose.

Although the turret remained largely unchanged, the structure on which it was mounted was very different to what had gone before. One of the major shortcomings of the earlier emplaced tanks (T18 and T24) was that the installation was vulnerable to heavy artillery fire. By 1931 military engineers at the Engineering Academy in Moscow had developed a ferro-concrete shelter to mount a tank turret, but it was only later that it was decided to use the T26. This was named the Type T pillbox (tank pillbox).

One of the T26 turrets installed in the Minsk fortified region. It is missing its main armament and turret hatch. (E. Hitriak)

A close up of the turret ring for the T26 turret which was fixed to the top of the concrete 'T' pillbox. (E. Hitriak)

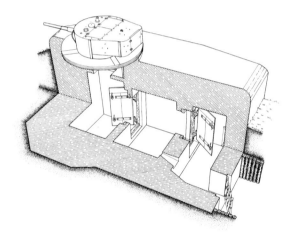

T26 Type 'T' pillbox cutaway.

The machine gun embrasure that was used by the radio operator to protect the entrance to the shelter. The steel flap could be locked in place. (E. Hitriak)

The bunker was divided into three sections. To the rear was the entrance* protected by a steel gate. An aperture enabled the radio operator inside to cover the entrance with small arms fire. When not in use the aperture could be covered with a hinged 10mm steel plate. Inside the main entrance was a corridor, which was constructed with a small opening that was designed to vent any shock waves away from the inner casemate door.

The corridor led to what could be loosely translated as 'the technical room'. The door to this room was constructed from wood with steel sheets for added strength. The technical room housed a switchboard/telephone that enabled communication with neighbouring pillboxes, the external observer and headquarters; messages within the shelter were conveyed by means of pipes. A radio was also installed, the antenna for which was fitted to the roof of the shelter. The ventilator (initially the KP-1 or

---

*It was also possible to gain access to the shelter through the turret hatches.

The rooms within the 'T' pillbox were secured with wooden doors that were fitted with a steel skin. (E. Hitriak)

One of the speaking tubes that was used to communicate within the shelter. (E. Hitriak)

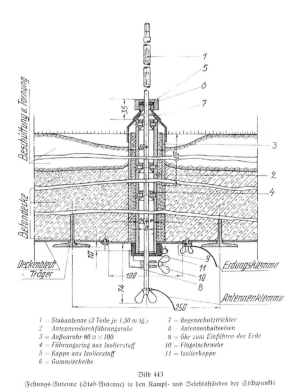

1 = Stabantenne (3 Teile je 1,50 m lg.)
2 = Antennendurchführungsrohr
3 = Außenrohr 60 ⌀ × 100
4 = Führungsring aus Isolierstoff
5 = Kappe aus Isolierstoff
6 = Gummischeibe
7 = Regenschutztrichter
8 = Antennenhalteeisen
9 = Öhr zum Einführen der Erde
10 = Flügelschraube
11 = Isolierkappe

Bild 443
Festungs-Antenne (Stab-Antenne) in den Kampf- und Befehlsständen der Stützpunkte und Stützpunktgruppen

A German drawing of the antennae that was fitted to the roof of the T26 shelter. (Taken from Denkschrift uber die Russische Landesbefestigungen, *courtesy of E. Hitriak)*

KP-2 but later the KP-3 or KP-4V) was also located here. It was hand operated and provided fresh air through a system of pipes, although the shelter was not gas-proof.* A further door led from the technical room to the fighting compartment directly underneath the turret. This was fitted with a ladder that linked the two and was also used to store extra ammunition.

The internal walls of the pillbox were covered with sheet metal that prevented concrete splinters from injuring the crew when the position was shelled and also helped to reduce the levels of concrete dust.

The entrance to the structure was protected by a small wooden extension, which could be covered with spoil. From here a revetted trench, some 40m (130ft) in length, led to the crew's living and sleeping quarters and a storage dugout where extra ammunition, provisions and fuel were kept. The position was manned by five or six men – two men occupied

*It was planned to make the pillboxes gas proof, but the work was not completed.

A steel rung ladder led from the pillbox through an access hatch to the turret's fighting compartment. (E. Hitriak)

the turret (commander and loader), one man was located under the turret to provide ammunition, one man operated the radio/covered the door and another operated the ventilator. Another man acted as observer.

The turreted positions were usually built just behind the main positions of the line and were often supported by other pillboxes. They were extremely well camouflaged to compensate for the fact that it was a stationary target and the turret armour was relatively thin, and only really provided protection against small arms fire.

It is unclear exactly how many T26 turrets were installed. In the Minsk UR, a front of about 140km (87 miles), nine tank turrets were installed and in the Polotsk UR, a front of 60km (37 miles), ten turrets were installed. There were plans to install a further forty turrets in the Stalin Line following a review of the defences in 1938. This had highlighted a number of serious shortcomings, particularly the lack of anti-tank weapons, but the order was cancelled following the defeat of Poland in 1939 and the subsequent decision to build a new series of defences along the new border. It was later decided that concrete pillboxes with 45mm anti-tank guns offered a better alternative than tank turrets and no further Type T pillboxes were constructed between 1938 and 1940.

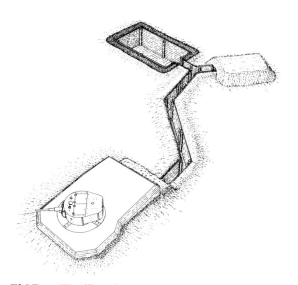

T26 Type 'T' pillbox showing supporting trenches.

This T26 tank appears to have been buried in the ground whole with only the turret visible. The engine deck and louvres can still be seen. (Imperial War Museum)

T26

Turret statistics:
Armour (thickness/angle):

Gun mantlet	Front	Side	Rear	Roof
–	15mm	15mm	15mm	10mm

Weapon statistics:

Armament:	1933: 1 × 45mm 1932 L/46
	2 × 7.62mm Degtarov MG
Traverse:	360°

Bunker statistics:

Front wall	Side wall	Roof	Round steel
1.5m	1.0m	1.2m	–

*A Soviet BT5 TOT turret installed in the Stalin Line
and captured by the Germans in 1941.
(US National Archives, courtesy of S. Zaloga)*

BT

At the same time as the T26 was being developed using the British Vickers tank, the first steps were being taken in the design of the BT series of 'fast' tanks which were based on the American Christie M1930. Numerous BT prototypes were developed but the most numerous was the BT5 Model 1933 which was armed with a 45mm gun. Approximately 5,000 were produced from 1932 until production stopped in 1935.

The lessons learned in the fighting with the Japanese on the border between Mongolia and Manchuria, which had led to a redesign of the T26, were also applied to the BT5. This led to the development of the BT7 1935. This had a very different hull design and the turret, although nearly identical to the BT5, was almost all welded.

Later, and in parallel with the T26 modernization programme, the BT7 was fitted with a new turret featuring sloping armour to provide greater protection for the crew without adding to the weight. The new model was given the designation BT7 Model 1937. Again, the old vertically configured turrets were used as fixed fortifications, although details are sketchy. One position fitted with a BT5 turret was seemingly mounted on the hull of a T28 medium tank. This example was found in 1998 on top of a hill in the middle of vast swamps in the former Karelian UR. The difficult access probably saved it from being cut up for scrap.

Other Models

After the invasion of the Soviet Union, and in spite of the failure of the Molotov and Stalin Line to stem the German advance, the Red Army still used tank turrets for defence. Many different turrets were now employed including T28, T34, T40, T60 and KV turrets. It is even believed that captured German turrets were used. Such improvised fortifications

This TOT is somewhat unusual in that it has the body of a T28 tank but is fitted with a BT5 turret. It was installed in June 1941 in the Karelian UR near Sosnov. The tank body, less its engine and suspension, was mounted on a concrete base. The crew could access the position through the normal hatches and a hole cut in the front of the vehicle. (Sergei Netrebenko)

BT

Turret statistics:
Armour (thickness angle):

Gun mantlet	Front	Side	Rear	Roof
–	6–13mm			

Weapon statistics:
Armament: 1 × 45mm Model 1932
1 × Degtarov MG

A somewhat unusual view of a T-28 turret that was used as a fixed fortification. For some reason the standard mantlet has been replaced by a new one.
(Sergei Netrebenko)

The front view of a KV1 turret, which was tested as an improvised, fixed fortification. This example is installed at the Red Army test site near Moscow.
(Russian Fortification Website)

A T44 turret mounted on a special steel base. Just visible in each corner are the lifting hooks. This example was located at the Red Army test site near Moscow.
(Russian Fortification Website)

were used to defend Moscow and Leningrad. Following the blockade of Leningrad in September 1941, the defenders had at their disposal several hundred damaged tanks. Some were simply buried in the ground but others had their turrets removed and were mounted on different shelters.

Test Facility
The Scientific Research Institute of Engineering Technical Equipment of the Red Army* was established in 1930 near Moscow and was where the various versions of Soviet pillboxes were tested up until 1950 when the facility was closed. The work undertaken at the Institute included tests on the first specially designed tank turret pillbox, the Type T,

developed in 1931. Later in 1941–42 an improved version of the Type T pillbox was developed and tested. This was larger than its predecessor and was fitted with a heating system and an extraction system for the noxious exhaust fumes, although it was still fitted with the original hand-cranked KP-4 ventilation system. By the time the design was accepted the tide of the war had changed and it is not thought that these structures were actually used.[1]

---

*Later called the Special Test Site for Fortified Areas.

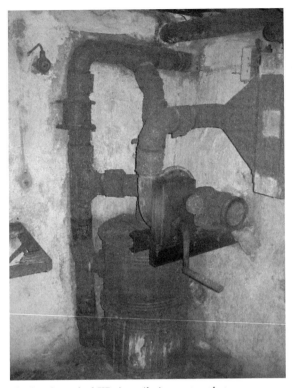

This T70 light tank turret has been fitted with a specially constructed welded steel 'nose' to house a machine gun. This example is installed at a Red Army test site near Moscow. (Russian Fortification Website)

The hand cranked KP-4 ventilation system that was installed in the shelter beneath the KV1 turret. This shelter is believed to be an example of the larger improved version of the Type 'T' pillbox that was developed in 1941–42. (Russian Fortification Website)

As well as tests on the base structures, most if not all of the turrets mentioned above were tested at this facility. In addition to these a number of rarities and unusual adaptations were assessed including the T44* and a version of the T70 which had its main armament removed and replaced with a specially constructed welded steel 'nose' to house a machine gun.

Postscript

After the war all the fortified regions of the 1930s (with the exception of the Karelian UR) were deemed to be unnecessary and in the 1950s work began to demolish the defences. The majority of the tank turrets were removed for scrap metal, but the concrete bunkers were often left and today it is still possible to find examples. Where tanks had simply been buried in the ground it was found to be extremely difficult to excavate the hull and at least one T18 has since been recovered and is on display at the Polish Army

Museum.[2] A T18 was also recently discovered in Karelia and this, together with three T18 turrets in the Far East, have been restored and can now be seen in one of a number of museums in the Soviet Union including one at the Central Museum of the History of the Great Patriotic War, Moscow.

Armoured Trains

As well as being used on concrete shelters, tank turrets were used on Soviet armoured cars and also to equip armoured trains.[†] The Red Army had a great tradition of using armoured trains which dated back to the Civil War. In the interwar period trains were once again used for mobile artillery and would often be fitted with tank turrets, including old T26 turrets and the multi-turreted T28. During the war more modern KV and T34 turrets were used.[‡] Other single coach units mounted with a T26 turret were used to carry a small detachment of troops for reconnaissance and scouting roles.

BELGIUM

Belgium only became an independent kingdom in 1831 following a revolt against the idea of a union

---

*Based on the T34/85 – (*see* Chapter 4 – Post War).

[†]The BA3 armoured car, for example, mounted the T26 turret.

[‡] An armoured wagon mounting two T34 76 turrets was developed with one mounted at either end of the unit. They generally formed part of a longer train.

A Soviet T18 found near Przemysl, Poland. This example was originally installed in the Molotov Line. The chassis was completely buried with only the turret visible. It was recovered from its position and is today on display at the Polish Army Museum, Warsaw, Poland. (S. Zaloga)

with the Netherlands that was imposed on them after the defeat of Napoleon. The position of the new kingdom was guaranteed under the terms of the Treaty of London in 1839 and was reaffirmed during the Franco-Prussian War of 1870. In spite of these guarantees, the government instigated a building programme, under the direction of Gen Brialmont, to fortify the strategically important cities of Antwerp, Liege and Namur.

Fortifications

In the years before the outbreak of the First World War the Belgian government instituted a programme of work to strengthen Brialmont's defences. It was hoped that this would deter any possible aggression by Germany, but its efforts were in vain. In August 1914 the German Imperial Army launched its Schlieffen Plan; an audacious attempt to wheel around the flank of the main French defences and capture Paris. German troops advanced through Belgium avoiding the fortifications, which were invested by subsequent waves of troops. Despite modernization the fortifications were not sturdy enough to withstand bombardment from modern ordnance and they crumbled under the fearful pounding from the huge German howitzers brought forward for the purpose. The failure of the great forts to withstand the German assault undermined the military's faith in the value of

such defences. However, this was restored later in the war following the battle of Verdun where the forts protecting the ancient city provided the backbone of the French defence.*

Determined to avoid a repeat of 1914 the Belgian government in the interwar period embarked on an ambitious building programme to create a series of fortifications that would deter her much larger neighbour from using Belgium as an avenue through which to attack France. Around Liege two main lines of defence were constructed: *Position Fortifiée de Liège* I and II. The former included the crowning glory of the Belgian defences, Fort Eben Emael, which dominated the Albert Canal. To the south, the city of Naumur was similarly defended and the defences of the port of Antwerp were strengthened. Some small-scale work was also undertaken to protect the exposed coastline, especially around the ports of Oostend and Zeebrugge.

Tanks

At much the same time the Belgian government decided that the army should be modernized. This programme included a plan to motorize the *Corps de Cavalerie* (Cavalry Corps). The tank chosen was

---

*The French forts had also been built by Brialmont, but had been strengthened with reinforced concrete that enabled them to better withstand the German shelling.

the Renault *Auto-Mitrailleuses de Combat (A.M.C) Modèle 1933 Type YR*, which was fitted with the APX1 turret with a 25mm gun. An order for twenty-five was placed but was subsequently cancelled after tests in France showed the tank to be unsatisfactory and production was stopped after the first batch of twelve had been completed.

In spite of the cancellation of the original order there was still a requirement for a cavalry tank and an order for twelve Renault *AMC Modèle 1935 Type R* ACG1s was placed (out of the twenty-five planned). The first of these was delivered in June 1937, but its arrival caused unease in government circles. Belgium had by now adopted a neutral stance and the delivery of tanks, especially from France, seemed to undermine that position. As a result, after the final batch of three was delivered in January 1938, the order was cancelled on the grounds that the French army had decided to procure the Somua 1935 model rather than the Renault ACG1.*

Meantime a separate order for twenty-five APX2B turrets was placed with *Ateliers de Puteaux* in France that were to be delivered in 1936. On delivery, work began to fit the Belgian 47mm 1936 model gun. The *Fonderie Royale de Canons* (FRC) or Royal Gun Foundry had little difficulty installing the main armament, but the 7.65mm Hotchkiss machine gun could not be fitted without reorganizing the turret. The left lateral periscope was moved towards the rear of the turret to make room for the machine gun and the hole left filled with armour plate. These modifications were made to twenty-three of the twenty-five turrets.[†] The two outstanding unmodified turrets were used to arm two concrete structures built at Sougné-Remouchamps, on the site of a fort that was no longer to be built.[‡]

The idea of using tank turrets as improvised fortifications was later adopted for coastal defence. With the cancellation of the order for the ACG1 it was decided to use the modified APX2B turrets in much the same way as those installed at Sougné-Remouchamps and thirteen turrets were mounted along the Belgian coast.[¶] The remaining ten turrets were fitted to the tanks, which were purchased from France in 1939.

APX2B Turret

The turret was formed by assembly of a cast body and laminated plates 25mm (1in) thick. On the rear face

there was a door, with two halves opening outwards. In the turret roof there was a second hatch that opened towards the front. The turret had two housings to take the main and coaxial gun. A small amount of ammunition was held in the turret itself including six armour piercing and six high explosive shells and five belts of ammunition for the MG. In addition there were five blocks each containing nine flares.

APX2B				
Turret statistics:				

Gun mantlet	Front	Side	Rear	Roof
–	25mm	25mm	17mm	14mm

Armour (thickness/angle):
Turret weight: 1,650kg (without weapons)

Weapon statistics:
Armament: 1 × FRC 47 mm 1936 model cannon
1 × Hotchkiss 7.65 mm light machine gun
Traverse: 360°

---

*Nine of the vehicles delivered were subsequently put in store at *Ateliers Carels* at Gand. In September 1939 eight of the tanks were restored and six took part in the fighting of May 1940. They did not perform well and only three remained on 28 May 1940.

[†] These modifications were still not found to be satisfactory and the FRC later decided to install Maxim light machine guns.

[‡] In 1931 money was released for building the *Position Fortifiée de Liege* 1 forts and as a result 30 hectares were purchased above the Amblève valley for Fort Sougné. Nothing happened until the middle of January 1935 when a company was contracted to carry out some deep drilling work. However, two weeks later the decision was taken to stop and all work ceased. The Defence Ministry spent the money that had been allocated for the project on mechanizing the cavalry. Belgium's return to neutrality and the desire of the government to fortify Belgium's southern border meant that the idea was revisited and a new study was undertaken early in 1936. Plans were finally agreed for the construction of Fort Sougné but only the turrets were installed.

[¶] The exact locations of all of the turrets is not known, but two were installed at Oostende, and one each at Mariakerke, Middelkerke, Lombardsijde, Bredenen, Den Haan, Zeebrugge, Blanghebergen, Heist and at Knokke.

Front view of one of the Belgian APX2B turrets mounted on a concrete shelter at Sougné-Remouchamps. The main and coaxial armaments have been removed. (Courtesy of F. Vernier)

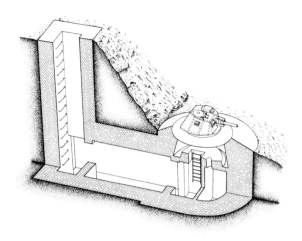

APX2B turret at Sougné-Remouchamps.

A view of the corridor that linked the access shaft and the chamber below the turret. The steel louvered door led to the integral ladder. (Courtesy of F. Vernier)

The shelters

The two shelters installed at *Heid des Gattes* near to the caves at Sougné-Remouchamps were classified as CS25 and CS A5 Bis* respectively. They were completely built into the rock and were identical in almost every respect. Access to the shelter was through a hatch that concealed a vertical shaft with integral ladder. At the bottom was a slightly offset steel louvered door that led to a corridor that was some 3m (10ft) long and 2m (6½ft) wide. This was home to a hand-operated ventilator, which provided fresh air and vented dangerous gases. At the end of the corridor was an airtight door that led to the

chamber below the turret. This was fitted with shelves and was where the ammunition was stored. The ammunition store could hold 96 armoured piercing shells and the same number of high explosive shells as well as 19 belts of MG ammunition and two drums of 24/31 R.Y.G. model 18I flares (120 in total).[†]

A ladder led from the store to the fighting compartment. At the very front of the shelter, under the turret, was a void which automatically collected spent cases and which was fitted with a vent to allow gases to escape via an airtight outlet flap. Above the fighting compartment was the turret that could rotate through 360 degrees. This was initially achieved by hand – 200 turns of the wheel were required for a single revolution. Later it was decided to add a motor, which enabled the turret to be rotated completely in less than two minutes. This required a power supply and as a result the shelter was connected to the civilian network. To ensure that the turret could operate independently an iron-nickel battery and a charging panel was fitted.

The tank turret was operated by a crew of five men: in the turret there was an NCO turret commander and gunner plus an assistant gunner, at the lower level there was a soldier preparing the ammunition whilst two men worked the ventilator.

*This prefix reflected the part of the defences where the structures had been built. In this case between Comblain and Sougné so CS.
[†] The shelter also had a Lebel rifle with 300 rounds of ammunition.

Because the tank turret shelters had no room to accommodate the permanent garrison, it was decided to build two guardrooms. These were constructed just prior to the outbreak of war in August 1939. The guardroom of the CS25 shelter was built into the ground using local stone topped by a reinforced concrete slab. This roof was covered over with earth to provide both added protection and for camouflage. Because the shelter was partially buried, special arrangements were made to prevent the walls from becoming damp. The guardroom had a main area serving as a rest room for the garrison, which was equipped with a table, four chairs and a coal-fired stove. Two further rooms, both accessed externally, were provided one to store coal and the other housing the latrine. The two windows of the building were covered with wire mesh to provide some protection against enemy fire, especially grenades. In total the structure cost 49,703 francs.

The guardroom of the CS A5 Bis shelter was built with sandstone and had a tiled roof in order to match the local building style. Like the CS25 guardroom it had a main living area, coal store and latrine. A tank was installed to hold rainwater. This meant that the drinking water requirement, which was difficult to supply because of the shelter's hillside position, could be reduced. The shelter cost 44,726 francs to build. Like the main fighting positions, the two guardrooms were supplied with electricity towards the beginning of 1940.

The thirteen turrets mounted on bunkers along the coast were broadly the same as those at Sougné-Remouchamps. Access to the shelter was though at hatch at the rear. This led to a vertical shaft fitted with rungs, which enabled the crew to descend to the munitions store below and to gain access to the fighting compartment directly below the turret. A platform for the crew enabled them to operate the weapons.

The turrets were mounted on a circular base plate that was secured to the main structure with bolts. The bunker was constructed from reinforced concrete, which was often faced with stone or brick to help it merge in with the background. The base structure was set into the sea wall so that only the turret was visible and camouflage paint schemes and other methods of breaking up the outline of the turret were also used to make the position as inconspicuous as possible. The

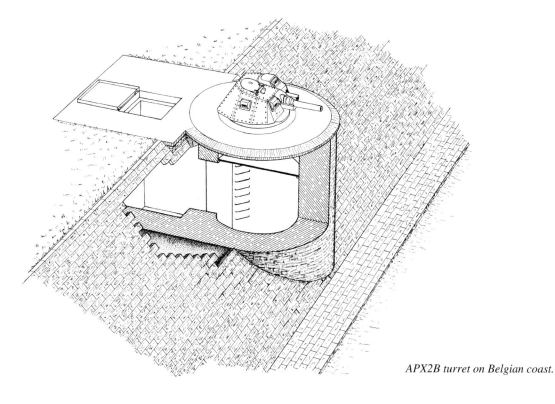

APX2B turret on Belgian coast.

turrets at Sougné-Remouchamps were camouflaged with wire netting covered with strips of raffia.

In Action

The title of this section is something of a misnomer, since none of the turrets that were installed were actually involved in any fighting. At the time of the German invasion in May 1940 the turrets at Sougné-Remouchamps were manned by men of the *3e escadron du 1er Lanciers* under Col B. E. M. Deleuze. The turrets were abandoned when the unit was forced to retreat toward Grâce-Berleur. The turrets mounted on the coast had an equally inauspicious service record, designed as they were to protect against a seaborne invasion that never came.

One of the APX2B turrets that were installed along the Belgian coast. This example has been camouflaged with a brick pattern in keeping with its surroundings. The turret was located at Den Haan, Belgium. (Alain van Geeteruyen)

Another APX2B turret that was positioned to protect the Belgian coast. This example was located at Lombardsijde, and was incorporated in the coastal batterie Ramien. Just visible in the background are barbed wire entanglements which stretch the length of the beach. (Alain van Geeteruyen)

They were manned by *11e Batterie du Ier Groupe du 5e Régiment d'Artillerie d'Armée* under Maj Chomé and were abandoned on 28 May 1940 without ever having been used.

Postscript

There is little evidence of the tank turrets today. Those installed along the coast were removed after the war with one now on display at the Belgium tank museum. At Fort Sougné it is possible to see one of the two APX turrets. However, the main armament and machine gun have been removed.[3]

FRANCE

In the immediate aftermath of the First World War Germany was impotent and posed no threat to European peace. Her armed forces were reduced or scrapped, the Rhineland was occupied and de-militarized, and the country was saddled with huge reparations. Secure in the knowledge that there was no immediate risk of invasion, France had no plans to fortify the border with her historic enemy. As the years passed, however, the situation changed. A comprehensive disarmament treaty proved elusive and in 1926 Britain removed her troops from the Rhineland.* In this new environment France no longer felt quite so assured and in that same year the government sanctioned the construction of a line of fortifications along the border with Germany, work on which began 1929.

Fortifications

This new line of defences was christened the Maginot Line, after the Minister for War, and was to stretch the entire length of the border with Germany.[†] Initially there was some debate about the form that these defences should take, but eventually it was decided to build a thin line of powerful forts. The backbone of the line was formed by the so-called *ouvrages*. These were large artillery casemates served by a subterranean network of tunnels, some fitted with light railways, and other facilities including generators, ammunition stores, living and sleeping quarters and even hospitals. These *ouvrages* were

reinforced with an array of smaller shelters for troops, anti-tank guns and machine guns. Among these smaller positions were a number of emplaced tank turrets and, on the same lines, a series of specially designed armoured cupolas.

In the late nineteenth century, Grüson of Germany had developed the *Fahrpanzer*, a light, transportable turret for a rapid-firing 5.3cm gun. This had been adopted by the Imperial Army to supplement the defences of their *Feste* or fortifications. But Germany was not alone in considering the usefulness of such a weapon. In France, in February 1890, the *Comités de l'Artillerie et du Génie*[‡] considered the production of a transportable cupola, similar to that made by Grüson. Indeed, the foundry at Le Creusot went so far as to undertake a pilot study. At about the same time, a prototype 57mm cannon was produced by Hotchkiss, but tests were inconclusive and it was not adopted. In 1907 the idea was revived with a plan for a transportable cupola for a machine gun. However, in June 1909, the *Haute Commission des Places Fortes*[¶] decided that it no longer considered there to be a requirement and the project was cancelled.

During the First World War a number of Grüson turrets were captured by the French and their usefulness assessed. The upshot of these tests was that in the interwar period the idea of a mobile armoured hood for a machine gun was considered once again. These were intended for the gaps in the *Régions Fortifées* or Fortified Regions, in particular for the machine-gun companies of the fortress infantry regiments, and for field positions, which were to be constructed when mobilization took place. The studies resulted in the development of the *Tourelle Démontable Modèle* 1935.

This was constructed in two sections: a fixed part that was intended to be placed in the ground, and a movable part. The structure could be transported manually and was designed to be partially buried, with only the turret appearing above ground. This was capable of withstanding a direct hit from anything up to 25mm in calibre. Access to the shelter was via a

---

*France retained a presence until 1930.
[†]And later also included the border with Italy together with works on Corsica.
[‡]Artillery and Engineering Committee.
[¶]High Commission on Fortresses.

hatch in the turret or via a rear door let into the upper section of the fixed part.

The turret was fitted with a pivot mount designed to accommodate a Hotchkiss machine gun. An armoured sheath protected the barrel of the machine gun from enemy fire. Observation was possible by means of a Type K periscope or observation slits. A fairly sophisticated aiming system made it possible to use the weapon at night.

To allow for the differing topography two types of turret were developed, a normal 150mm (6in) dome for flat terrain and a higher 250mm (10in) dome for uneven terrain. Subsequently, a height of 190mm (7in) became standard, regardless of where they were to be located. A few minor improvements were also made to the *Modèle* 35, with the new improved version known as the *Modèle* 1937.

During peacetime, the turrets were usually stored in depots belonging to the engineers, but on mobilization they were collected by the units to which they had been allocated. These units provided the weapons, transported them to their destination, and installed them in a hastily dug hole. According to tests carried out at Châlons in 1934, it took three and a half hours for four men to install a turret. This arrangement was not found to be particularly satisfactory and from 1935 standard concrete positions were constructed to accommodate the turrets. Sometimes the turrets were incorporated into a larger structure, or were provided with a shelter for the crew.

A number of turrets were to be permanently positioned. These were to be concealed from the enemy and protected from acts of sabotage inside specially built sheds. However, although a number of turrets were installed before mobilization, especially on the more heavily fortified parts of the line where it was easier to observe them, it does not seem that the sheds were built. In the *Nord département*, the turrets were not installed until mobilization with some of the concrete structures sealed with a removable concrete cap.

By 26 May 1938, 355 turrets had been built (of which 353 had been delivered to the regions and two

Another tourelle démontable, which was installed in the Maginot Line. A revetted trench leads to the entrance of the position. This example formed part of the defences at Schoenenberg and can still be visited today. (Courtesy of Jean-Louis Burtscher at www.Lignemaginot.com)

A tourelle démontable which formed part of the Maginot Line defences and which is still visible today at the small Rohrbach work. Often these turrets were installed in prepared concrete positions, but this one is a simple fieldwork. (Svein Wiiger Olsen)

retained for study), ninety were being manufactured (for delivery between the end of 1938 and May 1939) and forty were on order, of which thirty were to have a raised dome* for the Alps. The technical instruction dated 23rd February 1939 stated that the 1935 model turret was numbered up to 495, and the 1937 model from 496.

In 1938 plans were considered for an armoured hood mounting a 25mm anti-tank gun that was proof against 47mm weapons. Drawings were produced in early 1938 and there were plans for a prototype to be built later in the year with a view to producing 300 units, but war intervened before it could be brought into production.[4]

Tanks

The Renault FT light tank was developed in the First World War and for its time the tank's configuration was unique, mounting, as it did, a fully traversable turret. This, together with other innovations, earned the FT the distinction of being the first modern tank. Its innovative design and diminutive size meant it was produced in large numbers and exported around the world and also, was widely copied. In the years following the end of the First World War it was employed in numerous smaller conflicts including the Spanish Civil War.

FT17

The FT17's position as the mainstay of the French tank corps was eventually surrendered to the new

TSF tank used as observation point (1937)
Allocation of FT tanks to the fortified regions

Regions	TSF tanks delivered in August 1934	FT TSF blockhaus delivered in Sept. 1937
1st RM	–	31
2nd RM	–	35
6th RM	16	20
20th RM	6	20
7th RM	5	15
Totals	27	121

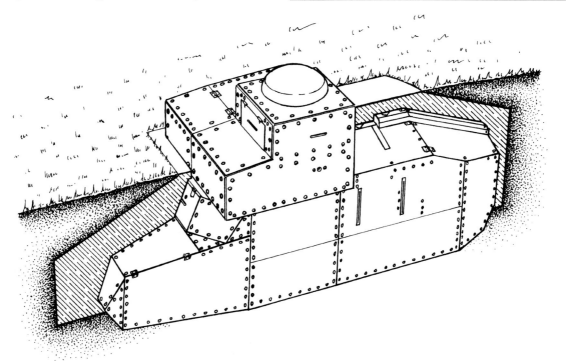

Renault FT TSF tank in the Maginot Line.

*To allow firing in particularly difficult conditions.

The Char signal TSF was a radio tank version of the FT17. The 'turret' was used by the French as an armoured observation post in the Maginot Line defences. This example is still visible today at Fermont, near Longuyon. (Courtesy of Jean-Louis Burtscher at www. Lignemaginot.com)

Turrets from obsolete FT17 tanks were also used to strengthen the Maginot Line defences. This example is still visible today at the small Rohrbach work. (Author)

generation of tanks including the Renault R35, Hotchkiss H35 and H39 and the Somua S35. A number were still used to equip front line units but most were relegated to second line duties or were placed in stores. The decision to mothball the bulk of the FT17s coincided with the study to assess the value of armoured hoods and as a cost-effective, short-term expedient, it was decided to use surplus FT17 turrets as fixed fortifications.

As early as August 1934 tanks were being delivered to the different fortified regions for emplacement. Initially these were mainly Renault FT TSF tanks. This was specially designed to mount a radio with the turret replaced by a fixed armoured cab for an observer. The whole of the tank, minus its engine, track system and other non-essential equipment, was buried in the ground so that only the armoured cab was visible. Sometimes the tanks were encased in concrete, but others were simply buried in the ground. Alternatively, the armoured cab of the tank was mounted on a concrete casemate. Positions were also constructed using standard FT17 tanks buried and encased in concrete, which were used either as observation points* like the TSF, or as machine-gun posts, the latter being found particularly in the Sarre Defensive Sector. In the *Nord département* turrets were also installed on small concrete blocks.[†] The use of tank turrets was seen as a cheap, though not as effective, alternative to the specially designed CORF[‡] observation points.[¶]

---

*These turrets had their machine gun or cannon replaced with an armoured plate with a small aperture.
[†] One of these turrets, recovered at Villecloye, in the Montmédy Fortified Sector, can be seen at the Musée de Fermont.
[‡] *Commission d'Organization des Régions Fortifées* or Commission for the Organization of the Fortified Regions.
[¶] Turret mantlets from FT17 tanks were also removed and reused as machine-gun firing slots for casemates.

*Renault FT17
tank in the
Maginot Line.*

FT 17

Turret statistics: *
Octagonal or Omnibus turret (sheet or armour plate)
Armour (thickness/angle):

Gun mantlet	Front	Side	Rear	Roof
16mm	16mm/77°	16mm/75°	16mm/75°	8mm/25 & 0°

Berliet or Round Omnibus turret (cast and forged)

Armour (thickness/angle):

Gun mantlet	Rounded plate	Roof (cast top section)
16mm	22mm	16mm

Diameter (turret ring): 106cm

Weapon statistics:
Armament: 1 × 37mm SA Canon or 1 × 7.5mm Reibel Model 1931 MG
Traverse: 360° hand operated
Elevation: +35° −20°

---

* Three turret types were developed:
1. Cast turret with machine gun.
2. Renault octagonal riveted turret. This was introduced to overcome production difficulties with the original cast turret.
3. Berliet designed a turret based upon the original prototype, but made it in two sections with the top section being cast and the lower section constructed from rounded steel plate. The turret was much heavier than the octagonal turret but it was more heavily armoured and gave much better protection. The turret was fitted with a 37mm gun.

3 The Second World War

Part 1 – Typology

During the campaign in France and the Low Countries and later during the invasion of the Soviet Union the Germans encountered tank turrets used as fixed fortifications. Few in number and often outflanked, these defences did little to stem the German *blitzkrieg* and were largely ignored by troops in the vanguard. Later the structures were examined in more detail and their potential assessed, but at that time, despite the undoubted merits of using turrets in this way, the idea had no practical application and was simply noted and filed for future reference. At much the same time the German military, motivated by the experiences gained in the early campaigns, instituted a much more general review of the effectiveness of fortifications. One of the findings of the study concerned the shortcomings of steel observation and weapons cloches, which had been used extensively in the West Wall. Engagements with positions of the Maginot Line, albeit limited, and subsequent tests on these fortifications, demonstrated that these cloches were vulnerable to direct fire. Moreover experience had shown that they were expensive to produce and consumed valuable raw materials that might be better used in the production of other weapons.

The upshot of this review was the development of the *ringstand* or open observation position. This had many similarities to the Italian *tobruk* that had first been encountered by the British and Commonwealth forces in Libya at Bardia and Tobruk (hence its name) and although it is not clear whether the *ringstand* was based on the Italian model, it was given the same name by the Allies. These observation posts were integrated into larger shelters, but were also constructed as individual positions. One of the most widely produced was the *Ringstand* 58c. This was essentially an eight-sided construction with circular opening in the centre that was level with the ground. The opening could accommodate a light mortar or could be fitted with a ring to mount a machine gun. Alternatively, the position could be used without alteration. An entrance at the rear led to a revetted trench which provided safe access to the shelter.

A later model, the *Bauform* 67, which was based on the *Ringstand* 58c and whose layout it adopted, was designed to mount tank turrets.* The development of this shelter, although not the direct result of Hitler's decision to invade the Soviet Union, was undoubtedly heavily influenced by this resolution, and not simply because the Red Army made extensive use of this expedient in the Molotov and Stalin Lines, although these turrets did enjoy some success. More significantly, the fighting on the Eastern Front forced Germany to begin fortifying the coast of occupied Europe and, importantly, led to a major rethink about tank design. This resulted in the development of a new generation of fighting vehicles and at the same time the creation of a large stockpile of obsolete German models.

The decision to invade the Soviet Union gave Britain a valuable respite and although in no position to embark upon a full-scale invasion of Continental Europe it could launch small-scale commando raids. To counter this threat work began in December 1941 to fortify key installations on the coast and in September 1942, following the abortive landing at Dieppe the previous month, Hitler ordered an extensive construction programme to turn Europe into an impregnable fortress. The greatest effort was concentrated on those sections of the coastline most

---

*The main differences were that the access corridor included a recess for ammunition racks and the combat area had a slightly larger diameter at 1.97m (6ft).

vulnerable to attack and these permanent defences were supplemented by smaller works including tank turrets mounted on concrete shelters. In more remote areas the defences were less numerous and emplaced tank turrets, because they were largely self-contained and because they offered all-round fire were widely used.*

The turrets that were to be used on these shelters initially came from captured tanks, principally from France, but following the invasion of the Soviet Union, a new source of turrets became available and these were not simply taken from captured Red Army tanks. Soon after Operation *Barbarossa* was launched the Germans encountered the first T34 tank, arguably the best medium tank of the Second World War. Almost overnight, the T34 rendered obsolete the mainstay of the *Panzer* divisions (*Panzer* I and II and Czech 35(t) and 38(t) tanks) that had swept all before them in the campaigns of 1939 and 1940. Steps were now taken to design and build a new tank that it was hoped would restore German superiority. This ultimately led to the development of the Panther medium tank that first appeared at the battle of Kursk in 1943.[†] The introduction of the Panther, together with the Panzer VI Tiger, saw the gradual phasing out of the older models which soon joined those that had been captured in the opening campaigns of the war. These tanks were now either relegated to second line duties, or had their turrets removed and their chassis used as an improvised anti-tank or self-propelled gun platform.

The huge array of tank turrets now available for use

Steps leading from the entrance to the main fighting compartment of a panzerstellung at Aalborg airfield, Denmark. (A. Johansen)

Another view of the tank turret position at Aalborg airfield, Denmark. This shows the opening into which the tank turret would be mounted. Just to the right it is possible to see one of the ammunition niches. (A. Johansen)

as fixed fortifications prompted a review of the of the numbering system and the single *Bauform 67* model was split into twenty or so *Bauformen* numbered from 231 to 251, although the original designation was still used right until the end of the war as a generic descriptor. The first twelve designs,[‡] from 231 to 241, covered obsolete German turrets.[¶] The remainder, *Bauformen* 242–251, broadly dealt with captured turrets, although included within the series were designs for both Panzer III and IV turrets and for two prototype turrets which had been developed for the VK3001 and 3601. Bookending these series were *Bauformen* 226–227 and 259–260, which dealt with specially designed armoured hoods and armoured car turrets respectively.

Despite the large number of turret types utilized, generally speaking each shelter had the same layout, although the precise dimensions varied according to the type of turret mounted. The shelters were to have walls and ceilings constructed from reinforced concrete 40cm (15in) thick and a floor 20cm (7½in) thick, although this varied according to the weapon

---

*In the interwar period Belgium had found tank turrets used in this way to be a cheap and effective way of protecting the coast and these were subsequently absorbed into the 'Atlantic Wall'.
[†] So impressed were the Germans by the T34 that the initial design for the Panther was almost a carbon copy of the Soviet tank.
[‡] Twelve because *Bauform* 232 had 'a' and 'b' versions.
[¶] Exceptionally *Bauform* 235 was for the French R35.

mounted and geological conditions.* The shelters were thus proof against light anti-tank and anti-aircraft weapons and machine gun fire. The internal dimensions of the position were formulated so that, as a bear minimum, an average man could stand upright, but, save for a stove, this was the only concession to the crew's comfort. It was not possible to fit gas proof doors or a ventilation system because there simply were not the resources to supply such huge quantities. Nevertheless, units were encouraged to make improvisations to ensure that the shelters were proof against such attacks.

Regardless of the fact that standardized designs had been developed and the structures were to be built from reinforced concrete, they were designated as field works rather than as permanent fortifications. As such, the designs were to be used as a simple template and the actual structure was to be built according to local conditions, hence the wide variety of structures that can be found. Moreover, along the Atlantic Wall, in addition to the standard designs, a number of local designs were used. A note from *Der Chef der Heeresrüstung und Befehlshaber des Ersatzheeres* (the Chief of Military Armaments and Commander of the Reserve Army) to the *General der Pioniere und Festung* (General in Charge of Engineering Works and Fortifications) in October 1943 made clear that no formal documentation existed for the construction of shelters to mount the Renault FT17, the Renault R35 and the Somua S35 turret. These were to be installed, it explained, according to local instructions issued by the *Inspekteur für die Landesbefestigung West* (Inspector of Fortifications West).[1] The designs were often inspired by *Bauform* 67, or reinforced versions thereof, or were commonly constructed in a simple U-shape.

As well as the specially designed *Bauformen* and the local variants, turrets were also integrated into larger permanent fortifications like the *Doppelschartenstände*. These bunkers were fitted with a single 5cm KwK but had a double embrasure that enabled the crew to enfilade both flanks. The tank turrets were fitted at the front of the emplacement to cover the beach or at the back to provide protection at the rear.[†] Plans were also drawn up to mount turrets on pre-prepared wooden shelters and temporary wooden pedestals.[‡] Initially, these wooden structures were only suitable for mounting the smaller

A *Doppelschartenstand* mounting a 5cm KwK at Vasterville plage. The gun could enfilade both flanks and the tank turret, just visible at the front, could sweep the beach to the front. (Service Historique Marine)

(and lighter) turrets. So in October 1944 there were only plans to mount the following: *F Pz DT* 4803, 4804, 4806 and 4808; *Panzer* I, *Panzer* II, *Panzer* 35(t) and *Panzer* 38(t) turrets. Later, more substantial shelters were developed and ultimately a wooden shelter for a Panther turret was designed and used.[2]

The turrets for the different shelters were supplied by *Oberkommando des Heeres* (OKH) and were, insofar as was possible, ready for installation. The turrets were mounted on their base plates and were supplied with all the necessary accessories and internal fittings, which were packed in cases and dispatched separately. The turrets and cases of accessories were given unique identification marks and numbers so that there was no danger of a mix up. All the necessary documents, including construction drawings, templates (to ensure that the anchor bolts were correctly positioned on the shelters) and anchor bolts, were supplied by *OKH Inspektion der Festungen* (Fortress Inspectorate). When finished with these documents were to be returned to the respective *Heimat Festungspionierpark* (Home Fortifications Engineering Depot) together with any fittings that had not been used. Finally, operating instructions for the turrets were also supplied in the form of D Regulations (D1600, D1601 and so on).[3]

---

*For example the concrete thickness could be reduced when the shelter was built in rock.
[†] See section on *Sockellafetten* for further details.
[‡] In 1942 a simple log shelter mounting a T34 turret was included in *Bildheft Neuzeitlicher Stellungsbau*.

The turrets that were to be mounted on shelters were either taken from the tank largely unaltered or were modified so that they were better suited for their new role. Often foreign turrets had their weapons removed and replaced with a German model to simplify the provision of ammunition. Exceptionally, where the turrets were to be employed using machine guns (MG34 or MG42) rather than their original weaponry, these were to be supplied by the local unit. These modified turrets were referred to as *Festungspanzerdrehturm* (F Pz DT).

The turrets were mounted on the various bunkers by means of a simple turret race affixed to the bunker or by an armoured plate fitted with a turret race. Sometimes this was simply the top section of the tank from which the turret had been taken. The turrets were rotated manually and the targeting system (as with a lot of bunkers) utilized a simple 'dial' system or images of key landmarks (lighthouse, churches, houses, and so on) with their approximate ranges usually painted on the inside of the bunker.

Because the tank turrets were static, camouflage was essential, especially from the air. Indeed, the design authority stipulated that the same amount of effort should be expended on camouflage as was invested in protection. A suitable camouflage paint scheme was to be applied and an attempt made to disguise the position by changing the silhouette. Mounts were welded to the turret sides into which metal rods were to be inserted. These were cut to different lengths, to avoid giving the impression of symmetry, and were to have wire stretched from each

and a camouflage net or matting attached. Care had to be taken to ensure that the camouflage did not impair the operation of the weapons or the observation from the turret. Moreover, it was stressed in the guidance that when camouflaging the structure against observation from the air that the turret was not made more conspicuous at ground level. As such, any covers were to be kept as low as possible and certainly not greater than 30 degrees.

In order to make the turrets less conspicuous and to provide further protection, the shelters were, where possible, to be buried in the ground. The resulting spoil was to be piled irregularly around the turret so as not to look too uniform and draw attention to the position. If all round operation was not required it was also suggested that the spoil be heaped to the rear to break up the turret outline. Alternatively the turret could be installed below the skyline so that it did not stand out against the horizon. The installation instructions also stressed that the turrets were not to be built on or near prominent landmarks that would draw attention to the position, although it was recognized that this might mean compromising the turret's all round operation.

Where possible the ground immediately surrounding the turret was to be strengthened to counteract the suction caused by the gas pressure when the weapon was fired. This *sogplatte*, or suction plate, could be made from concrete, bricks or in some instances by simply using a wire mesh. If concrete was used it had to be roughed up to ensure that it was not too conspicuous.

Because the tank turrets were static it was important that they were heavily camouflaged like this Panzer 38(t), which was installed on the island of Corsica. (Imperial War Museum)

In all, some twenty-four different tank turrets were used or were considered suitable for use as fixed fortifications, as were two armoured car turrets together with a further three armoured hoods specially designed for the role. The turrets were taken from German tanks and from captured armoured fighting vehicles (thirteen in total) from four different nations. The specifications of each of the different turret types is given below, together with commentary where possible.[4]

CAPTURED TANK TURRETS

British

After the British withdrawal from the Continent at Dunkirk in May 1940, the Germans captured nearly 200 British Cruiser tanks and a number of A12 Matildas.[5] However, despite the widespread use of captured French tank turrets, none of these appear to have been used to strengthen the Atlantic Wall. Later the turrets from a number of tanks captured by the *Afrika Korps* in the desert campaign and after the abortive Dieppe landings of August 1942 were used as improvised fixed fortifications, but the practice was not widespread. The reason for this is unclear, but one possibility is the difficulty in sourcing ammunition.

Churchill Mk III

The first action that the Churchill tank took part in was Operation *Jubilee*, the amphibious assault on the French port of Dieppe. On 19 August 1942 thirty tanks of the 14th Canadian Armoured Regiment (the Calgarys) with their supporting infantry were sent ashore in a rehearsal for a later full-scale invasion of occupied Europe. The operation was a disaster. One of the tanks of the regimental headquarters did not leave its landing craft and two others sank in deep water. The remaining twenty-seven struggled ashore and a number managed to clear the sea wall and reach the promenade, but with the exit routes blocked they went no further. After some fierce fighting and with no prospect of relief or evacuation the crews of the tanks fought an heroic rear guard action before surrendering.

Only a few of the tanks were disabled by enemy fire, most had lost tracks or became bogged down in the shingle and were captured intact, providing valuable intelligence for the Germans. One Mk III (Blondie) was restored to full running order and was tested by the Germans (and was not found to be particularly impressive when compared to the modern German and Russian models). Other tanks were used for target practice to assess the effectiveness of German anti-tank weapons.

At least one of the Mk III turrets mounting the larger 6-pounder was used by the Germans as an improvised pillbox, which was located at *Stützpunkt* 2, plateau d'Epremesnil, Montivilliers la Rive near Le Havre. It is not believed that any other turrets were used in this way, probably because of the lack of ammunition. Relatively few tanks were involved in the attack and those that were sent ashore were a mixture of Churchill Mark Is and Mark IIIs (as well as three special flamethrowers), which mounted 2-pounder and 6-pounder guns respectively. But most significantly during the landing, the Calgary Regiment expended much, if not all, of its ammunition.

In an interesting twist, 'Cougar', one of the first Churchills ashore at Dieppe, was engaged by a dug-in French tank used as a pillbox. Recognizing the danger, the crew of the Churchill reacted immediately. 'At once the turret swung round, and a two-pounder round smashed its way into the enemy machine. There was an explosion, and the French tank disintegrated, fragments of torn metal flying high into the air.'[6] If this is correct, Cougar can be credited with destroying the first German *panzerstellung*. But it was not the regiment's last engagement with this type of fortification, because a little under two years later the Calgarys came up against emplaced Panther turrets in the Hitler Line in Italy. These were an altogether different proposition (*see* Chapter 3, Part 3 *below*).

Matilda

During the course of 1941 the British and Commonwealth forces in the Western Desert launched a series of attacks against the German *Afrika Korps*. These were unsuccessful and the enemy captured a large number of Matilda tanks. Some of these were used against their previous owner in later engagements but others were seemingly dug in and used as improvised strong points in the defensive line around the Halfaya Pass and Capuzzo. This expedient might have been

A number of Churchill tanks were captured after the ill-fated Dieppe raid of 1942. One of the Mark III turrets with its 6-pounder gun was installed as part of the defences of Stützpunkt 2, Plateau d'Epremesnil, Montivilliers la Rive, France. (Unknown)

Churchill Mk III

Turret statistics:
Armour (thickness/angle):

Gun mantlet	Front	Side	Rear	Roof
–	88mm/0°	76mm/0°	76mm/0°	19mm/90°

Turret weight: – Weapon height: *circa* 380mm
Overall height: *circa* 830mm Diameter: *circa* 1,670mm

Weapon statistics:
Armament: 1 × 6 pdr. OQF
1 × BESA 7.92mm
Traverse: 360°
Elevation: +20° −12.5°

Locations:

Atlantic/West Wall	Total
1	1

adopted because the Matildas had been damaged beyond repair, but equally it might have been because the Germans had insufficient diesel to keep the tanks running – their own vehicles ran on petrol. The fluid nature of the fighting and the harsh desert environ-ment also undoubtedly influenced the decision to use the tanks in the hull down position rather than con-structing a concrete shelter. To dig the tanks in was relatively quick and only required men and shovels.

A British Matilda tank turret. which was captured by the Germans in the fighting in North Africa and emplaced at the Halfaya Pass. Two British soldiers are removing the unused ammunition. (Imperial War Museum)

French

In May 1940 when Hitler launched his attack in the west, France was able to field over 3,000 tanks of varying designs (excluding instructional or experimental vehicles and vehicles that had been mothballed). A number of these tanks were destroyed in the month long campaign before France finally surrendered, but many others were captured intact. These were evaluated and in spite of the precipitate collapse of the French forces, it was recognized that a number of the tanks were as good as, if not better than, their German counterparts.* These tanks were, with a few alterations (for example, the replacement of the semi-spherical commanders hatch with a split hatch in common with other German models) absorbed into second line units and used for internal security tasks. This ensured that the mainstay of the *Panzer* divisions was not diverted to secondary tasks but was available for the next operation – the invasion of Britain.

The failure of Göring's *Luftwaffe* to defeat the RAF in the Battle of Britain led to the postponement and ultimately the cancellation of Operation *Seelöwe* (*Sealion*) and instead Hitler turned his attention east. Notwithstanding the successes in Poland and the west this decision caused a certain amount of trepidation amongst the German High Command not least because Napoleon's all-conquering *Grande Armée* had come unstuck in Russia a little over a hundred years earlier. Hitler was not swayed by these concerns and contended that 'you only had to kick the door in and the whole rotten edifice [of Communist rule]

---

*At the time of the German invasion of France, the Somua S35 was rated by some as the best tank in the world.

Matilda

Turret statistics:

Armour (thickness/angle): Cast turret

Gun mantlet	Front	Side	Rear	Roof
–	75mm	75mm/0°	75mm/0°	20mm/90°

Overall height: 990mm   Diameter: 1,217mm

Weapon statistics:

Armament: 1 × 2 pdr OQF
1 × BESA 7.92mm MG
Sight: No 33 Mark II
Traverse: 360°
Elevation: +20° −20°
Range: 1,830 metres
Muzzle velocity: 853 m/sec
Penetration performance: 915m = 40mm

Locations:

Western Desert	Total
2	2*

would come crashing down'. Persauded but not convinced, the High Command pressed ahead with plans for Operation *Barbarossa*, but it was clear that if the *Wehrmacht* was to prevail every available resource, including captured *materiel*, would need to be employed. Already the best of the captured French tanks had been assimilated, but the remainder were considered heavy and slow, designed as they had been for infantry support rather than *blitzkrieg,* or were, like the First World War vintage FT17, largely obsolete. As such many had their turrets removed and were transformed into munitions tractors or driver training vehicles or were modified to mount larger anti-tank guns or light field howitzers. This freed up a large number of turrets that were placed in store, but which were soon to enjoy a new lease of life as improvised strong points.

It is unclear exactly how many French turrets were used in this way, but nearly 300 are quoted as being available for use.[†] The majority of these were taken from the Renault FT17, the Renault R35 and the Hotchkiss H35, both of which were fitted with the APX R turret. A limited number of turrets were also taken from the Somua S35 and the Char B1 bis tanks and a further forty-one turrets from various other models were available for installation as fixed fortifications, although official sources stated that none of them were released for use.[7]

The turrets that were released were employed exclusively along the Atlantic Wall and were used largely unaltered. Certainly they generally retained their original weaponry, although the designation was changed to more closely align with German nomenclature (see Table 1 below). The turrets were sometimes mounted on shelters derived from the

---

*There are photographs of at least two different turrets used as fixed fortifications.

[†] Official sources state that relatively few (less than thirty) were released for use, but photographic evidence gives the lie to this statement. Report dated 5 May 1944 in T. Jentz, '*Panzerstellung* – Part Three', *AFV News*, Vol. 9 No.5 (September 1974), pp.10–11.

U-Shaped Shelter – French APXR turret mounted on a reinforced concrete shelter.

Bauform 67 and indeed a standard design (*Bauform* 235) was developed for the Renault R35, although it is unclear whether any drawings were completed or structures built. Usually French turrets were mounted on non-standard positions which were constructed according to local instructions issued by the *Inspekteur für die Landesbefestigung West*.[8] There was a basic U-shaped design and variations thereon, (see above) or, on occasions, the whole tank was simply buried in its entirety so that just the turret was visible. A compromise between this and a complete concrete shelter was also developed and in many respects was similar to the expedient adopted by the French in the Maginot Line. The hull of an FT17, minus its running gear, was buried in the ground and encased in concrete. The French turrets were also

integrated into larger bunker designs such as the *Doppelschartenstand* mounting a 5cm KwK.* Finally, in a last desperate attempt to deter a possible invasion, tanks were simply stationed on the coast.

Char B1 bis
Approximately 365 Char B1 bis had been built by Renault before the outbreak of war. A number of these were captured intact by the Germans following the defeat of France and their potential usefulness was appraised. It was concluded that although the Char B1 bis was a very sophisticated tank, its poor performance (it had a top speed of just 28km/h) and the limitations of the one-man turret meant that it was

---

*See section on *Sockellafetten* for further details.

Table 1 Turret armament and German designation

APX1CE	Somua S35	47mm SA35	47mm KwK35(f) L/34
APX 4	Char B1 bis		
APX R	Hotchkiss/Renault	37mm SA38	37mm KwK38(f) L/33
	Hotchkiss H35	37mm SA18 and SA18 M37	37mm KwK18(f) L/21 or 37mm KwK144(f)
	Renault R35		
Cast/Rivetted	Renault FT17		

Note: All the turrets were fitted with the 7.5mm Reibel Model 1931 machine gun, which was given various designations: 7.5mm MAC31(f), 7.5mm MG Modell 31 or MG 311(f)*.

A view of one of the U-shaped shelters used to mount captured French tank turrets. These were exclusively employed along the Atlantikwall. The imprint for the base plate is just visible around the opening at the top. (Maciej Sledzinski)

since German records make no explicit reference to them but it is assumed that the number is well into double figures.[‡] In addition to these, a number of tanks were simply positioned at key locations on the coast as improvised strong points.

FT17

Other Designation: F.Pz.DT4807

The Renault FT light tank was developed in the First World War and uniquely mounted a fully traversable turret. Its innovative design and diminutive size meant it was produced in large numbers and exported around the world and was widely copied. During the interwar period the FT17 was gradually phased out of service with the French Army and as has been seen a number of turrets were used to strengthen the defences of the Maginot Line.[¶] Yet even at the outbreak of the Second World War 536 were still

only suitable for second line duties.[†] A number of tanks had their turrets removed to become driver training vehicles (*Panzerkampfwagen* B-2 (f) *Fahrschulefahrzeug*),[9] while a further sixteen tanks were fitted with 10.5cm field howitzers as a self-propelled gun (10.5cm leFH18/3 (Sf) *auf Geschützwagen* B-2(f).

It is difficult to say with any certainty how many turrets were available for use as fixed fortifications

---

*Where a machine gun was fitted to the FT17 this was the main armament.

[†] A number were sent to the Channel Islands to serve as a mobile reserve against any potential invasion. R. Heaume, 'Panzers in Guernsey', *Channel Islands Occupation Review* (1979), pp.38–42.

[‡] It might be that these turrets were absorbed into the number of Somua S35 turrets quoted as being available, the two being broadly the same – *see* section on Somua S35.

[¶] *See* Chapter 2 – Interwar.

Char B1 bis

Turret statistics:
Armour (thickness/angle): APX4 cast turret

Gun mantlet	Front	Side	Rear	Roof
56mm/round	56mm/0°	46mm/22.5°	46mm/22.5°	30mm/72.5–90°

Weapon statistics:
Armament: 1 × 47mm SA35
                   1 × 7.5mm Reibel Model 1931 machine gun (this was mounted coaxially behind a separate
                   mantlet giving it limited independent traverse +/-10°)

Sight: Rotating commander's cupola fitted with periscope binoculars and two episcopes. Telescopic sight in
machine gun mounting, common to both guns. Two episcopes in turret sides. Sighting vane externally on turret roof.

Traverse: 360° (manual)
Elevation: +18° −18°
Muzzle velocity: 733 m/sec

A French Char B1 bis tank used as a strong point to defend a beach on the France-Belgium border. The installation was undoubtedly rushed since no effort has been made to bury the body of the tank. It was captured by Canadian forces in September 1944. (Canadian National Archives)

being used to equip French armoured units and some saw action in the fighting of May 1940.* A further 1,168 tanks in various states of repair were either in store or in use for airfield protection and were captured by the Germans when France capitulated. Those that were serviceable were used for second line duties in occupied France and the Channel Islands with the remainder available for use to strengthen the Atlantic Wall.[10]

As early as April 1941 a decision was taken to use 100 FT17 37mm turrets for defence of the French coast.[11] The number finally installed undoubtedly exceeded this figure because as many as 80 turrets were installed in the Channel Islands alone. Just prior to the Allied invasion in May 1944, a further sixty turrets were still detailed as being available (although confusingly, in light of the significant numbers already used, none were quoted as having been released).[12]

The turrets were mounted on purpose-built shelters, or sometimes a stripped-down hull with turret was buried in the ground and encased in concrete. Exceptionally, the whole tank was simply buried in the ground so that only the turret was visible, or, on occasion, the tanks were simply positioned at key locations and acted as improvised strong points. Both types of turret were used on the different shelters – the cast turret and the riveted octagonal design – which were fitted with either the

*In the invasion of Poland the Germans also encountered FT17s, although most were used as static defensive positions or with armoured train units.

An FT17 turret installed to protect the Brittany coast. It is an octagonal riveted design with the main armament seemingly removed. The shelter is unusual with the concrete poured in a series of sections. German soldiers are busily spreading earth and laying turfs to camouflage the structure. (ECPA)

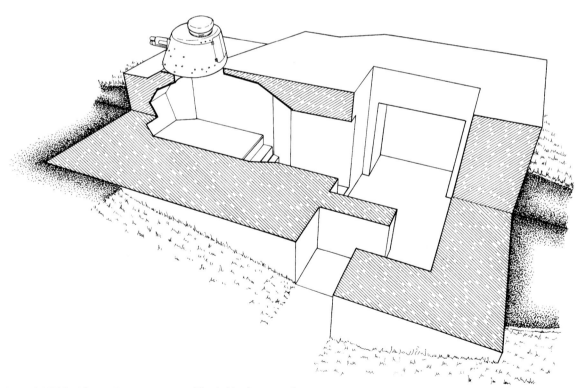

French FT17 with running gear removed buried in the ground.

FT17

Turret statistics:
See FT17 entry in Chapter 2 – Interwar

Weapon statistics:
Armament: 1 × 37mm SA 18 or 1 × 7.5mm
                   Reibel Model 1931 machine gun
Traverse: 360° (manual)
Elevation: +35° −20°

37mm SA 18 gun or the 7.5mm Reibel Model 1931 machine gun. Unusually, some turrets were fitted with new front plates so that the German MG34 or MG42 could be mounted.[13]

Renault R35 and Hotchkiss H35 (H38 or H39)*
Both the Renault R35 and the Hotchkiss H35 were fitted with the APX R turret and as such in the context of emplaced tank turrets they can be grouped together. The APX R turret had initially been developed by Atelier de Puteaux in 1935 for use by Renault on its infantry support tank, hence the APX-R designation, but it was also later adopted by Hotchkiss for use on the H35, which had been selected as the French cavalry tank.

The Renault and Hotchkiss models were built in far greater numbers than any other French tanks, although estimates of the number of tanks available to

---

*Neither the French nor the Germans differentiated between the different versions.

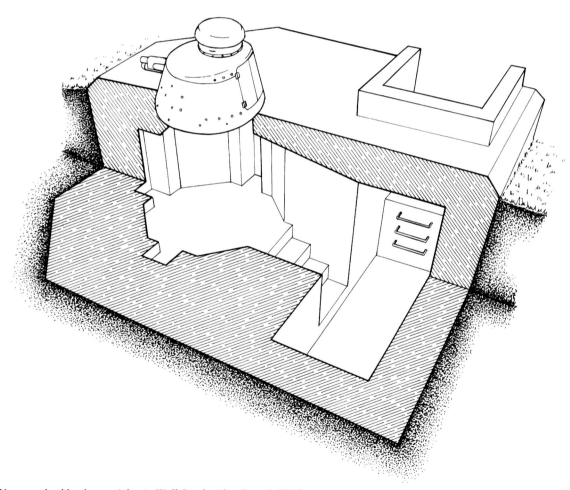

Non-standard bunker on Atlantic Wall fitted with a French FT17 turret.

the French Army in May 1940 vary. It is believed that there were somewhere in the region of 870 to 945 Renault R35s and around 800 Hotchkiss tanks in service. In spite of losses it is estimated that around 800 R35s and a significant proportion of H35s were captured by the Germans when France surrendered in June of that year.[14] Many of these, especially the Renault and Hotchkiss tanks armed with the long-barrelled 37mm S.A. 38, were issued to second line units and even at the end of May 1943 official sources still quoted 355 Hotchkiss and 58 Renault tanks as being employed in this role.

A significant proportion of the remainder had their turrets removed and were converted into artillery tractors or munitions carriers – the *Artillerie Schlepper* 35R(f) and 38H(f) or *Munitionsschlepper* 35R(f) and 38H(f). Other tanks were similarly altered, but were fitted with anti-tank guns. In the period from May to October 1941 some 174 of the 4.7cm PaK(t) *auf Panzerkampfwagen* 35R(f) *ohne Turm* were produced with a further twenty-six converted as command vehicles.[15] The larger 7.5cm PaK40 was fitted to the Hotchkiss chassis and twenty-four examples of the 7.5cm PaK40(Sf) *auf Geschutzwagen* 39H(f) were produced. A further forty-eight chassis were converted to mount light field guns in what became known as the 10.5cm leFH18(Sf) *auf Geschutzwagen* 39H(f).[16]

These conversions generated a large stockpile of surplus turrets that were made available for use along the Atlantic Wall, although seemingly not all of them were used or indeed issued. Those that were issued were mounted on various shelters and, in common with other French models, a number of tanks were simply used as static pillboxes.[17]

An interesting postscript to this section is that a number of APX R turrets were mounted on bunkers in Indo-China after the war (*see* Chapter 4 – Post War).

Bauform 235 Renault R35
Other Designation: F.P.DT4808
In addition to the widespread use of the APX R turret with its original 37mm main armament, plans were formulated to adapt these turrets to mount twin MG 42 (or possibly twin MG37(t)) machine guns. It is unclear what, if any, progress was made in the development and installation of this design.

A German soldier stands guard near a Renault R35 turret. The position was located in front of the Blue Waves Café in Marseilles. (ECPA)

Another view of the R35 turret in Marseilles clearly showing the original commander's cupola, main and coaxial armament and lifting hooks. (ECPA)

The turret of a Hotchkiss H38 located near Le Havre, Normandy. The turret baseplate bolted to the concrete shelter is clearly visible. (ECPA)

Somua S35

Some 416 Somua S35 medium tanks were available to the French Army in 1940. Of these 297 were captured by the Germans[18] following the fall of France. This was arguably the best French tank of the period and after some minor modifications they were issued to German units. Most were used for training or were deployed in the rear to counter partisans, often being loaded onto armoured trains. A number had their turrets removed and were issued as *Farschulefahrzeug* (driver training vehicles),[19] but, unlike other French tanks, no other major conversions were undertaken. This would suggest that relatively few turrets were free for use as fixed fortifications and it may be that the number quoted as being available included turrets taken from the Char B1 bis. The Char B1 bis was fitted with the APX4 turret, which externally was very similar to the APX1 CE turret. To confuse the situation still further a number of Char B1 bis tanks (*circa* 100) were fitted with APX 1 CE turrets because of a shortage of the original.

Panhard Armoured Car[20]

Other Designation: F.Pz.DT4811

At the outbreak of the war France had somewhere in the region of 360 Panhard Armoured cars in service.

Renault R35 and Hotchkiss H35 (H38 or H39)

Turret statistics:
Armour (thickness/angle): APXR cast turret

Gun mantlet	Front	Side	Rear	Roof
25mm/round	45mm/0–25°	40mm/30°	40mm/30°	12mm/90°

Weapon statistics:
Armament: 1 × 37mm SA18 or 1 × 37mm SA38 (longer barrelled version)
1 × 7.5mm Reibel Model 1931 machine gun coaxially mounted

Sight: Rotating cupola with visor. Telescopic sight coaxial with guns. Three periscope binoculars (or alternatively three episcopes with vision slits) mounted on front face and one on each side wall.

Traverse: 360° (manual)
Muzzle velocity: SA18 – 425 m/sec
SA38 – 767 m/sec

Availability:

No. of turrets available	No. of turrets released
156	24

Note: includes R 35 and H35 turrets

Bauform 235 Renault R 35[21]

Turret statistics:
Armour (thickness/angle): Cast turret (APX R)

Gun mantlet	Front	Side	Rear	Roof
45mm round	45mm/0–25°	40mm/30°	40mm/30°	12mm/90°

Weapon statistics:
Armament:	2 × 7.92mm MG42
Traverse:	360° (manual)
Range:	4,500m
Muzzle velocity:	740m/sec
Rate of fire:	1,200 rounds/minute

Bunker statistics:

Earth excavation	Concrete	Formed steel	Round steel
~80m³	~16 m³	–	~1.00 tonne

Ventilation: The installation was ventilated by means of a manually operated fan HES10 installed in the anteroom.
Munitions storage: 45,000 rounds.

A Somua S35 turret sited at a road intersection near Marseilles, France. The commander's cupola has received a direct hit and sits upside down next to the turret. (US National Archives courtesy of S. Zaloga)

These were armed with a 25mm gun and 7.5mm Reibel Model 1931 machine gun. A significant proportion of these were captured by the Germans and were either used in their original role or were altered to run on railway lines to protect them against attack by partisans. In 1943 a number of armoured cars had their turrets removed and were replaced with the German 5cm KwK L/42 gun set in a rigid superstructure. The surplus turrets were made available for use as fixed fortifications, although it is unclear how much further than the allocation of an official serial number this work progressed.[22]

Somua S35

Turret statistics:
Armour (thickness/angle): APX 1 CE cast turret*

Gun mantlet	Front	Side	Rear	Roof
56mm/round	56mm/0°	46mm/22.5°	46mm/22.5°	30mm/72.5–90°

Note: Dimensions quoted are for the APX4 in the absence of accurate data for the APX1CE.

Weapon statistics:
Armament: 1 × 47mm SA35
                       1 × 7.5mm Reibel Model 1931 machine gun (this was mounted coaxially behind a separate mantlet giving it limited independent traverse +/-10°).
Sight: Rotating commander's cupola fitted with periscope binoculars and two episcopes. Telescopic sight in machine gun mounting, common to both guns. Two episcopes in turret sides. Sighting vane externally on turret roof.
Traverse: 360° (manual)
Elevation: +18° −18°
Muzzle velocity: 733 m/sec

Availability:

No. of turrets available	No. of turrets released
25	5

Locations:

Atlantic/West Wall	Total
5	5

Panhard Armoured Car

Turret statistics:
Armour (thickness/angle):

Gun mantlet	Front	Side	Rear	Roof
26mm/round	26mm/24°	15mm/26°	15mm/30°	7mm/82°

Weapon statistics:
Armament: 1 × 7.92mm MG34 or 1 × 7.92mm MG42
Traverse: 360° (manual)
Range: 4,500m
Muzzle velocity: 740m/sec
Rate of fire: 1,200 rounds/minute

Italian

At the outbreak of the Second World War in Europe, Italy did not declare war on the Western democracies, despite signing the Pact of Steel military alliance with Germany in May 1939. However, the *Wehrmacht's* stunning victories in the spring of 1940 prompted Mussolini to ally himself with Hitler. Thereafter the Italian army went on the offensive with campaigns in

*CE – *circulaire élargie* or widened turret ring.

France, North Africa and the Balkans. However, the Italian armed forces, despite the propaganda, were not prepared for war and after a number of embarrassing reverses Mussolini was forced to seek the help of his larger ally. Initially, Italy's fortunes improved; Greece was defeated and the *Afrika Korps* advanced to Egypt, but gradually the tide of the war turned; Axis forces were forced to retreat on the Eastern Front and were defeated in North Africa.

In July 1943 the Allies invaded Sicily and soon after, Mussolini was deposed and placed under arrest. In September the Allies landed on the Italian mainland and Italy formally surrendered. That same month Hitler, realizing the enormity of the situation, ordered his forces south to protect the Third Reich's 'soft underbelly'. In so doing Germany also captured a significant number of tanks and the main tank production facilities based in the north of the country. These tanks were hopelessly outdated by the standards of the day, but at that stage in the war they offered a useful addition to the German arsenal. Some were used to equip German armoured divisions or in the case of the L3 tankette were simply dug in and used as improvised strong points. Not surprisingly in the light of the low esteem in which these tanks were held, a significant number of turrets were set aside to be mounted on bunkers. These were to be constructed exclusively in Italy and the turrets were to be adapted to accommodate German ordnance.

Bauform 242 M42(i)

Other Designation: F.Pz.DT4815

Around 100 of the *Carro Armato* M15/42 were captured by the Germans and a number of these tanks were released for use by German *Panzer* units and by the end of 1944 a few were still in service. The remainder were earmarked for use as fixed fortifications. The turrets were to have their original 47/40 gun removed and replaced with the German 3.7cm KwK L/45, perhaps to simplify the supply of ammunition or, possibly, the German 3.7cm gun was considered more effective. There were plans to install 100 turrets in the *Voralpenstellung*, but it is unclear whether this work was completed.[23] Certainly no plans appear to have been drawn up, nor does the work to replace the main gun seem to have started and a status report of 26 March 1945 makes no mention of them.

Bauform 242 M42(i)

Turret statistics:[24]
Armour (thickness/angle):

Gun mantlet	Front	Side	Rear	Roof
37mm (round)	12mm–37mm/16°	25mm/22°	25mm/22°	14mm/85°

Overall height: 700mm
Diameter: 1,250mm

Weapon statistics:
Armament: 1 × 3.7cm KwK L/45
Traverse: 360°
Range: 3,500m (although effective range was only 1,500m)
Muzzle velocity: Pz.Gr   565m/sec
    Sprg.Gr   435m/sec

Availability:

No. of turrets available	No. of turrets released
100	0

An Italian P40 turret fitted with a German 7.5cm KwK L/24 gun. The turret was captured by the Americans at the Rheinmetall proving ground, Hillersleben. The photograph was taken by the late Col G. B. Jarrett in the summer of 1945.
(G. B. Jarrett collection, US Army MHI courtesy of S. Zaloga)

Bauform 249 P40(i)
Other Designation: F.Pz.DT4814

Following Hitler's decision to occupy Italy in 1943, the German army captured not only a significant number of P40 tanks but also the FIAT-Ansaldo works where the tank was produced. The armour on the P40 was considered to be extremely effective and there were plans to equip a number of German armoured regiments with them. This proposition was not without its difficulties, the main one being the unreliable diesel engine, which it was hoped to replace with a petrol model. However, the work to adapt the P40 was less than successful and a number of tanks without engines were used as improvised strong points as part of the Gustav line defences and at Anzio.[25]

Later the idea of using the turret as a fixed fortification was considered. Already in April 1944 plans had been drawn up for the base plate to mount the P40 turret,[26] and in the following August detailed plans for the shelter were completed.[27] However, as with the desire to absorb the P40 into the ranks of the *Panzer* divisions, this idea was problematical. The original Italian 75/34 gun was only considered to have moderate performance and so it was planned to replace the main and coaxial armament (8mm Breda

Model 38 MG) with the German 7.5cm KwK L/24 and an MG42. By 27 February 1945 46 turrets had been finished and one completed turret was sent to the Hillersleben test facility for trials. This was mounted on a specially designed concrete shelter. The entrance at the rear led to an anteroom that housed the hand operated ventilation system. A flight of steps led from here to the main fighting compartment below the turret. The floor here was raised on wooden decking that not only served to improve the crew's footing but also served as a repository for spent machine gun shells. Spent cases from the main armament could be jettisoned through a small opening in the 40cm- (15in) thick wall to a chamber at the rear. A small wooden box was provided that could be moved under the turret to aid observation for the crew.

Just before Christmas 1944, with none of the concrete shelters finished, plans were drafted for a wooden framework or *schnelleinbau* (rapid installation) to mount the P40.[28] The wooden structure was built in two sections. At the bottom was the *fundament*, or base. On top of this was the *holzsockel*, or wooden body, onto which the *fundamentring* was secured with eight bolts, which in turn accommodated the turret race and turret. The *holzsockel* was built from machined timber into which an opening on the right was made below the turret, which led to the *hülsengrube*, an open pit, where spent shells could be safely jettisoned. The base was constructed from roughly hewn logs. Piles were driven into the ground and were braced with horizontal beams. Access to the shelter was via a revetted trench that led to an opening in the base.

One hundred of the turrets were to be installed in the *Voralpenstellung*,[29] but, as with the M15/42, it is unclear whether this work was completed and again the status report of 26 March 1945 makes no mention of them.

Soviet

On 22 June 1941 Hitler launched Operation *Barbarossa*, the invasion of the Soviet Union. On that momentous day some 3.6 million soldiers supported by 3,600 tanks and 2,700 aircraft crossed into Soviet occupied

---

Bauform 249 P 40(i)

Turret statistics:[30]
Armour (thickness/angle):

Gun mantlet	Front	Side	Rear	Roof
60mm/round	60mm/15°	45mm/25°	40mm/25°	20mm/82–90°

Weapon height:	*circa* 280mm
Overall height:	*circa* 700mm
Diameter:	1,640mm

Weapon statistics:

Armament:	1 × 7.5cm KwK L/24
	1 × MG42
Sight:	TZF5b
Traverse:	360°
Elevation:	+23° −10°
Muzzle velocity:	Pz.Gr 325m/sec
	Sprg.Gr 420m/sec
Penetration performance:	100m = 70mm

Bunker statistics:

Length	Width	Height
5.45m	4.65m	2.77m

Ventilation: The installation was ventilated by means of a manually operated HES10 fan installed in the anteroom.

Availability:

No. of turrets available	No. of turrets released
100	0

Locations:[31]

Italy	Total
100	100

Poland. This force, the largest in European military history, was split into three army groups each directed against a specific target – Moscow, Leningrad and Kiev – with the aim of destroying the Red Army. The formations facing Hitler's *Wehrmacht* were, on paper at least, as impressive with 2.9 million men, 10–15,000 tanks and 8,000 aircraft. However, much of the equipment was obsolete and Stalin's purges in the 1930s had decimated the officer corps. In spite of these handicaps, the Red Army bravely resisted the onslaught but initially at least, proved no match for the German *blitzkrieg* and in a series of huge encirclements the Germans crushed the Soviet forces of the western military districts and in so doing captured huge quantities of men and *materiel*.

As they had in earlier campaigns, the Germans were keen to utilize the spoils of war, but found that many of the tanks had either been so badly damaged that they were unusable or had been rendered useless with the removal of essential parts by both Soviet and German forces. Moreover, such was the strain on German repair facilities that they could barely maintain German tanks, let alone refit captured Soviet models, and so thousands of tanks were simply left on the battlefield as the Germans advanced.

The expeditious advance also meant that, as in the west, there was little time to study the enemy's defences, like the use of emplaced tank turrets, which were employed in both the Molotov and Stalin Lines. However, as the tide of the war began to turn, consideration was given to the hitherto unthinkable prospect of retreat, the value of such positions was reappraised and as early as 1942 a timber construction designed to mount the Soviet T34 turret appeared in a German manual of field fortifications.* Later concrete shelters were developed to mount Soviet tank turrets taken from the BT7, KV1, T34 and T70 tanks.† These all seem to have been mounted on larger concrete shelters that incorporated not only a fighting compartment and entranceway but also an ammunition store. This might have been motivated by the increased size and weight of these turrets or might have been prompted by the demands of the Eastern Front where the vast open spaces meant that such positions needed to be capable of independent operation.

In common with the majority of the German *panzerstellungen*, the shelters for the T34 and the T70

had walls 40cm (15in) thick. By contrast the structures mounting the KV 1 and T34 (improvised) turrets had thicker walls at 60cm (23in). The reason for this is unclear although it might be that, as elsewhere, it was an attempt to compensate for the lack of steel reinforcing rods. Aside from this, the layout of these structures was fairly typical with a revetted communication trench leading to the main entrance, which in turn led to the ammunition store and fighting compartment that was reached via four steps. The positions were also fitted with a recess for spent shell cases. The shells were jettisoned into this cavity via a small opening in the wall below the turret; two wooden hatches, one at the top and one at the front provided access from the outside.

Somewhat surprisingly, in light of the numbers of tanks captured, less than 200 captured turrets appear to have been made available for use in this way and even fewer were seemingly released for installation. This might have been partly due to the fact that wherever possible the superior Soviet tanks were used by front line units (see Table 2 below).

BT 7

Table 2 – Captured Soviet tank in German service

Available as at:	31 May 1943	30 December 1944
Pz Kpfw T-26(r)	1	2
Pz Kpfw T-70(r)	4	2
Pz Kpfw KVI(r)	2	–
Pz Kpfw KVII(r)	1	–
Pz Kpfw T-34(r)	50	39

Note: It is eminently possible that these figures do not represent the true picture since some tanks were undoubtedly used but did not feature in official reports because the situation at the front was so confused.

---

*This appeared in *Bildheft Neuzeitlicher Stellungsbau* which was originally published in 1942 and reprinted in March 1943.
†Other models were undoubtedly used as improvised fortifications but formal plans were not drawn up. Often tanks were simply buried in the ground as strong points.

The BT 7 tank was one of a series of 'fast' tanks developed to support the Soviet cavalry. By the time of the German invasion this tank was already obsolete and the Soviets had mounted turrets from older versions on concrete shelters. Nevertheless, significant numbers were still used to equip front line units and many were captured in the early part of the campaign. Two of these were released for use in a static role (probably on the Eastern Front), although no formal plans appear to have been drawn up for a shelter to mount the turret. Other BT7s, whose running gear or engine had been damaged beyond repair, were simply dug into the ground to protect strategically important installations.[32]

A captured Soviet KV I turret fitted with a 76.2mm gun at the Rheinmetall proving ground, Hillersleben. The turret does not appear to be mounted on a bunker and was clearly previously used by German forces as evinced by the German cross on the side. It retains its original white camouflage. (G. B. Jarrett collection, US Army MHI courtesy of S. Zaloga)

BT7

Turret statistics:[33]
Armour (thickness/angle):

Gun mantlet	Front	Side	Rear	Roof
–	13mm	13mm	13mm	10mm

Weapon statistics:
Armament: 1 × 4.5cm KwK(r) (Soviet Model 35)
1 × MG(r) 7.62mm DT
Traverse: 360°
Elevation: +40° −4°

Bunker statistics:

No. of turrets available	No. of turrets released
2	2

Bauform 251 KV1 (Normalserie)

The Soviets had begun to develop heavy tanks in the early 1930s and at the outbreak of the war the Red Army was equipped with the KV series of tanks, named after Marshal Klimenti Voroshilov, the People's Defence Commissar. The existence of the KV 1 and other Soviet heavy tanks came as a real shock to the Germans because at this stage in the war they had nothing comparable. Fortunately for the Germans the KV1 suffered from a number of teething troubles and were poorly deployed being thinly dispersed among armoured units and as such lost some of their potency. These factors combined meant that in spite of their undoubted superiority a number of tanks fell into enemy hands. With their thick armour and powerful 7.62cm gun they were quickly pressed into service against their previous owner.

Later, with the advent of much larger and much more powerful tanks, a number of KV1 turrets were made available for use as fixed fortifications. As far as it is possible to establish they were all mounted on a standard concrete shelter and all of them were installed along the eastern front.

Bauform 244 T34 (Behelfsmäßig)
Other Designation: F.Pz.DT 4805

The T34 was the new medium tank of the Soviet army. Like the KV1 its appearance on the battlefield came as a shock to the German High Command not least because of its advanced features including sloping armour. However, like the KV1, it too suffered from teething problems and was poorly deployed. Consequently, a significant number of them were captured and many were integrated into the *Panzer* divisions, albeit often in second line duties so as to avoid confusion in battle.

Later in the war, as the German forces on the Eastern Front were forced onto the retreat, a large number of turrets were made available for use as

Bauform 251 KV 1 (*Normalserie*)

Turret statistics:
Armour (thickness/angle):

Model	Gun mantlet	Front	Side	Rear	Roof
KV1A	60 + 25mm	75 + 25mm	75mm	75mm	35mm
KV 1B	100mm	75 + 35mm	75 + 30mm	75mm	35mm
KV 1C*	105mm	120mm	120mm	120mm	40mm

Turret weight:	5,500kg	Weapon height:	*circa* 540mm
Overall height:	*circa* 880mm	Diameter:	*circa* 1,600mm

Weapon statistics:
Armament: 1 × 7.62cm KwK (r) L/30.5
                 2 × MG (r) 7.62mm DT
Sight: 2 × manually operated periscopes 3 x 14°
                 4 × VGB 487 periscopes for all-round observation
                 1 × TZF 43/1(t) telescopic sight for aiming
Traverse: 360°
Elevation: +25° −9°

	7.62cm KwK(r)	MG (r)
Range:	7,300m	4,000m
Muzzle velocity: Pz. Gr	612m/sec	740m/sec
Spr. Gr	635m/sec	
Rate of fire:	12 rounds/min	800 rounds/min

Penetration performance: 200m = 52mm
                           600m = 49mm
                           1,000m = 44mm
                           1,500m = 39mm

Bunker statistics:

Earth excavation	Concrete	Formed steel	Round steel
150m³	52m³	–	3.1 tonne

Length	Width	Height
5.76m	5.68m	2.98m

Ventilation: The installation was ventilated by means of a manually operated HES10 fan installed in the anteroom. The exhaust fumes from the gun were extracted through a fan set in the roof of the turret, driven by a built in 70-watt motor with 12-volt battery.

Munitions storage: The following could be stored in the ammunition recesses:
7.62cm KwK (r)   = 240 rounds in 40 boxes
MG(r)   = *circa* 21,000 rounds in 14 boxes and ca 3,000 rounds in cartridge belt bags

Availability:

No. of turrets available	No. of turrets released
6	0

Locations:[34]

East	Total
10	10

---

*KV 1 Model 42.

Bauform 244 T34 (*Behelfsmäßig*)

Turret statistics:
Armour (thickness/angle): as per T34

Weapon statistics:

Armament:	1 × 5cm KwK L/42	
	1 × MG 42	
Traverse:	360°	

	5cm KwK L/42	MG 42
Range:	4,800m	4,500m
Muzzle velocity: Pz.Gr	685m/sec	740m/sec
Sprg.Gr	450m/sec	
Rate of fire:	15 rounds/min	1,200 rounds/min
Penetration performance:	100m = 50mm	
	600m = 43mm	
	1,000m = 36mm	
	1,500m = 28mm	

Bunker statistics:

Length	Width	Height
5.78m	5.70m	2.97m

Ventilation: N/K
Munitions storage: 5cm KwK = 352 rounds
MG42 = 24,000 rounds

Availability:

No. of turrets available	No. of turrets released
158	0

---

fixed fortifications. The vast majority of these were to be modified to take the German 5cm KwK L/42. The logic behind this decision is not entirely clear. It is certainly true that the Soviet 7.62cm L11 gun that was originally fitted to the T34 was less than satisfactory, but this does not seem reason enough to dispense with it and fit a smaller calibre weapon. More likely, it was replaced because it would have been difficult to source enough ammunition for these turrets as well as for those tanks serving with front line units.* Moreover, because the 5cm KwK L/42 had only recently been phased out of service there were plenty of spare guns available and the provision of ammunition would not have been a problem.

Plans were drafted for a shelter to mount the modified turret and these were broadly the same as those used to mount other Soviet turrets, although the main entrance and the access hatch to the spent cartridge bin were in parallel rather than adjacent to each other. However, there is little evidence to suggest that any of these turrets were actually installed save for vague plans to use the F Pz DT 4805 in the West Wall.[35]

Bauform 248 T34 (Normalserie)
In addition to the plans to use T34 turrets fitted with the 5cm KwK L/42 a limited number of unaltered turrets were released for use and were all seemingly employed on the Eastern Front. As early as 1942 the

---

*As at the end of May 1943 official sources quoted fifty T34s as being in service with front line units.

A technical drawing depicting a concrete shelter mounting a T34 (Normalserie) turret. (Bundesarchiv)

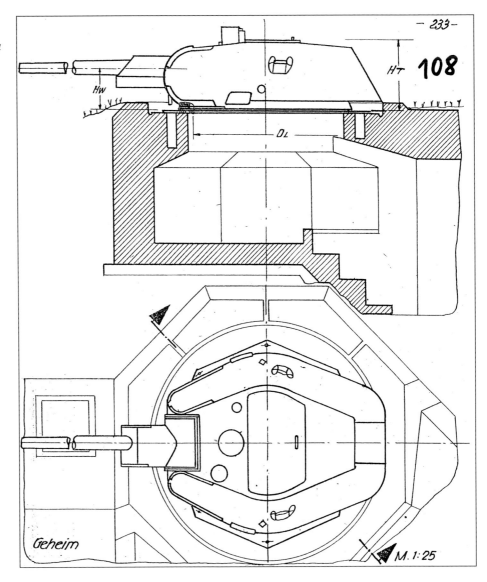

manual of German field works[36] included a design for a timber shelter surmounted by a T34 turret. Later, plans were developed for a concrete structure, but this proved problematic. A note from *Der Chef der Heeresrüstung und Befehlshaber des Ersatzheeres* to *General der Pioniere und Festungs* in October 1943 noted that a number of defects had come to light during firing tests and that the shelter would have to be redesigned.[37] This may go some way towards explaining why only four of these turrets were seemingly released and installed by the end of the war.

Bauform 243 T70 (Normalserie)

The Soviet T70 was a light scout tank that was developed to replace the slower T60. However, by the standards of the day even as a reconnaissance vehicle its gun was considered too small and the single man turret was recognized as being a major handicap. A number of these tanks were captured by the Germans and some were used by German units, indeed two

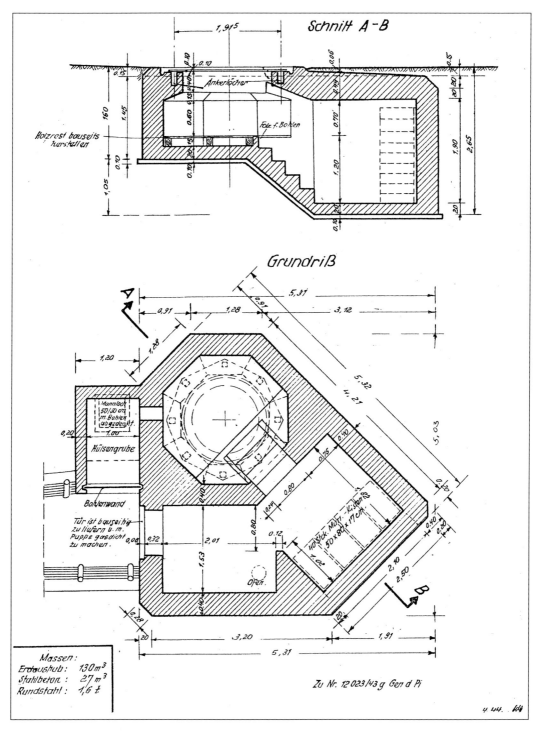

A drawing of the concrete shelter that mounted the T34 turret (Baufrom 248). The shelter included an ammuntion store, fighting compartment, spent shell bin and entrance way with oven. (Bundesarchiv)

Bauform 248 T34 (*Normalserie*)

Turret statistics:
Armour (thickness/angle):

Model	Gun mantlet	Front	Side	Rear	Roof
T34A	45/25mm	45mm	45mm	40–45mm	16mm
T34B	45/25mm	45/17mm	45/17mm	45mm	16mm
T34 B Cast	45/25mm	60–70mm	60–70mm	60–70mm	20mm

Turret weight:	ca 3,000kg	Weapon height:	*circa* 510mm
Overall height:	ca 750mm	Diameter:	*circa* 1,440mm

Weapon statistics:

Armament:	1 × 7.62cm KwK L/41,5 or L/30,5(r)
	1 × MG(r) 7.62mm DT
Sight:	1 × manually operated periscope 3 × 14°
	2 prisms (cast turret) or 2 periscopes (welded turret)
	1 × TZF 43/1(t) telescopic sight for aiming
Traverse:	360°
Elevation:	+32° −6°

	7,62cm KwK L/42	MG (r)
Range:	L/41,5 7,600m	*circa* 4,000m
	L/30,5 7,300m	

Muzzle velocity:	L/41,5		
	Pz.Gr	662m/sec	740m/sec
	Sprg.Gr	680m/sec	
	L/30,5		
	Pz.Gr	612m/sec	
	Sprg.Gr	635m/sec	

Rate of fire: 12 rounds/min

Penetration performance:	L/41,5	200m = 59mm
		600m = 54mm
		1,000m = 49mm
		1,500m = 44mm
	L/30,5	200m = 52mm
		600m = 49mm
		1,000m = 44mm
		1,500m = 39mm

Bunker statistics:

Earth excavation	Concrete	Formed steel	Round steel
130m³	27m³	–	~1.6 tonne

Length	Width	Height
5.32m	5.31m	2.75m

Ventilation: The installation was ventilated by means of a manually operated HES10 fan installed in the anteroom. The exhaust fumes from the gun were extracted through a fan set in the roof of the turret, driven by a built in 70-watt motor with 12-volt battery.

Bauform 248 T34 (*Normalserie*) cont'd

Munitions storage:
The following could be stored in the ammunition recesses:

7.62cm KwK (r)   = 240 rounds in 40 boxes
MG(r)   = *circa* 18,000 rounds in 12 boxes and *circa* 3,000 rounds in cartridge belt bags.

Availability:

No. of turrets available	No. of turrets released
14	4

Locations:

?	East	Total
19	4	23

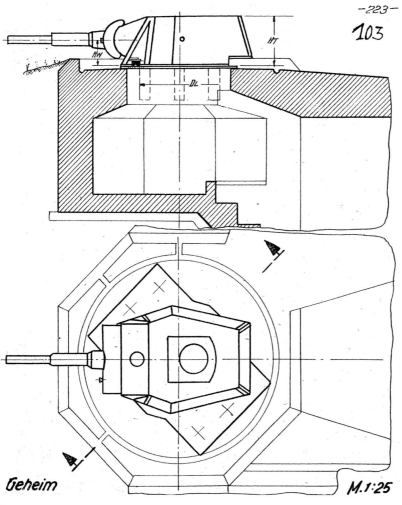

A technical drawing depicting a concrete shelter mounting a T70 (*Normalserie*) turret. (*Bundesarchiv*)

were still quoted as being in use at the end of 1944. Others had their turrets removed and were used as artillery tractors.[38] * The surplus turrets were released for use as fixed fortifications that were to be constructed on the Eastern Front. The structure that the turret was to be mounted on was broadly the same as the examples used to mount other Soviet turrets, but rather than a bespoke base plate the turret was mounted on a base section taken from the tank and affixed to the concrete structure with six bolts.

GERMAN TANK TURRETS

In June 1941 Hitler launched Operation *Barbarossa*. The Führer's battle-hardened troops swept across that portion of Poland that had been ceded to Stalin in 1939, and on deep into the Soviet Union. But the stunning victories in the first months of the campaign were tarnished by the fact that it was clear that the German armed forces were not superior to the Soviets in all fields, and certainly not in terms of tanks. The appearance of the T34 and KV heavy tanks was a tremendous shock to the Germans and almost overnight rendered obsolete many of the tanks that had formed the backbone of the campaigns in France and the Low Countries. Technical problems with these ground-breaking tanks as well as tactical naivety meant that the inferior German models enjoyed further success, but it was clear that urgent steps would need to be taken if Hitler's forces were to prevail in this battle of ideologies. This wake-up call led to the development of the Tiger I and Panther tanks and gradually many of the older models were relegated to second line duties. Others had their turrets removed and were fitted with anti-tank or light field guns and used as self-propelled guns or were used as command vehicles or artillery and ammunition tractors. The surplus turrets, just as had been the case with many of the captured tanks earlier in the war, were released for used as improvised fixed fortifications.

Production Models

Bauform 233 Panzer I (Normalserie)
From the second half of 1940 until early 1941 the *Panzer* I *Ausf* A and *Ausf* B were phased out of

service. A number had their turrets removed and were converted into self-propelled guns with the addition of a 4.7cm PaK anti-tank gun. Later, in the spring of 1942, a further batch of obsolete *Panzer* Is were remodelled for use as load carriers by fitting a large steel box in place of the turret. Finally, in early 1943, an order was issued stipulating that all remaining *Panzer* Is were to be converted to '*Munition-sschlepper ohne Aufbau*' (ammunition tractors without superstructure).[39] The turrets removed from these vehicles and from the earlier conversions were freed for use as fixed fortifications.

A significant proportion of these turrets were used largely without alteration; the only external change of note was the addition of four lugs so that camouflage nets could be applied. This, and any other modification work, was undertaken at the *Heeres-Zeugamt* (Army Stores Depot) in Magdeburg and the 250 turrets completed were classified as the TI (MA). A further thirty-one turrets were to be modified by *Artillerie Werkstatt die Kommandantur Hill* (Garrison HQ workshop) but only eleven of these TI (H) turrets were completed.[40]

Detailed plans for a standard concrete shelter to mount the *Panzer* I turret were drawn up in March 1943. The bunker was typical of its type with access from the side leading to an anteroom and then up a flight of steps to the fighting compartment below the turret which sat on an octagonal steel plate affixed with eight bolts. The floor of the fighting compartment was fitted with wooden duck boards and a drain under this ensured any water drained away without affecting the workings of the structure. Drainage channels on the top of the shelter directed water away from the turret to the rear, which was slopped at an angle of 10 degrees.[41]

Bauform 231 Panzer I (Behelfsmäßig)
Other Designation: F Pz DT 4803
In addition to the standard *Panzer* I turrets that were used, an even greater number were modified so that they were better suited to their new role. The original mantlet was removed and replaced with a 20mm (¾in) thick plate with openings for the main weapon

---

*A number of T60 tanks were also used as artillery tractors, but it is unclear whether the surplus turrets were used for fixed defences.

Bauform 243 T70 (*Normalserie*)

Turret statistics:
Armour (thickness/angle):

Gun mantlet	Front	Side	Rear	Roof
60mm	35mm	35mm	35mm	10mm

Turret weight:	*circa* 1,600kg	Weapon height:	300mm
Overall height:	560mm	Diameter:	940mm

Weapon statistics:

Armament:	1 × 4.5cm KwK246(r) L/46 (Soviet Model 38)
	1 × MG(r) 7.62mm DT
Sight:	1 × TZF 43/1(t) telescopic sight for aiming
	1 × VBG486 periscope for all round observation
Traverse:	360°
Elevation:	+20° −5°

Bunker statistics:

Earth excavation	Concrete	Formed steel	Round steel
110m³	26m³	–	1.5 tonne

Length	Width	Height
4.78m	4.66m	2.74m

Ventilation: The installation was ventilated by means of a manually operated HES10 fan. The exhaust fumes from the gun were extracted through a fan set in the roof of the turret, driven by a built in 70-watt motor with 12-volt battery.

Munitions storage:

The following could be stored in the ammunition recesses:

4.5cm KwK	= 300 rounds in 30 boxes
MG(r)	= *circa* 18,000 rounds in 12 boxes and a further 3,000 rounds in cartridge belts

Availability:

No. of turrets available	No. of turrets released
11	11

Locations:

East	Total
13	13

A Panzer I turret located near Nafplio on the Greek coast. The twin machine guns and commander's hatch have been removed. Since this photograph was taken the turret has been removed. (K. Faros, courtesy of T. Tsiplakos)

(either an MG34 or MG42) and the sight. The two vision slits in the turret side were dispensed with and were covered by 20mm (¾in) steel plates which were welded over the openings as ventilation ports, or *luftschächte*. The turret roof access hatch, with its various rest positions, also served to ventilate the turret, but while this expedient saved the crew from asphyxiation it exposed them to the potential danger of enemy fire. As with the standard model four small pipes were welded onto the lower edge of the turret, which housed the rods to which the camouflage screens were affixed.

The modifications to the mantlet meant that the internal set-up of the turret had to be radically re-engineered with a complete reworking of the way the weapons were arranged. The machine gun – whether it be MG34 or MG42 – was positioned to the right of the turret and was mounted on a weapon support. This consisted of a pedestal, gun cradle and sliding carriage. The pedestal, which was fixed to the turret with screws, mounted the gun cradle, which was secured with two bolts. A sliding carriage, onto which the machine gun was secured, was spring mounted in the gun cradle. After the machine gun had been inserted a Bowden cable was attached to the trigger (to allow remote firing). Separate supports for both the MG34 and MG42 were provided; the unused one

An F.Pz.DT 4803 (Panzer I) turret installed in the West Wall. The machine gun mounting and turning mechanism are clearly visible inside the turret. The original side vision slits have been removed and replaced with armoured plates to provide better ventilation. (US National Archives courtesy of S. Zaloga)

being stored in a holder attached to the roof.[42] The machine gun to be used had to be supplied by the crew, as did the optics for the periscope that was located in the access hatch.

To the left of the machine gun was the elevating gear and an indicator that showed the angle of

Bauform 233 Panzer I (*Normalserie*)

Turret statistics:
Armour (thickness/angle):

Gun mantlet	Front	Side	Rear	Roof
15mm/round	15mm/10°	13mm/22°	13mm/22°	8mm/82°–90°

Turret weight:	*circa* 450kg	Weapon height:	*circa* 135mm
Overall height:	*circa* 345mm	Diameter:	*circa* 924mm

Weapon statistics:

Armament:	2 × 7.92mm MG13
Sight:	1 × TZF2
	1 × sighting bar
Traverse:	360°
Elevation:	+ 20° −10°
Range:	4,500m
Muzzle velocity:	700m/sec
Rate of fire:	800 rounds/minute

Bunker statistics:

Earth excavation	Concrete	Formed steel	Round steel
~80m³	~16m³	–	~1 tonne

Munitions storage: 45,000–60,000 rounds

Availability: *

No. of turrets available	No. of turrets released
646	511

Locations:

Denmark	Atlantic/ West Wall	Southeast (Balkans)	East	Schools/ Experimental	Total
20	3	161	76	1	261

elevation of the weapon and a support to hold the sight. Just below was the support for the ammunition box. On the right was an arm for the weight balance, to stop the weapon and support being tail heavy, and further over was the traversing wheel, which was fitted with the trigger for the machine gun. Engaging the traversing gear, the turret, which was mounted on a base ring of ball bearings secured with six brackets, could be rotated through a full 360 degrees. A turret traverse clamp fitted to the support ring made it possible to secure the turret in any given position.

All of the modification work was completed by Schichau of Elbing. The first 250 were designated as the TI(S). The later examples that were additionally fitted with a periscope, or *beobachtungsspiegel*, were classified as theTI(S) *Ausführung* B.[43]

*These turrets were also used for the *Bauform* 231, F Pz DT 4803 (*see above*)

Bauform 231 Panzer I (*Behelfsmäßig*)

Turret statistics:
Armour (thickness/angle):

Gun mantlet	Front	Side	Rear	Roof
–	35mm/8°	13mm/22°	13mm/22°	8mm/82°–90°

Turret weight:	*circa* 450kg	Weapon height:	*circa* 145mm
Overall height:	*circa* 345mm	Diameter:	*circa* 925mm

Weapon statistics:
Armament: 1 × 7.92mm MG34 or 1 × 7.92mm MG42
Sight: 1 × TZF2 **or** TZF4b/1
                 1 × periscope
Traverse: 360°
Elevation: + 20° -12°
Range: 4,500m
Muzzle velocity: *circa* 750m/sec
Rate of fire: 800–1200 rounds/minute

Bunker statistics:

Earth excavation	Concrete	Formed steel	Round steel
~80m³	~16m³	–	~1 tonne

Ventilation: Natural   Munitions storage: 45,000 – 60,000 rounds

Locations:

Denmark	Atlantic/ West Wall	Italy	East	Total
97	143*	91	32	363

*95 of these turrets were planned to be installed in the West Wall.[44]

Bauform 232a Panzer II Flamingo (Normalserie)
Before the outbreak of the Second World War it was recognized that it would be desirable to have an armoured vehicle armed with a flamethrower that could be used against enemy bunkers and fortified positions. This led to the development of the *Panzerkampfwagen II Flamm* (or Flamingo). Production began in May 1940 and the last tank of the initial series was completed in February 1941. The flamethrower tank saw action on the Eastern Front but the highly flammable fuel, which was stored inside the vehicle, and the thin armour proved to be an explosive combination and it was withdrawn from service in 1942.

The surplus turrets were released for use as fixed fortifications with modification work to prepare them for their new role undertaken by Schichau of Elbing. The principal change was the addition of six lugs welded to the outside of the turret to take the camouflage nets.

Bauform 232b Panzer II Flamingo (Behelfsmäßig)
After the completion of the initial production run, a second batch of tanks armed with flame-throwers was begun in August 1941, but in spite of minor improvements the vehicle was not a success and production ceased in March 1942. The surplus chassis

---

Bauform 232a Panzer II Flamingo (*Normalserie*)

Turret statistics:
Armour (thickness/angle):

Gun mantlet	Front	Side	Rear	Roof
–	30mm/0°	30mm/12°	30mm/30°	8mm/84°–90°

Turret weight:	*circa* 1,000kg	Weapon height:	*circa* 205mm
Overall height:	*circa* 420mm	Diameter:	*circa* 1,000mm

Weapon statistics:
Armament: 1 × 7.92mm MG34
Sight: 1 × KZF2
1 × periscope
Traverse: 360° (The MG could be traversed independently +/−15°)
Elevation: +20° −10°
Range: 4,500 metres
Muzzle velocity: ca 700m/sec
Rate of fire: 800 rounds/minute

Bunker statistics:

Earth excavation	Concrete	Formed steel	Round steel
~80m³	~16m³	–	~1 tonne

Ventilation: Natural   Munitions storage: 45,000–60,000 rounds

Availability:

No. of turrets available	No. of turrets released
25	25

Locations:

Norway	East	Schools/ Experimental	Total
4	20	1	25

---

were used to mount captured Soviet 7.62cm anti-tank guns and the turrets released for use as fixed fortifications.[45] In preparation for their new role these turrets were given a major overhaul by Schichau of Elbing. As well as the addition of tubes welded to the turret sides to enable camouflage nets to be fitted, the ball-mounted machine gun was removed and replaced with an armoured plate that could accommodate a sight and either an MG34 or MG42 (which were to be supplied by the unit manning the turret). The commander's hatch was also scrapped and the opening sealed with a welded armour plate. In a number of instances the front vision slits were similarly modified. Directly above the machine gun a raised armoured box was fitted to provide ventilation.

Plans for the bunker to mount the turret were drawn up in March 1943 and was fairly typical in layout. It was accessed from the side from a revetted

A Panzer II Flamingo (Normalserie) turret that was installed in Stavanger, Norway. Not long after the photograph was taken the structure was demolished to allow for local redevelopment. Thankfully, the turret was saved and taken to a local museum. (Erik Ettrup)

trench that led to a small anteroom. Steps led from here up into the fighting compartment on top of which was the turret and octagonal base plate, which was secured with eight bolts. The floor of the fighting compartment was fitted with wooden duckboards. A drain under the floor channelled any water to the lower anteroom the floor of which was sloped at 2

degrees towards the external trench where a soak-away was fitted. Drainage channels on the roof directed any precipitation away from the turret to the rear which was sloped at ten degrees.[46]

Bauform 234 Panzer II (Behelfsmäßig)
Other Designations: F Pz DT 4806 or *Drehhaube* IIa (Rotating hood IIa

Plans were formulated to use *Panzer* II turrets fitted with twin MG 42 machine guns rather than the 20mm main armament. The idea does not appear to have progressed beyond the concept phase.

Bauform 236 Panzer II (Normalserie)
Mit Bugpanzerdach – with front superstructure as baseplate

In addition to plans to use *Panzer* II turrets fitted with twin machine guns there were also plans to use unmodified turrets, which became available in large numbers after the invasion of the Soviet Union. The main armament of the *Panzer* II was hopelessly ineffective against Soviet armour and in June 1942, a little over a year after it entered production, it was decided that half of the *Ausf* F chassis were to be used to mount the PaK 40 and just over a year later it was decided that all the chassis were to be used in this

A Panzer II Flamingo (Behelfsmäßig) turret located near Lista, Norway. The front vision slits have been sealed and the MG ball mount removed. Small tubes have been welded to the turret for attaching camouflage. (Erik Ritterbach)

Bauform 232b Panzer II Flamingo (*Behelfsmäßig*)

Turret statistics:
Armour (thickness/angle):

Gun mantlet	Front	Side	Rear	Roof
–	30mm/0°	30mm/21°	30mm/30°	10mm/84°–90°

Turret weight:	*circa* 1,000kg	Weapon height:	*circa* 205mm
Overall height:	*circa* 420mm	Diameter:	*circa* 1,000mm

Weapon statistics:

Armament:	1 × 7.92mm MG34 or 1 x 7.92mm MG42
Sight:	1 × Pz Z F 7a
	1 × periscope
Traverse:	360°
Elevation:	+12° −10°
Range:	4,500 metres
Muzzle velocity:	*circa* 750m/sec
Rate of fire:	800–1,200 rounds/minute

Bunker statistics:

Earth excavation	Concrete	Formed steel	Round steel
~80m³	~16m³	—	~1 tonne

Ventilation: Natural   Munitions storage: 45,000–60,000 rounds

Availability:

No. of turrets available	No. of turrets released
63	63

Locations:

Norway	East	Total
31	32	63

way. The surplus *Ausf* F turrets were freed up for use as fixed fortifications and these were supplemented with repaired turrets that were taken from older marks.

MAN of Nürnberg was contracted to convert fifty-eight *Panzer* II turrets of which forty-nine were completed and were classified as TII(M). A further seventy-two turrets, of which only forty were completed, were to be converted at the FAMO Werk at Ursus near Warsaw and its sister plant in Breslau. In addition a number of new turrets were completed at the Ursus works and these, together with the converted turrets, were grouped together and were given the designation TII(FAM). A number of other turrets were converted by Skoda and *Artillerie Werkstatt die Kommandantur Hill Süd* and were consolidated into the TII(P) series.*[47]

Plans for the shelter were drawn up in March 1943 and shared many of the features with other structures in

---

*Twenty-nine were ordered but only twenty-eight TII(P) turrets were completed for both *Bauform* 236 and 237.

Bauform 234 Panzer II (*Behelfsmäßig*)

Turret statistics:
Armour (thickness/angle):

Gun mantlet	Front	Side	Rear	Roof
15 or 30mm/ round*	15 or 30mm/ round*	15mm/21°	15mm/21°	10mm/77°–90°*

*Depends on which mark of turret was used

Overall height: *circa* 590mm Diameter: *circa* 1,160mm

Weapon statistics:
Armament: 2 × 7.92mm MG42
Traverse: 360°
Range: 4,500m
Muzzle velocity: *circa* 740m/sec
Rate of fire: 1,200 rounds/minute

Bunker statistics:

Earth excavation	Concrete	Formed steel	Round steel
~80m³	~16m³	–	~1 tonne

Ventilation: The installation was ventilated by means of a manually operated HES10 fan.
Munitions storage: 45,000 rounds

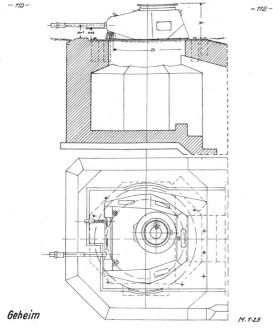

Geheim

A technical drawing depicting a concrete shelter mounting a Panzer II turret mit Bugpanzerdach. (Bundesarchiv)

the series. The turret was mounted on a section of the tank superstructure, or *Bugpanzerdach*, which was fixed to the shelter with eight bolts. For reasons that are not entirely clear the base plate was orientated in reverse so that the section that normally faced towards the rear faced the front. Drainage channels directed water away from the turret to the rear where the roof was constructed with a slope of approximately 10 degrees.

Directly below the turret was the fighting compartment. This was fitted with wooden duckboards that served as a makeshift repository for the spent shell cases. Any water that entered the fighting compartment would also collect here before being channelled through a drain to the lower level where the floor was angled at 2 degrees to direct water out of the shelter to the soak away at the entrance. Access to the fighting compartment was via a flight of steps from the anteroom inside the entrance. This in turn led to a revetted trench at the side.[48]

Bauform 67 – Panzer II mit Bugpanzerdach mounted on reinforced concrete shelter.

Bauform 237 Panzer II (Normalserie)
(Mit achteckigem Fundament – With Octagonal Base Ring*)*

The history of how the *Panzer* II turrets came to be released for use as fixed fortifications is detailed in the text above relating to the *Bauform* 236, because the turrets shared common origins.

Some eighty-seven turrets were adapted by *Heeres-Zeugamt* of Magdeburg for use in this role and were given the designation TII(MA). Other turrets were modified by Skoda and *Artillerie Werkstatt die Kommandantur Hill Süd* and were combined in the TII(P) series.* In addition some 335 new turrets were completed by FAMO at their Ursus plant. These were used on both this shelter and the *Bauform* 236 and were given the designation TII(FAM).[49]

Plans for a shelter fitted with an octagonal base plate were drawn up in December 1942 and, with the exception of the turret mounting, the design was broadly the same as that for the *Bauform* 236.[50]

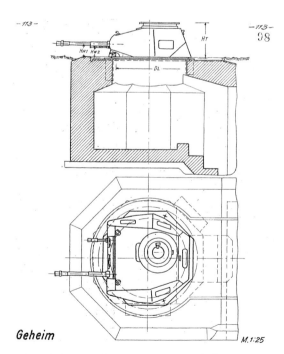

Geheim

M.1:25

A technical drawing depicting a concrete shelter mounting a Panzer II turret mit achteckigem Fundament. (Bundesarchiv)

---

*Twenty-nine were ordered but only twenty-eight were completed TII(P) for both *Bauform* 236 and 237.

Bauform 236 Panzer II (*Normalserie*)

Turret statistics:
Armour (thickness/angle):

Gun mantlet	Front	Side	Rear	Roof
15 or 30mm/ round*	15 or 30mm/	15mm/21° round*	15mm/21°	10mm/77°–90°*

*Depends on which mark of turret was used.

Turret weight:	*circa* 800kg	Weapon height (KwK):	*circa* 240mm
Overall height:	*circa* 590mm	Weapon height (MG):	*circa* 200mm

Weapon statistics:

Armament:	1 × 2cm KwK 30
	1 × 7.92mm MG 34
Sight:	1 × TZF4
	1 × sighting bar
	8 × periscopes in cupola
Traverse:	360°
Elevation:	+20° −10°

Bunker statistics:

Earth excavation	Concrete	Formed steel	Round steel
~80m³	~16m³	–	~1 tonne

Ventilation: Natural

Munitions storage:
2cm KwK 30	=	2,800 rounds
MG 34	=	19,000 rounds

Availability:

No. of turrets available	No. of turrets released
739	485

Locations:

Denmark	Norway	Italy West Wall	Atlantic/ (Balkans)	Southeast	East Experim.	Schools/	Total
7	46	17	191	58	217	2	538

Note: In official records the shelters mounting the *Panzer* II turret (*Bauform* 236 and 237) are grouped together.

Bauform 238 Panzer II (Behelfsmäßig)
Other Designations: F Pz DT 4804 or *Drehhaube* II
The cancellation of the *Panzer* II *Ausf* F programme and the decision to use the chassis as a self-propelled anti-tank gun platform meant that a number of *Panzer* II turrets were available for use as fixed fortifications. These were used as the basis for both the *Bauform* 236 and *Bauform* 237 but were also used for the F Pz DT 4804. The majority of the 100 turrets were taken from the stockpile of *Ausf* F turrets but in

A Panzer II (Normalserie) turret captured by American forces in August 1944. This example was located in Marseilles near the historic Fort St Nicolas that guarded the entrance to the harbour. (US National Archives courtesy of S. Zaloga)

A Panzer II turret fitted with a 3.7cm KwK L/45 gun at the Rheinmetall proving ground, Hillersleben. The main entrance to the bunker is clearly visible and has been temporarily provided with a wooden door. (G. B. Jarrett collection, US Army MHI courtesy of S. Zaloga)

addition fourteen turrets were taken from older marks.

Unlike the majority of the *Panzer* II turrets used, the *Bauform* 238 required a major reworking of the turret which was undertaken by Schichau of Elbing and FAMO at their Ursus works.[51] The most

significant change was the replacement of the 2cm KwK with a 3.7cm KwK L/46.5 gun. This was positioned in the centre of the mantlet where the visor hole had been located. The original 2cm KwK was removed and the resulting hole used to mount the TZF 4/1 gunsight. The MG34 was retained, but where the machine gun was dispensed with the hole was filled with an armour plug. The original cupola was removed and replaced with an armoured plate with nine ventilation slits and a larger hole for a periscope. At the base of the turret six lugs were welded onto the turret to secure the camouflage netting and four additional lifting lugs were also affixed to the turret (in addition to the two originally fitted) two on either side. In common with general improvements made to the Panzer III and IV turrets the front right visor was removed.[52]

Bauform 239 Panzer II VK 901 (Normalserie)

The VK901* or *Panzer* II *Ausf* G was a further development of the basic *Panzer* II. The initial prototype was completed late in 1939, but numerous

---

*VK or *Versuchskonstrucktion* (experimental construction) is followed here by a three-digit number. The first digit related to the weight and the last two to the classification.

Bauform 238 Panzer II (*Behelfsmäßig*)

Turret statistics:
Armour (thickness/angle):

Gun mantlet	Front	Side	Rear	Roof
15 or 30mm/ round*	15 or 30mm/ round*	15mm/21°	15mm/21°	10mm/77°–90°*

*Depends on which mark of turret was used

Turret weight:	*circa* 950kg	Weapon height (KwK):	*circa* 240mm
Overall height:	*circa* 510mm	Weapon height (MG):	*circa* 200mm
Diameter:	*circa* 1,160mm		

Weapon statistics:

Armament:	1 × 3.7cm KwK L/46.5
	1 × 7.92mm MG 34
Sight:	1 × TZF 4/1
	1 × periscope
	1 × improvised sighting bar
Traverse:	360°
Elevation:	+15° -9°
Range:	6,800m (KwK)
Muzzle velocity:	750m/sec
Rate of fire:	20 rounds/minute (KwK)
Penetration performance:	600m = 33mm
	1,500m = 22mm

Bunker statistics:

Earth excavation	Concrete	Formed steel	Round steel
~80m³	~16m³	–	~1 tonne

Ventilation: Natural   Munitions storage:

3.7cm KwK L/46.5	= 360 rounds
MG 34	= 45,000 rounds

Locations:

Atlantic/ West Wall	Southeast (Balkans)	Total
60*	40	100**

*The majority, if not all, of these were destined for the West Wall where twenty-five turrets were allocated to Fest Pi Kdr XXI and eventually twenty-four were installed and ready for action: thirteen by Fest Pi Stab 21 and eleven by Fest Pi Stab 27.[53]
**None of these turrets are quoted as being used in the east, but at least one example was installed in Poland, northeast of Krakow, and until recently could still be seen.

A Panzer II VK901 turret armed with a 2cm KwK 38 gun. This example was installed in front of the seaside hotel called Kurhotellet on the Danish island of Fanö. (Frihedsmuseet)

modifications delayed production and there is no evidence to suggest that the tank actually saw service. The surplus turrets were released for use as fixed fortifications with MAN of Nürnberg commissioned to undertake the modifications. The company finished seventeen of the turrets each of which was fitted with the TZF 10 binocular telescopic sight. Additionally, *Artillerie Werkstatt die Kommandantur Hill* undertook work to modify ten further turrets, which were fitted with the TZF4 telescopic sight.[54]

Plans for the shelter were drawn up in March 1943[55] and it was broadly the same as most other examples in the series. The main access was at the side from a revetted trench that led to a small anteroom. Steps led from here up into the fighting compartment. This had a raised floor to take spent shells and which also concealed a drain that channelled water away without affecting the operation of the weapon. The waste water was discharged on to the lower floor, which was angled at 2 degrees to ensure that all the water found its way to the soak away outside.

The turret was mounted on a section of the original superstructure (including the hatches), which was secured to the top of the shelter with ten bolts. It was fitted in such a way that the two hatches, which were more vulnerable to enemy fire, faced towards the

rear. Drainage channels ensured that any rainwater or melted snow was conveyed away from the turret to the rear, which was sloped at 10 degrees.

Bauform 245 Panzer III
7.5cm KwK L/24
By the summer of 1942 it was realized that the *Panzer III* armed with its 5cm gun was increasingly ineffective against the new generation of enemy tanks. It was therefore decided to replace the main armament with the short-barrelled 7.5cm L/24 gun. Initially turrets from the *Ausf* L (and also a few *Ausf* Js) were modified. Later it was decided to complete the production of the *Ausf* M turrets with 7.5cm L/24 guns bringing the total completed to 700. These tanks played a valuable role in both North Africa and on the Eastern Front but it soon became clear that in spite of the addition of this more powerful weapon the *Panzer III*'s days were numbered. In April 1944 designs for a *fundamentring*, which was fitted to the shelter and onto which the turret was mounted, were finalized and in July plans for a concrete shelter were finished.

The concrete shelter for the Panzer III was fairly typical. A revetted trench led to the shelter that housed the HES10, hand-operated ventilator. To the right was the main fighting compartment, which was dominated by a pedestal that sat directly below the

Bauform 239 Panzer II VK 901 (*Normalserie*)

Turret statistics:
Armour (thickness/angle):

Gun mantlet	Front	Side	Rear	Roof
30mm/round	30mm/9°	15mm/25°	15mm/25°	12mm

Turret weight:	860kg	Weapon height:	*circa* 190mm
Overall height:	*circa* 580mm	Diameter:	*circa* 1,190mm

Weapon statistics:

Armament:	1 × 2cm KwK38
	1 × 7.92mm MG 34
Sight:	1 × TZF10 or 1 x TZF4
	8 periscopes in cupola
Traverse:	360°
Elevation:	+20° −10°
Range:	4,000m (KwK)
Muzzle velocity:	800m/sec
Rate of fire:	450 rounds/minute (KwK)
Penetration performance:	100m = 22mm
	1,000m = 11mm

Bunker statistics:

Earth excavation	Concrete	Formed steel	Round steel
~80m³	~16m³	–	~1 tonne

Ventilation: Natural   Munitions storage:
                              2cm KwK 38   = 2,800 rounds
                              MG 34   = 24,000 rounds

Availability:

No. of turrets available	No. of turrets released
27	27

Locations:

Denmark	Atlantic/ West Wall	Schools/ Experimental	Total
16	10	1	27

turret. To the side was the *hülsengrube*, an open pit, where spent shells could be safely jettisoned down an inclined shaft. This was fitted with a small chimney on the top that vented the fumes outside and was accessed through two hatches, one on top and one at the front, adjacent to the main entrance.

In January 1945 plans were drawn up for a wooden structure to mount the *Panzer* III turret for rapid installation (*schnelleinbau*). This was built in two sections: the *holzsockel*, or wooden body, onto which the *fundamentring* was secured with eight bolts, sat on top of the *fundament*, or base. The *holzsockel* was built from machined timber and was constructed with an opening in the side below the turret that led to the *hülsengrube*. The base was constructed from piles driven into the ground, which were braced with horizontal beams. Access to the shelter was via a revetted trench that led to an opening in the base.

Some twenty-one Panzer III turrets with 7.5cm guns were dispatched in March 1945 to Bruck an der Leitha in northern Austria to protect Vienna, but the city fell to Red Army forces on 13 April before the

turrets had arrived. The other turret was installed at the Hillersleben test facility.

Bauform 245 Panzer III
5cm KwK L/42
As early as March 1942 the *Oberkommando des Heeres* considered phasing out the *Panzer* III in favour of the Panther. In the summer of the year production of the *Ausf* M was scaled down and soon after a number of hulls were set aside for use as self-propelled guns (*Sturmgeschütz* 40 *Ausf* G and

Bauform 245 Panzer III 7.5cm KwK L/24

Turret statistics:
Armour (thickness/angle):

Gun mantlet	Front	Side	Rear	Roof
50mm	50mm	30mm	30mm	12mm

Note: the angle of the armour plate depended on the turret type used.

Weapon statistics:
Armament:　　　　　　　1 × 7.5cm KwK L/24
　　　　　　　　　　　　1 × MG 34
Sight:　　　　　　　　　5 vision slits in cupola
Traverse:　　　　　　　360°
Elevation:　　　　　　　+20° −10°
Range:　　　　　　　　6,200m
Muzzle velocity:　　　　Pz. Gr　　　385m/sec
　　　　　　　　　　　Spr. Gr　　　420m/sec
Rate of fire:　　　　　　12 rounds/min
Penetration performance:　100m =　　41mm
　　　　　　　　　　　　600m =　　38mm
　　　　　　　　　　　1,000m =　　35.5mm
　　　　　　　　　　　1,500m =　　32.5mm

Bunker statistics (concrete):

Length	Width	Height
5.67m	3.62m	2.80m

Ventilation: The installation was ventilated by means of a manually operated HES10 fan.
Munitions storage:
7.5cm KwK L/24　　　　= 216 rounds in 108 boxes

Locations:

East	Total
22	22

A Panzer III turret fitted with a 7.5cm KwK L/24 gun at the Rheinmetall proving ground, Hillersleben. In the background is an Italian P40 turret fitted with the same main armament. (G. B. Jarrett collection, US Army MHI courtesy of S. Zaloga)

Sturmgeschütz 40 *Ausf* F/8). Later front-line *Panzer* IIIs sent to the rear for an overhaul were also converted into self-propelled guns. This created a sizeable stockpile of *Panzer* III turrets for use as fixed fortifications.[56] In April 1944 plans were drawn up for the octagonal base plate to mount a *Panzer* III turret and in July detailed drawings of a concrete structure to accommodate the turret were completed. Plans were also drawn up for a wooden structure and a detailed description of the construction is included in the entry for *Bauform* 245 *Panzer* III 7.5cm L/24.

In February 1944, work to modify ten of the tank turrets that had been released for this purpose began. In March 1945 one turret was dispatched to Bruck an der Leitha on the Austrian border with Czechoslovakia and a further seven to Riesa to the north west of Dresden. However, none of these turrets seemingly arrived in time for installation.[57] The only turret that was completed was at the Hillersleben test facility.

Note: There is anecdotal evidence to suggest that Panzer III turrets armed with the original 3.7cm KwK and MG34 were also to be used as fixed fortifications,

but it has proved impossible to corroborate this.[58] Mention is also made of the use of the Panzerkampfwagen III (Fl) turret, but again no further evidence to support this has been found.[59]

A Panzer III turret fitted with a 5cm KwK L/42 at the Rheinmetall proving ground, Hillersleben. The main entrance with steel door can just be seen in the foreground. The structure to the side with the chimney is the hülsengrube for spent shells. (G. B. Jarrett collection, US Army MHI courtesy of S. Zaloga)

Bauform 245 Panzer III 5cm KwK L/42

Turret statistics:
Armour (thickness/angle):

Gun mantlet	Front	Side	Rear	Roof
50mm	50mm	30mm	30mm	12mm

Note: the angle of the armour plate depended on the turret type used.

Weapon statistics:
Armament: 1 × 5cm KwK L/42
                             1 × 7.92mm MG 34
Sight: Five vision slits in cupola
Traverse: 360°
Elevation: +20° −10°
Range: 4,800m
Muzzle velocity: Pz.Gr   685m/sec
                             Sprg.Gr   450m/sec
Rate of fire: 15 rounds/min
Penetration performance: 100m   =   50mm
                             600m   =   43mm
                             1,000m =   36mm
                             1,500m =   28mm

Bunker statistics:

Length	Width	Height
5.67m	3.62m	2.80m

Ventilation: The installation was ventilated by means of a manually operated HES10 fan.
Munitions storage:
5cm KwK L/42   = 216 rounds in 108 boxes

Availability:

No. of turrets available	No. of turrets released
110	0

Locations:

East	Total
8	8

Bauform 246 Panzer VK 3001* (Normalserie)
In January 1937 Henschel was commissioned to design a tank in the 30-ton class. It was to be armed with a 7.5cm KwK L/24 gun and protected by a turret with 50mm thick armour. An order for eight tanks was made, but only four hulls and six turrets, which were produced separately at the Krupp-Grusonwerk in Magdeburg, had been completed when priority was given to the development of the Tiger tank.[60] The six turrets were made available for use as fixed fortifications and were largely unaltered save for the addition of lugs to mount camouflage netting.

Bauform 246 Panzer VK3001 (*Normalserie*)

Turret statistics:
Armour (thickness/angle):

Gun mantlet	Front	Side	Rear	Roof
50mm/round	50mm/10°	50mm/15°	50mm/13°	15–20mm/83–90°

Turret weight:	2,500kg	Weapon height:	330mm
Overall height:	1,000mm	Diameter:	1,520mm

Weapon statistics:
Armament: 1 × 7.5cm KwK L/24
           1 × MG 34
Sight: 1 × TZF 9 telescopic sight for aiming
        10 × periscope for all round observation (7 in commanders cupola, 3 in the turret roof)
Traverse: 360°
Elevation: +20° −10°

	7.5cm KwK L/24	MG 34
Range:	6,200m	4,500m
Muzzle velocity: Pz. Gr	385m/sec	755m/sec
Spr. Gr	420m/sec	

Rate of fire: 12 rounds/min
Penetration performance:
100m	=	41mm
600m	=	38mm
1,000m	=	35.5mm
1,500m	=	32.5mm

Bunker statistics:

Earth excavation	Concrete	Formed steel	Round steel
180m³	55m³	–	3.30 tonne

Length	Width	Height
6.30m	7.65m	2.96m

Ventilation: The installation was ventilated by means of a manually operated HES10 fan installed in the anteroom. The exhaust fumes from the gun were extracted through a fan set in the roof of the turret, driven by a built in 70-watt motor with 12-volt battery.
Munitions storage:
The following could be stored in the ammunition recesses and in the turret:
7.5cm KwK L/24 = 168 rounds in 21 boxes
MG34 = *circa* 18,000 rounds in 12 boxes and 3,000–3,300 rounds in cartridge belt bags.

Availability:

No. of turrets available	No. of turrets released
6	6

Locations:

Atlantic/ West Wall	Total
6	6

A VK3001 turret armed with a 7.5cm KwK L/24 gun, which was positioned at Omaha Beach and formed part of the defences of Widerstandsnest 68. Clearly visible are the lugs around the base that were used to attach the camouflage. (US National Archives, courtesy of S. Zaloga)

VK3001 turret mounted on reinforced concrete shelter with integral section of sea wall.

The design of the shelter to mount the turrets was slightly more problematical. A memorandum from *Der Chef der Heeresrüstung und Befehlshaber des Ersatzheeres* to *General der Pioniere und Festung* in October 1943 noted that work on the shelter to mount the VK3001 turret had not been finished, and a completion date could not be given![61] This might have been partly due to the weight and size of the turret, because the concrete shelter that was eventually commissioned was a departure from the standard design with a larger anteroom near the entrance, a separate ammunition storeroom and thicker walls at 60cm (2ft).

In spite of this delay, in May 1944 the six VK3001 turrets were finally ready to be emplaced; four were installed in the Atlantic Wall and the final two turrets, which had initially also been earmarked for the Atlantic Wall, were sent to the store at the Fortifications HQ Homburg. At the beginning of March 1945 they were passed to *Fest Pi Stab* 27 for installation in the West Wall.[62]

Bauform 247 Panzer VK 3601 (Normalserie)

In the summer of 1939 Krupp was contracted to develop a turret with 100mm (4in) of armour that could mount a 10.5cm gun. Later in May 1941 this contract was cancelled and instead an order was placed with the company to produce six turrets that could mount a weapon with improved armour penetration capability. However, by July 1941 it was recognized that it would be impossible to supply the necessary quantity of tungsten for the armour piercing shells and the decision was taken not to continue with the project. Krupp was now ordered to simply complete the six turrets so that they could be used as fixed fortifications. Work began on plans for a shelter to mount the turret, but development was beset with problems were never seemingly resolved[63] and Allied bombing raids on Essen, where the turrets were stored, finally ended any prospect of using them.[64]

Bauform 250 Panzer IV

It is somewhat surprising, given the widespread use of this expedient, that the turret of the *Panzer* IV was not used more extensively as a static pillbox. Over 1,000 turrets fitted with the 7.5cm L/24 gun were produced but few were made available for use as improvised fixed fortifications. One turret was installed at the Hillersleben test facility and in May

---

* The VK3001 and 3601 (or *Versuchskonstrucktion*) tanks were experimental constructions. The first two digits referred to the weight of the vehicle (30 and 36 tonnes respectively) and the last two digits to the vehicles classification.

Bauform 247 Panzer VK3601* (*Normalserie*)

Turret statistics:
Armour (thickness/angle):

Gun mantlet	Front	Side	Rear	Roof
100mm/0°	100mm/10°	80mm/0°	80mm/0°	26mm/90°

Weapon statistics:

Armament:	1 × 7.5 KwK
Sight:	1 × KgZF2
Traverse:	360°

Availability:

No. of turrets available	No. of turrets released
6	0

Bauform 250 Panzer IV

Weapon statistics:

Armament:	1 × 7.5cm KwK L/24
	1 × 7.92mm MG34
Traverse:	360°

Availability:

No. of turrets available	No. of turrets released
2	0

A Panzer IV turret fitted with a 7.5cm KwK L/24 at the Rheinmetall proving ground, Hillersleben. The photograph was taken by the late Col G. B. Jarrett in the summer of 1945. (G. B. Jarrett collection, US Army MHI courtesy of S. Zaloga)

1944 two repaired turrets were detailed as being stored at the *Heeres-Zeugamt*, Vienna, but there are no details of their release or indeed of any *Panzer* IV turrets being installed on any front.[65] Part of the reason for this might have been that the *Panzer* IV formed the backbone of the *Panzer* Divisions and was still in production until the end of the war. But the same could be said of the Panther turret and this was employed almost universally. This then leaves the possibility that the armour of the Panzer IV was considered too thin and as such it was not well suited to static employment.

Bauform 240 Panzer 35(t) (Normalserie)
Umbau auf 3.7cm KwK 38(t) und MG37(t) – rebuilt with 3.7cm KwK 38(t) and MG37(t)

A considerable number of *Panzer* 35(t)s were confiscated from the Czechs following the German occupation in March 1939. Many of these were considered unfit for service and of those that were used the majority were lost in battle. The few tanks that survived were converted into *Artillerie Schleppers* (artillery tractors) with the removal of the turret and covering the opening. The surplus turrets, together with a number salvaged from tanks returned for repair, were made available for use as fixed fortifications.

These turrets were still fitted with their original armament – a 3.7cm KwK34(t) L/40 and a 7.92mm MG37(t) – but these were to be removed and replaced with the mantlet from the Panzer 35(t)'s sister tank, the Panzer 38(t). Skoda, the original tank manufacturer, was contracted to undertake the work and it was completed at the company's Pilsen works. In spite of this modification the turret was still described in official documents as being *normalserie*.

Plans for the shelter were drawn up in March 1943, and its layout was broadly the same as the others in the series.[66] The modified turret sat on top of an octagonal base plate which was secured to the top of the shelter with eight bolts. Immediately below the turret was the main fighting compartment with its raised wooden floor. This was reached via steps from the entranceway, which led in turn to the main trench system. As with all the shelters in this series the possibility of water seeping in was a major concern. The upper surface was designed in such a way that rain was directed away from the turret and internally steps were taken to prevent flooding, including the fitting of a drain in the fighting compartment, slopping the floor in the entranceway and the digging of a soak away.

Bauform 240 Panzer 35(t) (Behelfsmäßig)
(Improvised version – main armament replaced with MG37(t))

As with the *normalserie*, the mantlet of the Panzer 35(t) *behelfsmäßig* was replaced with the frontispiece from the *Panzer* 38(t). However, on this version the main 3.7cm KwK 38(t) was omitted in favour of a further MG37(t) with telescopic sight. On 1 April 1945 Skoda was ordered to complete nine of these turrets for installation in Festung Brünn* The possibility of restoring the standard 3.7cm main gun was considered, but the pressing situation meant that this idea was dismissed and the turrets were to be

A rare view of a Panzer 35(t) turret. The main and coaxial armament have been removed. This example was installed at Kjevik in the Kristiansand area of Norway. (Erik Ritterbach)

installed as originally configured. It is unclear whether all or indeed any turrets were emplaced by the time the city fell to forces of the Red Army on 26 April 1945.[67]

Bauform 241 Panzer 38(t) (Normalserie)

A considerable number of *Panzer* 38(t)s were seized by the Germans when they occupied Czechoslovakia in March 1939. These played a key role in the fighting in Poland, France and the Low Countries and they were also employed during the invasion of the Soviet Union. However, the shortcomings of the tank soon became apparent against the superior Soviet models, like the T34, and in December 1941 a decision was taken to use the chassis as the basis for a self-propelled gun. The turret was removed and replaced with a simple prefabricated superstructure and either the Soviet 7.62cm anti-tank gun or the German 7.5cm Pak 40 was fitted to counter the heavily armoured Soviet tanks. Other tanks had their turrets removed and were fitted with an artillery piece as an infantry support vehicle, or were transformed into reconnaissance vehicles, armoured ammunition carriers or anti-aircraft gun platforms. The surplus turrets were made available for use as improvised fixed fortifications and this number was boosted with

the decision to switch production from the *Panzer* 38(t) *Ausf* G and instead concentrate on tank hunters like the Hetzer, because a significant number of turrets had already been built and were now no longer needed.[69]

In terms of operation and equipment the *Panzer* 38(t) turret was basically the same as those intended for use in tanks. The weapons and optics and the traversing and elevating gear were common to both.

The minor alterations to prepare the turrets for their new role was carried out at the Böhmisch-Mährische Maschinenfabrik (BMM)[†] in Prague, which was contracted to complete 225 turrets ready for installation using a mixture of new and old turrets. A further one hundred turrets were to be completed by the *Heeres Kraftfahrzeug Werkstatt* in Pschelautsch (Prelouc) in Böhmen (Bohemia) and another twenty-six at the *Heeres-Zeugamt* in Vienna.[70]

At least ten more turrets were seemingly released after this initial work because 361 turrets were

---

*A city in the Sudetenland of the former Czechoslovakia (modern day Brno).

[†]This was the new name given to the Czech manufacturer CKD by the Germans.

Bauform 240 Panzer 35(t) (*Normalserie*)

Turret statistics:
Armour (thickness/angle):

Gun mantlet	Front	Side	Rear	Roof
25mm/round	25–50mm/10°	16mm/14°	16mm/15°	8mm/81–90°

Turret weight: *circa* 1,500kg   Weapon height: *circa* 278mm
Overall height: *circa* 800mm   Diameter: *circa* 1,190mm

Weapon statistics:
Armament: 1 × 3.7cm KwK 38(t)
     1 × 7.92mm MG37(t) Brno
Sight: 1 × TZF 38(t)
     1 × MGZF38(t)
     1 × hand operated periscope (t) (No. 2301)
     4 × vision mirrors in commander's cupola
Traverse: 360° (Note: the turret mounted MG had a horizontal field of fire of 12° right and 10° left)
Elevation: +25° −10°
Range: 6,800m (KwK)
Muzzle velocity: 750m/sec
Rate of fire: 20 rounds/minute (KwK)
Penetration performance: 100m =   40mm
         600m =   33mm

Bunker statistics:

Earth excavation	Concrete	Formed steel	Round steel
~80m³	~16m³	–	~1,00 tonne

Ventilation: Natural   Munitions storage:
         3.7cm KwK 38(t)   =   396 rounds
         MG37(t)   = 24,000 rounds

Availability:

No. of turrets available	No. of turrets released
38	36

Locations:

Denmark	Atlantic/ West Wall	East	Total
30	5	3	38

A technical drawing depicting a concrete shelter mounting a Panzer 35(t) (Behelfsmäßig) turret where the main armament was replaced with twin MGs. (Bundesarchiv)

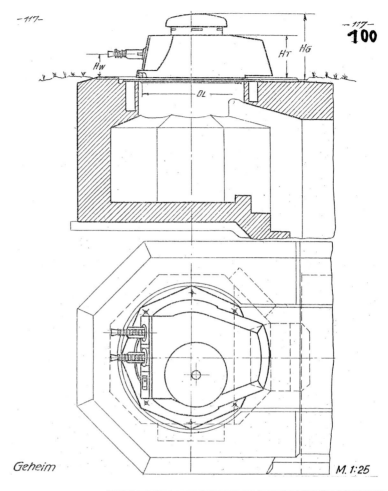

actually installed. These might have been taken from the turrets that were to be fitted with twin machine guns (*see Bauform* 241) or it might simply be that more of the turrets available were released for use from Army Stores Depots. Certainly at the end of March 1945 *OKH Inspektion der Festungen* called for tank turrets to be included in the anti-tank emergency armament programme and in April 1945 a number of *Panzer* 38(t) turrets arrived and were installed in German cities on the Eastern Front.

The turrets were to be fitted to both concrete and wooden shelters. Plans for the concrete shelter were drawn up in October 1942 and it was identical to the other standard designs.[71] Access to the shelter was via the entrance at the side which connected the position with the main trench system. The area just outside the entrance was also where the soakaway was located,

A Panzer 38(t) turret that was located near Lista, Norway. Both the 3.7cm KwK and machine gun have been removed. The base plate, which was taken from the tank's upper deck, can be clearly seen. (Erik Ritterbach)

240 Panzer 35(t) (*Behelfsmäßig*)

Turret statistics:
Armour (thickness/angle):

Gun mantlet	Front	Side	Rear	Roof
25mm/round	25–50mm/10°	16mm/14°	16mm/15°	8mm/81–90°

Turret weight:	*circa* 1,300kg	Weapon height:	*circa* 278mm
Overall height:	*circa* 800mm	Diameter:	*circa* 1,190mm

Weapon statistics:
Armament: 2 × 7.92mm MG37(t) Brno
Sight: 2 × MGZF38(t)
 1 × hand operated periscope (t) (No. 2301)
 4 × vision mirrors in commander's cupola
Traverse: 360° (Note: the MGs had a horizontal field of fire of 15° right and 8° left)
Elevation: +25° −12°

Bunker statistics:

Earth excavation	Concrete	Formed steel	Round steel
~80m³	~16m³	–	~1 tonne

Ventilation: Natural Munitions storage:
 MG37(t) = 45,000 rounds

Locations:

East	Total
9	9

which dispersed all the excess water from the position and ensured that the operation of the turret was not compromised. Steps took the crew from the entrance-way up to the fighting compartment below the turret. As with a number of tank turrets used in this way the original *Panzer* 38(t) superstructure was used and was secured to the top of the shelter with eleven bolts. The superstructure was reconfigured with the removal of the radio operator's hatch and was rotated through 180 degrees so that the section that normally faced towards the rear now faced forward.

The Panzer 38(t) was also mounted on a wooden framework[72] that was relatively straightforward to construct. Firstly, the construction area was staked out, then the turf and the top layer of soil were removed and kept for later use as camouflage. The bulk of the excavation work was now completed. If

necessary, and this was principally the case in marshy ground, posts were driven into the ground to provide a solid foundation. With the preparatory work completed, the main uprights could be lowered into the ground and secured with horizontal beams using a mixture of nails, wire and staples. Next, the roof was attached, which was covered in felt to waterproof the structure and finally the turret was installed before the whole was camouflaged.[73]

Uniquely, details have survived describing how the Panzer 38(t) turrets were transported to their final destination and some of the instructions on how they were to be operated. The turrets were supplied with their foundation plates and during transportation, squared timbers were placed beneath the plate to prevent damage to the turret basket. On arrival at its final destination the timbers were removed and the

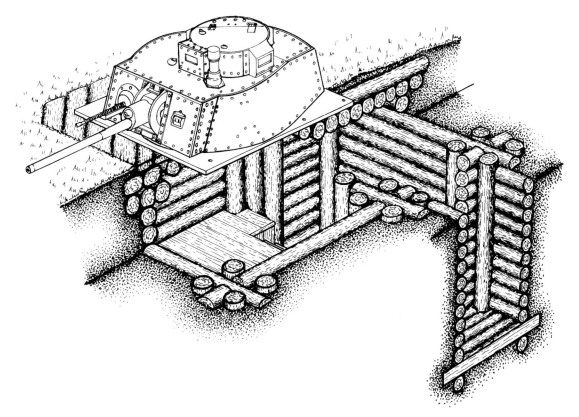

Panzer 38(t) Holzunterstand – Panzer 38(t) mounted on wooden shelter.

turret and baseplate were either hoisted into place on the shelter or, increasingly often, the turret had to be manoeuvred into place manually. The foundation plate was then bolted in place. Care had to be taken to ensure that the turret was level and that all the bolts had been tightened. Thereafter, the fixings needed to be regularly checked to ensure that they had not come loose. A wooden accessory box was also dispatched with the turret and bore the same identification marks as the turret. This included all the other equipment necessary for its effective operation.

Because no ventilation system was supplied it was essential that the turret hatch was left open when firing so that the crew was not overcome by dust and fumes. It was also suggested that the door to the shelter was left open, although both measures compromised the crew's safety.[74]

Bauform 241 Panzer 38(t) (Behelfsmäßig)
(Improvised version – main armament replaced with MG37(t))
As with the *Panzer 35(t)* a decision was taken to modify a number of *Panzer 38(t)* turrets and replace the main armament with a further machine gun and telescopic sight. In total eighty-four turrets were to be modified in this way.* A single experimental turret was certainly completed by May 1944 and four more turrets were ordered on 1 April 1945 and were to be completed by Skoda in Pilsen for installation in 'Festung Brünn'.† However, as the war in Europe entered its closing stages the possibility of reverting to the original configuration was considered and

---

*It is possible that a number of these turrets were in fact released as *normalserie* because a paper written in May 1944 quoted 351 as being released but a report dated March 1945 stated 361 were installed.
†Modern-day Brno.

Bauform 241 Panzer 38(t) (*Normalserie*)

Turret statistics:
Armour (thickness/angle):

Gun mantlet	Front	Side	Rear	Roof
25mm/round	25–50mm/10°	15–30mm/10°	15–30mm/10°	12mm/90°

Turret weight:	*circa* 1,570 kg	Weapon height:	*circa* 292mm
Overall height:	*circa* 730mm	Diameter:	*circa* 1,190mm

Weapon statistics:

Armament:	1 × 3.7cm KwK 38(t)
	1 × 7.92mm MG37(t) Brno
Sight:	1 × TZF 38(t)
	1 × MGZF 38(t)
	1 × TRbl F38(t)
Traverse:	360° (Note: the turret mounted MG had a horizontal field of fire of 12° right and 10° left)
Elevation:	+25° −10°
Range:	6,800m (KwK)
Muzzle velocity:	750m/sec
Rate of fire:	20 rounds/minute (KwK)
Penetration performance:	1,000m = 28mm
	1,500m = 22mm

Bunker statistics:
Concrete Shelter

Earth excavation	Concrete	Formed steel	Round steel
~80m³	~16m³	–	~1 tonne

Ventilation: Natural

Munitions storage:

3.7cm KwK 38(t)	=	396 rounds
MG37(t)	=	24,000 rounds

Length	Width	Height
N/K	4.27m	2.60m

Wooden shelter[68]

Earth excavation	Concrete	Wood*	Steel
~35 m³	–	~12.6 m³	–

Note: In addition the wooden shelter required 40 staples; 120m (393ft) of wire (2mm diameter); 10kg (22lb) of nails (75mm (3in) and 90mm (3½in); and 10m² (33ft²) roofing felt.

* Including: 385 metres (1,263ft) of 200mm (8in) diameter poles, 12m² (39ft²) of 30mm (1in) boards and 2m² (6ft²) of 50mm (2in) boards.

Bauform 241 Panzer 38(t) (*Normalserie*) cont'd

Ventilation: natural   Munitions storage: N/K

Length	Width	Height
3.90m	2.40m	2.50m

Availability:

No. of turrets available	No. of turrets released
435	351

Locations:

Denmark	Norway	Italy	Atlantic/ West Wall	Southeast (Balkans)	East	Schools/ Experim.	Total
20	75	25	9	150	78	4	361

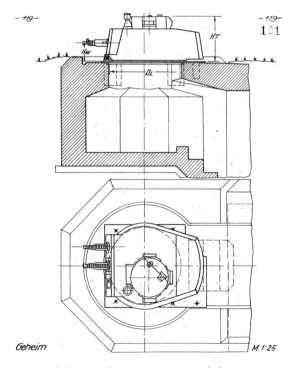

A technical drawing depicting a concrete shelter mounting a Panzer 38(t) (Behelfsmäßig) turret where the main armament was replaced with twin MGs. (Bundesarchiv)

accepted. Thus, the four turrets sent to the fortress commander in the city were supplied with a standard 3.7cm gun. It is unclear whether any turrets were emplaced before Brünn fell to the Red Army on 26 April 1945.[77]

Panzer V
See Chapter 3, Part 3.

Panzer VI
In the final months of the war there were plans to utilize Tiger and Königstiger turrets in fixed defences, but none appear to have been emplaced.[78] However, there is evidence to suggest that at least one disabled Tiger I belonging to s.Pz.Abt 504 was used as an improvised strong point at Seravezza (Lucca), Italy.

Specially designed turrets

Bauform 226 F Pz DT 4007
Other Designation: MG *Drehhaube* 4007
The F Pz DT 4007 was not, strictly speaking, a tank turret, but one of a series of armoured revolving hoods that were designed to provide a balance of firepower, protection and mobility. The plans for this particular version were drawn up in November 1943[80] and a trial production run of thirty turrets was

Bauform 241 Panzer 38(t) (*Behelfsmäßig*)

Turret statistics:
Armour (thickness/angle):

Gun mantlet	Front	Side	Rear	Roof
25mm/round	25–50mm/10°	15–30mm/10°	15–30mm/10°	12mm/90°

Turret weight:	*circa* 1,350 kg	Weapon height:	*circa* 292mm
Overall height:	*circa* 730mm	Diameter:	*circa* 1,190mm

Weapon statistics:
Armament: 2 × 7.92mm MG37(t) Brno
Sight: 2 × MGZF 38(t)
                   1 × TRbl F38(t)
Traverse: 360° (Note: the MGs had a horizontal field of fire of 15° right and 8° left)
Elevation: +25° −12°

Bunker statistics:

Earth excavation	Concrete	Formed steel	Round steel
~80m³	~16m³	–	~1,00 tonne

Ventilation: Natural   Munitions storage:
                               MG37(t)   = 45,000 rounds

Availability:[75]

No. of turrets available	No. of turrets released
84	N/K

Locations:

East	Total
4	4

completed and the turrets were all installed, but no further production was anticipated.[81]

The armoured hood was capable of mounting either an MG34 or MG42 but neither was supplied with the turret, rather the crew occupying the position was expected to provide the weaponry. Two gun supports were provided, one for each model of machine gun, with the support not in use stored in a holder located in the roof of the turret. The mounting allowed the gun to be elevated and depressed and the turret could be traversed manually by turning a handle. When not in use the hood could be locked in place by means of a clamp fitted to the turret ring.

The machine gun was aimed by using its own sights. General observation was through a periscope or via vision slits that could be closed when not in use. The periscope protruded through an opening in the roof. When retracted the opening could be covered with a lockable flap.

When the machine gun was in use a flexible tube ensured that the spent cartridges were safely discharged onto the floor.[82] No artificial ventilation was provided so it was important when using the MG34 that the entrance hatch, at the rear of the hood, was slightly ajar. More critically, when using the MG42 it was essential that the hatch be opened up

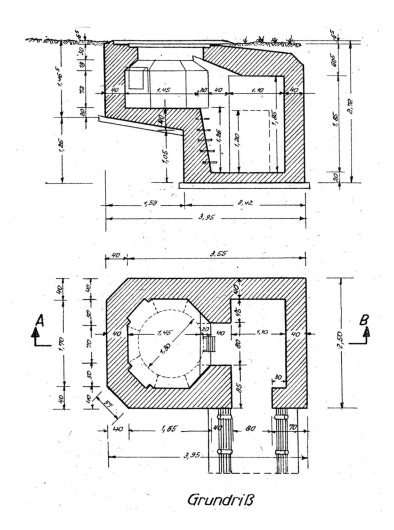

A technical drawing depicting a concrete shelter capable of mounting either the F Pz DT 4007 or 4010.
(Bundesarchiv)

Grundriß

completely to avoid the build up of gas, although this compromised one of the main objectives of the hood – namely crew protection.

The turret was constructed from steel plate that provided protection for the crew of two against small-arms fire and light shrapnel but was sufficiently light 325kg (716lb)) to be man portable, at least over short distances. Handles on the base plate meant that four to five men on either side could load or unload the hood and move it to its final position. This was either a prepared concrete or wooden shelter or, if neces-sary, on firm ground, although in loose or sandy soil a wooden framework was desirable. Once installed the hood could be camouflaged using the six lugs welded to the exterior.

Bauform 226 F Pz DT4010
Other Designation: MG *Drehhaube* 4010
See text above for Bauform 226 F Pz DT4007 – the 4010 turret was mounted on the same shelter.

Bauform 227 F Pz DT4011
Other Designation: MG *Drehhaube* 4011(f)*
The F Pz DT4011 had originally been used by France to strengthen the Maginot Line. Positions, sometimes constructed from concrete, were prepared into which the *tourelle démontable pour mitrailleuse* were to be installed in times of emergency. However, this work was largely in vain, as the German invasion plan specifically avoided a frontal attack on the border defences and as a result, many of these turrets fell into German hands after the fall of France in June 1940.

Bauform 226 F Pz DT 4007

Turret statistics:
Armour (thickness/angle):

Gun mantlet	Front	Side	Rear	Roof
–	15–25mm/45°	8–10mm/50–55°	8mm/55°	8mm/90°

Turret weight:	325kg	Weapon height:	*circa* 150mm
Overall height:	490mm	Diameter:	*circa* 1,275mm

Weapon statistics:

Armament:	1 × 7.92mm MG34 or 1 × 7.92mm MG42 (on special mount with gun support 5).
Sight:	Viewing slits were provided in the turret together with a periscope in the roof. The gun was aimed using the machine gun's own sights.
Traverse:	360°
Elevation:	+/−12°

Bunker statistics:

Earth excavation	Concrete	Formed steel	Round steel
70m³	15.5m³	–	0.92 tonne

Length	Width	Height
3.95m	2.50m	2.72m

Ventilation: natural   Munitions storage: 45,000–60,000 rounds of MG ammunition could be stored in the shelter.

Locations:

Atlantic/ West Wall	Italy	East	Total
10	10	10	30

It was not until much later in the war that consideration was given to using these turrets and only in July 1944 were plans for a concrete shelter to house the armoured turret drawn up.[84] The design broadly followed the general principles of the other armoured hoods but with adjustments made for the fact that the cupola was completely self-contained and came ready to install. The ground for the position was excavated and a rough concrete mix poured to act as a foundation and the anchor for the turret. Once positioned a 40cm (15in) thick circular concrete jacket was poured. Two flanges on the turret base section were bolted to the concrete surround allowing the turret, which sat proud of the ground, to rotate. A revetted communication trench led to a flight of steps, which in turn led to the main entranceway and the door to the armoured turret. A small opening at the bottom of the shelter was linked to a chamber that took the spent ammunition cases.

The turret was designed to take one man and a machine gun. The weapon was not supplied with the turret, but, like the other armoured hoods and the MG *Panzernest*, was supplied by the crew. The troops manning the position were also responsible for camouflaging the structure.

---

*The suffix (f) is in recognition of the fact that the turret had its origins in France.

Bauform 226 F Pz DT4010

Weapon statistics:
Armament: 1 × 7.92mm MG34 **or** 1 × 7.92mm MG42 (on special mount with gun support 6).
Sight: Viewing slits were provided in the turret together with a periscope in the ceiling.
                The gun was aimed using the machine gun's own sights.
Traverse: 360°
Elevation: +/−12°

Bunker statistics:

Earth excavation	Concrete	Formed steel	Round steel
70m³	15.5m³	–	0.92 tonne

Length	Width	Height
3.95m	2.50m	2.72m

Ventilation: No artificial ventilation was provided so when firing, it was essential that the ventilation slide in the ceiling was open. It was also advisable for the entrance hatch to be slightly open. When using the MG42 the hatch had to be opened up completely to prevent the build-up of noxious fumes and dust.
Munitions storage: 45,000–60,000 rounds of MG ammunition could be stored in the shelter.

Locations:

Denmark	Total
20	20

*In October 1944 an order was issued for nineteen turrets for the West Wall and before the end of the year work had begun on eleven of these. It is assumed that these were in addition to those installed in Denmark.[83]

In August 1944 detailed drawings for a wooden shelter to mount the armoured turret were completed.[85] The layout was much the same as the concrete model with a simple entranceway leading to the turret door. The turret was similarly secured to the wooden base with two bolts and a chamber below the floor was incorporated to capture the spent machine gun cartridges.

Armoured Cars

In addition to obsolete tank turrets, turrets were also taken from a number of German armoured cars and semi-tracked vehicles. These were mounted on concrete shelters and given the designations *Bauformen* 259 and 260. The turrets used were unique in that they were open-topped with only a folding wire mesh anti-grenade screen protecting the crew. Not surprisingly, this was a huge handicap when the turret was used in a static role.

Bauform 259 Stand für 2cm Hängelafette 38 aus Spähwagen
This turret had originally been fitted to the Sdkfz 234/1 eight-wheeled armoured car and later the Sdkfz 251/23 half track and the Sdkfz 140/1 (based on the *Panzer* 38(t) chassis). A number were also fitted to some versions of the Sdkfz 250/9 half track. The turret resembled that mounted on the Sdkfz 222 armoured car, but this version had thicker front armour and was a six-sided rather than a ten-sided construction.

According to a German report of 5 April 1945 twelve of these turrets were delivered to the Eastern Front and were installed as part of the defences of Frankfurt an der Oder.[88]

A technical drawing depicting a concrete shelter mounting an F Pz DT4011. (Bundesarchiv)

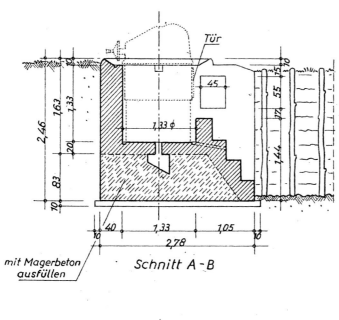

Schnitt A - B

mit Magerbeton ausfüllen

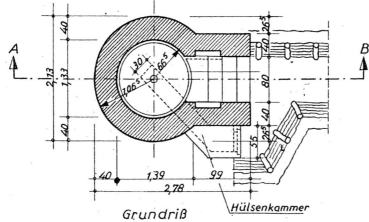

Grundriß

Hülsenkammer

Bauform 260 Stand für 2cm SKL 38 aus Spähwagen mit Ringschild

Other Designation: F Pz DT4901 or MG *Drehhaube* 4901

These turrets were taken from the Sdkfz 222 armoured car. Almost 1,000 of these were produced between 1936 and 1943 before it was replaced with the Sdkfz 250/9 half track. The turret was fitted with either a 20mm KwK30 or KwK38 with a coaxially mounted MG34 machine gun. The turret had ten sides and the armour was uniformly 8mm (under 1in). A number of the original turrets were fitted to the Sdkfz

Bauform 227 F Pz DT4011

Turret statistics:

Overall height:	420mm	Diameter:	1,330cm

Weapon statistics:

Armament: 1 × 7.92mm MG42

Sight: The turret had all round observation via a periscope (3 × 14°).
The gun was aimed using the machine gun's own sights.

Traverse: 360° (The weapon could additionally be traversed on its own mount 8° either side.)

Elevation: +/− 14°

Bunker statistics:

Earth excavation	Concrete	Formed steel	Round steel
~38m³	~6m³	~3m³	~0.4t

Length	Width	Height
2.78m	2.13m	2.46m

Ventilation: The only ventilation for the turret when firing was by means of the entrance and the turret hatch, which had to be opened slightly.

Munitions storage: 3,000 rounds of MG ammunition in 10 boxes could be stored in the installation.

Locations:

No evidence exists detailing if any of these turrets were installed.

Bauform 259 *Stand für 2cm Hängelafette 38 aus Spähwagen*

Turret statistics:

Armour (thickness/angle):

Gun mantlet	Front	Side	Rear	Roof
10mm/40°	30mm/40°	8mm/40°	8mm/38°	Open

Weapon statistics:

Armament: 1 × 2cm KwK 38 L/55 in *Hängelafette* (or swinging mount)
1 × 7.92mm MG 42

Sight: 1 × TZF3a

Traverse: 360°

Elevation: +70° -4°

Bunker statistics:[87]

Earth excavation	Concrete	Formed steel	Round steel
~85m³	~18m³	–	~1.00 t

Length	Width	Height
4.40m	2.80m	2.72m

Ventilation: Natural   Munitions storage:
2cm KwK 38 L/55 = 2,400 rounds
MG 42   = 19,500 rounds

Bauform 260 *Stand für 2cm SKL 38 aus Spähwagen mit Ringschild*

Turret statistics:[89]
Armour (thickness/angle):

Gun mantlet	Front	Side	Rear	Roof
8mm/35°	8mm/35°	8mm/35°	8mm/35°	Open

Diameter: 1,450mm

Weapon statistics:
Armament: 1 × 2cm KwK38 L/55
           1 × 7.92mm MG42
Sight: 1 × TZF3a
Traverse: 360°
Elevation: +87°−4°

250/9, but as early as May 1944 fifteen turrets were reported as being available to be installed on concrete shelters.[90] A little under a year later it was reported that fourteen of these turrets had been installed, although no details are provided as to where they were used.[91] By April 1945 a further fifty of these turrets had been despatched to the Eastern Front and were to be deployed around Frankfurt an der Oder,[92] although it is unclear whether they were actually installed.

A significant number of the original turrets armed with the 2 cm KwK30 were also released for use and again the bulk of these were sent to the Eastern Front (140 of the 150 installed). This was given the designation F Pz DT 4903.

Table 3 Old and new *Bauform* numbers and alternative designations

Bauform		Revolving hoods	Alternative designation
New	Old		
226	77	F.Pz.DT 4007 and F.Pz.DT 4010	MG *Drehhaube* 4007/4010
227	–	F.Pz.DT 4011	MG *Drehhaube* 4011(f)

Bauform		Tank turret designation	Alternative designation
New	Old		
231	67	*Panzer Kampfwagen Turm* I (*Behelfsmäßig*)	F.Pz.DT 4803
232a	67	*Panzer Kampfwagen Turm* II (Flamingo)	
232b	67	*Panzer Kampfwagen Turm* II (Flamingo) (*Behelfsmäßig*)	
233	67	*Panzer Kampfwagen Turm* I	
234	67	*Panzer Kampfwagen Turm* II (*Behelfsmäßig*)	F.Pz.DT 4806 *Drehhaube* IIa
235	67	*Panzer Kampfwagen R35*	F.Pz.DT 4808
236	67	*Panzer Kampfwagen Turm* II (*Mit Bugpanzerdach*)	
237	67	*Panzer Kampfwagen Turm* II (*Mit achteckigem Fundament*)	
238	67	*Panzer Kampfwagen Turm* II (*Behelfsmäßig*)	F.Pz.DT 4804 *Drehhaube* II
239	67	*Panzer Kampfwagen Turm* II (VK901)	
240	67	*Panzer Kampfwagen Turm* 35(t)	

241	67	*Panzer Kampfwagen Turm* 38(t)	
242	—	*Panzer Kampfwagen Turm* M42(i)	F.Pz.DT 4815
243	—	*Panzer Kampfwagen Turm* T70(r)	
244	—	*Panzer Kampfwagen Turm* T34(r) (*Behelfsmäßig*)	F.Pz.DT 4805
245	—	*Panzer Kampfwagen Turm* III (5cm/7.5cm)	
246	—	*Panzer Kampfwagen Turm* VK3001	
247	—	*Panzer Kampfwagen Turm* VK3601	
248	—	*Panzer Kampfwagen Turm* T34(r)	
249	—	*Panzer Kampfwagen Turm* P40(i)	F.Pz.DT 4814
250	—	*Panzer Kampfwagen Turm* IV	
251	67 d	*Panzer Kampfwagen Turm* KVI	
259	—	2cm *Hängelafette* 38 *aus Spähwagen*	
260	—	2cm SKL 38 *aus Spähwagen mit Ringschild*	F.Pz.DT 4901

Part 2 – Locations

ATLANTIC WALL

France (Including the Channel Islands)

The Atlantic Wall was instigated in 1941 at the behest of Hitler and eventually ran for almost 3,000 miles from Norway in the north to the Spanish border. The most vulnerable section of the wall, and therefore the most heavily fortified, was in France, and in particular around Calais where the Channel is at its narrowest and where the threat of invasion was considered greatest. This stretch of coastline was replete with casemates for artillery, anti-tank guns and machine guns as well as command bunkers and troop shelters. Away from this concentration the defences, with one important exception, were on a smaller scale and were more thinly spread. The exception was the Channel Islands. Hitler was determined that this small, but psychologically important piece of the British Isles would not easily be recaptured by the Allies and in October 1941 he issued a directive to turn the Channel Islands into an impregnable fortress. The principal islands – Alderney, Guernsey and Jersey – were disproportionately equipped with artillery batteries, anti-aircraft

installations and coastal defences. The same was true for the numbers of emplaced tank turrets, with over one hundred installed on the three main islands.

The tank turrets, which were all taken from obsolete French models captured in 1940, were employed in different roles according to need. Some were used independently to provide the main focal point of defence, for example in and around ports, some formed part of larger defensive positions while others were used to provide close-in support for some of the larger installations like artillery batteries.

Alderney
Although Alderney was the smallest of the three Channel Islands to be fortified by the Germans, for its size it had a greater concentration of defences than Jersey and Guernsey. To protect the island there were sixteen emplaced tank turrets (seven tank turrets with 3.7cm gun and machine gun (probably APXR turrets) and nine tank turrets with 3.7cm gun only (probably Renault FT17s)), which were largely concentrated around the coast. In addition the Germans had a mobile reserve of twelve to fifteen tanks (mostly FT17s) that were stored at three tank parks. At one of

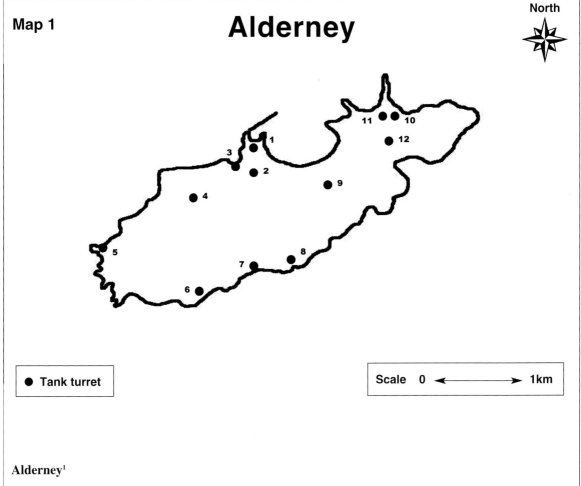

Alderney[1]

1. Resistance Nest 'Hafen' Harbour area – 3 tank turrets. One of these was in a two-tiered emplacement on the tip of the breakwater. The tank turret was positioned above a machine gun with 180 degree traverse.[2]
2. Strongpoint 'Hafen Süd York Hill – 1 tank turret.
3. Resistance Nest 'Dohlenfeste' Fort Doyle – 2 tank turrets
4. Resistance Nest 'Müllerhof' Bonne Terre – 1 tank turret
5. Resistance Nest 'Steinfeste' Fort Clonque – 1 tank turret
6. Resistance Nest 'Süd' Les Couriaux – 2 tank turrets

7. Flak Battery 'Millionär' and DeM Station Quatre Vents – 1 tank turret
8. Strongpoint 'Südhafen' Cachalière – 1 tank turret
9. 88mm Flak Battery 'Höhe 145' Mannez Garenne – 1 tank turret
10. Corblets Bay – 1 tank turret
11. Lager 'Norderney' Saye Bay – 1 tank turret
12. Strongpoint 'Graue Häuser' (South) Coast Guard Cottages – 1 tank turret

[1]Festung, Alderney, *The German Defences of Alderney* by T. Davenport.
[2]Pantcheff states that the turret was fitted with a 2cm gun but this seems unlikely since all the turrets on the island seem to have been of French origin and fitted with 3.7cm guns. P51 Pantcheff.

An FT17 with riveted octagonal turret and 3.7cm KwK 144(f) gun. This example was installed at Resistance Nest Archirondel, Jersey. (CIOS, M. Ginns)

these, Strongpoint *Rosenhof* (Rose Farm), the tanks were simply dug in to strengthen the defences.[1]

Guernsey

Although not having the same concentration of fortifications as Alderney, Guernsey nevertheless had an impressive array of artillery batteries, anti-aircraft installations, strong points* and resistance nests.[†] These defences were mostly located to the west, north and east of the island; cliffs to the south making any attack from that direction unlikely. To protect the batteries and provide added firepower to the coastal positions a number of tank turrets were installed. Somewhere in the region of 30 tank turrets, all taken from captured French tanks, were used. There were circa 20 FT17 turrets supplemented by a number of APX R turrets.[2]

Jersey

By far the largest number of tank turrets were installed on Jersey; sixty-one in total. The majority of the turrets, as was the case on the other islands, were taken from old French Renault FT17s with a few more modern APXR turrets.[‡] These were located along the coast with particular concentrations in the north, east and south-east of the island which the Germans believed were the least likely avenues for an Allied attack.

Immediately after the war British forces removed

most of the fixed weapons on the Channel Islands. Those that were not scrapped, including many of the tank turrets, were taken away in the 1950s in the post-war scrap-metal drive. A number of tank turrets did survive however. At least one FT17 turret on Jersey is in the hands of a private collector, and another, an octagonal turret that originally protected Fort Aubin, is on display at the Occupation Museum, St Ouen. Additionally, two of the APXR turrets can still be seen in their original locations protecting Elizabeth Castle and another at Les Creux, St Brelade. Two further examples can be seen on Guernsey where one turret (taken from Les Nicolles, the Forest) can be

---

*The German strong point or *stützpunkt* was designed for all-round defence and tended to include a series of emplacements, including bunkers mounting various weapons, troop/munitions shelters and command posts and was either an artillery or infantry strong point. The positions were all linked by trenches and the perimeter was protected by mines and barbed wire.
† The resistance nest or *widerstandsnest* was the smallest type of defensive position which was sometimes a self-contained position or formed part of a larger defence zone or fortress. Though difficult to make generalizations they would often consist of an anti-tank gun position supported by machine gun and mortar positions linked by trenches and protected by barbed wire and mines.
‡ Broken down as follows: thirty-six FT17s with MG; sixteen FT17s with 3.7cm KwK; and nine APX R with 3.7cm KwK and MG.

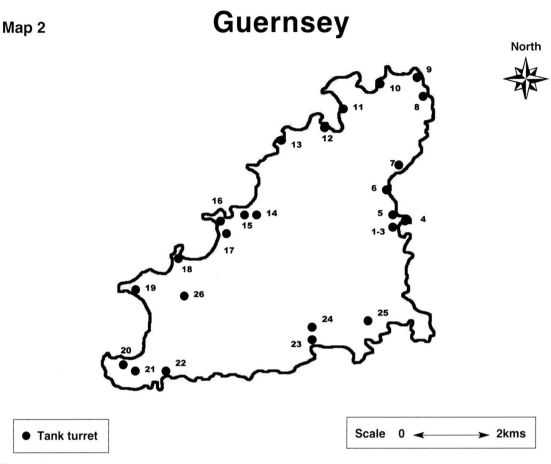

Guernsey

North

Map 2

● **Tank turret**

Scale 0 ⟷ 2kms

Guernsey[3]

1. Widerstandsnest (Resistance nest) Albert Pier – 1 tank turret with MG
2. Widerstandsnest Viktoria Pier – 1 tank turret with MG
3. Widerstandsnest Hafenreserve (White Hart Hotel) – 1 tank turret with 3.7cm PaK
4. Widerstandsnest Nordmole (White Rock) – 2 tank turrets with MGs
5. Widerstandsnest Peterseck (Salerie corner) – 1 tank turret with MG
6. Widerstandsnest Schonbucht-Mitte (Vale Road) – 1 Renault FT17 with MG
7. Widerstandsnest Richardseck (junction of Grandes Maisons Road and Bulwer Avenue) – 1 FT17 tank turret [Belle Greve Bay between Houge a la Perre and Mont Crevelt (p13 Occupation Review 22)]
8. Widerstandsnest Schwarzenbeg (Bordeaux) – 1 tank turret with MG
9. Stutzpunkt (strongpoint) Nebelhorn (Fort Doyle) – 1 tank turret with MG
10. Widerstandsnest Dohlenfels (L'Ancresse Bay) – 1 tank turret with 3.7cm Pak and MG [p12 Occupation Review 22 see also map on page 27]
11. Widerstandsnest Garen – 1 tank turret with MG
12. Widerstandsnest Houmet (Rousse) – 1 FT17 tank turret with 3.7cm PaK (photo), 2 tank turrets. [FT17 Houmets Lane, (nr Rue de Picquerel), Vale (pg 23, *Then and Now* – photo)]
13. Widerstandsnest Fischcerberg (between Pecqueries Bay and Portinfer) – 2 tank turrets with 3.7cm PaK.

14. Widerstandsnest Cobogels (Le Guet) – 1 tank turret with MG.
15. Widerstandsnest Lowenfels (Albecq) – 1 tank turret with 3.7cm Pak
16. Stutzpunkt Rotenstein (Fort Hommet) – 1 tank turret with MG [Fort Hommet, Vazon (p83 (map) Occupation Review 24)]
17. Widerstandsnest Rundturm (Vazon Bay) – 1 tank turret with MG (built into the sea wall)
18. Widerstandsnest Krossen (Fort Le Crocq – 1 tank turret with MG (built into the sea wall)
19. Stutzpunkt Lagenberg Naval Tower MP2 (Fort Saumarez, L'Eree) – 1 tank turret with 3.7cm Pak APX [Perelle bay overlooking Lihou Island
20. Widerstandsnest Unter Westberg (La Rue de la Varde) – 1 tank turret with MG
21. Widerstandsnest Westberg Riegel (La Rue des Pointes) – 1 tank turret with MG
22. Widerstandsnest Schutzenhof (Les Tielles) – 1 tank turret
23. Widerstandsnest Grune Bucht (Petit Bot Bay) – 1 tank turret with 3.7cm Pak
24. Widerstandsnest Nicolaus (Les Nicolles) – 1 tank turet with MG
25. Widerstandsnest La Fosse (Moulin Huet) – 1 tank turret with MG
26. Batterie Mirus (pg 203, *Then and Now* – photo)

---

[3]*A Guide to German Fortifications on Guernsey.*

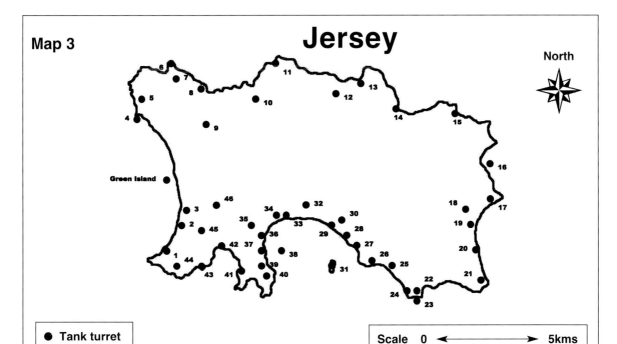

Map 3

Jersey

North

Green Island

● **Tank turret**

Scale 0 ⟵⟶ 5kms

Jersey[4]

1. L'Oeilliere; ‡(pg 49 Occ rev 26 Resistance Nest L'Oeilliere consisted of a Type 631 casemate for 4.7cm Pak 36(t) anti tank gun backing onto another casemate for a 10.5cm (K331(f) beach defence gun. The tank turret sat in between and could be reached by means of a ladder from within the complex); p135 Jersey's German Bunkers – diagram

2. La Carriere; ‡

3. Les Brayes; ‡

4. L'Etacquerel; †

5. Artillery Battery Moltke × 3; ‡ (Grid reference 547554 on the cliff top at Les Landes, St Ouen pg84 Occ rev 26)

6. and **7.** Plemont 1 × FT17 ‡ at bottom of cliff and 1 × APX at top of cliff;

8. Greve de Lecq;*

9. Artillery Battery Ludendorff; ‡ (grid ref 579533 – at junction of La Cache de l'Eglise and La Rue de La Cour – pg 82 occ rev 26)

10. Jute; ‡ (La Hougue Mauger, St Mary (now with private collector) (p121 Jersey's German Bunkers Archive Book No 9)

11. Sorel B; †

12. Jasmin × 2; ‡

13. Bonne Nuit; ‡

14. Bouley Hafen; †

15. Rozel 2 × Hafen and 1 × Fort; ‡

16. Archirondel (on unfinished breakwater); †

17. Gorey Hafen;*

18. Wiederstandsnest Krossen (Fort Le Crocq – 1 tank turret with MG (built into the sea wall)

19. Fort William; ‡

20. Le Hurel; †

21. La Rocque B × 2 (FT17† covering the main road and an APX turret facing the sea);

22. and **23.** La Rocque A × 3 – 2 × FT ‡ (One positioned near the gateway of Platte Rocque House disguised as a water pump. This covered the east-west coast road (CIOS Occ review 1977 p 20 (Map), 22–23) One positioned at the end of the breakwater in the autumn of 1944 to cover the port, beaches and the rest of the 'resistance point'. (CIOS Occ review 1977 p 20 (Map), 22–23)). 1 × APX turret positioned half way along the small pier;

24. Le Hocq; †

25. La Motte B; ‡

26. Grand Charriere; †

27. La Plage; †

28. South Hill Unten; †

29. Grand Hotel; †

30. Artillery Battery Endrass; ‡ (grid ref 643493 – Westmount, west of St Helier and 250 metres from St Aubins Bay – pg 83 occ rev 26)

31. Elizabeth Castle Süd;* [Still there – Zimmermann II pg 87 map pg 113 picture]

32. Artillery Battery Fritsch ‡ (grid ref 510623) north of The Grove at the top of Mont Cambrai/Mont Felard in St Lawrence – one static tank turret. Pg 80 Occ Rev 26

33. Third Tower; ‡

34. La Haule [pg 83 Then and Now – photo]; †

35. Artillery Battery Derfflinger; ‡

36. Bahnhof Aubin;*

37. Hafen Aubin × 2; ‡

38. Fort Aubin × 2; ‡ (One rusted away by 1986 the other was recovered by the CIOS and ultimately put on display at Artillery Batterie Moltke) 1 × APX (Removed to the CI Military Museum in St Ouen's Bay)

39. Noirmont Manor; ‡

40. Artillery Battery Lothringen × 2; ‡ (Grid reference 607466 Noirmont, St Brelade p85 Occ Rev 26) [The two tank turrets were sited on either side of the spine road and covered the open ground to the north of the perimeter fence. Note the author mentions that these were not mounted on the usual Tobruk type shelter, but were mounted on a small concrete construction which are still visible today. (Batterie Lothringen Archive Book No 10)]

41. Schmugglersdorf (Ouaisne); †

42. Beau Rivage; †

43. Battery;* (At Les Creux, St. Brelade and is still there)

44. Artillery Battery Roon; ‡ (Grid reference 571480, La Moye Point – p97 Occ rev 22) Now on display outside the Underground Hospital

45. Artillery Battery Hindenburg; ‡ (grid ref 576491 (off La Route Orange on the ground now covered by Elizabeth Avenue) pg 96 Occ Rev 22)

46. Peters Baracken 3 5 (3 3 FT17 with MG311 (f) and 2 3 FT 17 with 3.7cm KwK 144 (f))

Note: Green Island One 5cm Kwk 39 L/60 developed for the Panzer III (p88, *German Fortifications in Jersey*, M. Ginns)

*APX

†FT 17 with 3.7cm KwK 144(f)

‡FT17 with MG311 (f)

[4]Order of Battle Chart of 319 Infantry Division – letter M. Ginns 23 February 2000.

seen at the Guernsey Occupation Society Museum, Les Houards and another is on display at the Bunker Museum, St Peter Port.

Normandy

French tank turrets were also widely used on the mainland. It would of course be impossible to list every one, but by concentrating on key areas it is possible to give a flavour of how these turrets were employed and on occasion how they fared in battle. Those turrets installed in Normandy, and in particular on the five beaches chosen for the D-Day landings,* offer a unique opportunity in this regard because so much has been written about the landings.

Utah Beach

This was the code name for the most westerly of the five landing beaches that lay along the eastern coast of the Cherbourg peninsula. Here men of the 4th US Infantry Division under Maj General Raymond O. Barton were to land on the gently sloping beaches to the south of Les Dunes de Varreville. The village was protected by *Widerstandsnest 10* to the north and *Stützpunkt 9* to the south. The former consisted of a number of casemates and field works as well as two tank turrets armed with 37mm guns, which were located on the coast so as to be able to cover the beach. *Stützpunkt 9* also included a number of tank turrets in its arsenal with three emplaced to cover the beach – one at either end and another in the middle with a tunnel leading to a shelter at the rear – and a further two turrets approximately 100m further back.

A French Renault FT turret mounted on a U-shaped shelter. It was installed at Varreville-Nord – Utah Beach and in the distance is the American 'Gooseberry' breakwater. (Service Historique Marine)

An APXR turret mounted at Quinéville north of Utah Beach. The turret retains its original commander's hatch. A rudimentary camouflage pattern has been applied. (US National Archives)

All were French turrets with 37mm guns – probably APXRs.[†]

The strong point was clearly a major obstacle to any successful landing and it was heavily bombed and shelled prior to the landing with, as was subsequently discovered, a considerable amount of success. The reason that this did not become evident until later was due to the fact that the landing force drifted a mile to the south of its original target. This brought the men of the Ivy Division up against the defences of *Widerstandsnest 5* at La Grande Dune. Being only a resistance nest it was less well defended than the strongpoint at Varreville reflecting the fact that it only had a single road leading from the beach, which was flanked by inundations that made exploitation difficult. The defences consisted of a single casemate[‡] and miscellaneous other defences including one tank turret. Thankfully for the men of

---

*Codenamed Utah, Omaha, Gold, Juno and Sword. Utah and Omaha were the focus of American operations, while the other three beaches were to be used by British and Canadian units.

[†] Slightly to the north of Utah Beach *Widerstandsnest 11* had two further emplaced French tank turrets and *Stützpunkt 12* was equipped with four turrets; three covering the beach and one further to the rear.

[‡] The main bunker at La Grande Dune is now home to the Utah Beach Museum and is still flanked by a Renault FT 17 tank turret.

8th Infantry Regiment leading the assault, these defences had also been successfully targeted as part of the preliminary bombardment. Indeed the barrage was so successful that it left the defenders of the 3rd Battalion *Infanterie Regiment* 919 under Lt Arthur Jahnke completely shell-shocked and when the ramps were lowered on the first wave of landing craft not a single shot was fired. Eventually the young officer* and his men regained their composure and with the few weapons at their disposal they tried to repel the invasion force. The damaged 88mm gun hit one Sherman before it was put out of action, and Cpl Friedrich in the tank turret kept firing his machine gun cutting down a number of engineers before it was put out of action by a direct hit from a tank in the second wave. This effectively ended the German resistance on the beach. Engineers continued to clear obstacles while the infantry and tanks moved inland and by the end of the day almost 25,000 men were ashore at a cost of less than 200 casualties.

Omaha Beach

Ten miles or so along the coast was Omaha Beach, which lay between Port en Bessin, and the mouth of the River Vire. This stretch of the Normandy coastline was a far more daunting prospect for an invasion force. It had many more natural obstacles for the attacker to overcome and there was also a seawall. To make matters worse this stretch of beach had been heavily fortified with fourteen *Widerstandsnester*.

An FT17 that formed part of the defences of Utah Beach at Sainte Marie du Mont. The turret is of a riveted design and sits on a smaller version of the U-shaped reinforced concrete shelter. The turret is still in place today and can be found near the Musée du Débarquement. (Author)

A GI examines an APXR turret mounted at the Le Grand Vey, which covered the estuary of the Vire and the entrance to the Carentan Canal. The original commander's cupola has been replaced with a split hatch. (US National Archives)

These were principally located near the coast to cover the beach exits between the dunes. At Vierville there were three resistance nests, while exits on the beach in front of St Laurent sur Mer were protected by four more. A further three nests covered the exits from the beach at Colleville.

Of the three resistance nests covering the exit from the beach in front of Vierville sur Mer – *Widerstandsnester 71, 72* and *73* – only resistance nest 72 included a tank turret; an obsolete Renault FT17. Unusually it formed part of a casemate with double embrasure for 50mm KwK (*See* page 128). Four more turrets formed part of the defences of St Laurent sur Mer; two as part of *Widerstandsnest 66* and two as part of the defences of *Widerstandsnest 68*.[†] These positions flanked the valley leading up to St Laurent and were built on two levels; on the beach itself and on the plateau above. One turret was positioned on each level. A further turret was to be installed at the top of the beach as part of the defences of *Widerstandsnest 66* on 5 June 1944 but was not

---

*Jahnke was a veteran of the Eastern Front and had only recently been awarded the Iron Cross for his bravery.
[†] One of these was embedded in the side of the cliff and was fitted with a VK3001 turret.

completed.* Just along the coast at Colleville were a further two tank turrets. Both of these were French APX turrets and were installed in *Widerstandsnester 60* and *61* respectively. The turret in *Widerstandsnester 61* did not overlook the beach but was mounted to the south east of the position and was most likely positioned to protect against an outflanking attack from the side or rear.

These positions, as they had been at Utah Beach, were bombed and shelled prior to the initial landing, but the bombardment was not as effective as it had been for 4th Division as a combination of low cloud and over-cautious air crews saw the majority of the ordnance miss the target or remain in the bomb bay of the aircraft. Consequently, when the defenders emerged from their shelters they found the defences were largely intact and they were able to wreak havoc on the men of 116th Regiment of 29th Infantry Division and 16th Regiment of 1st Infantry Division and their supporting tanks. It is unclear what, if any, impact the seven tank turrets had in the fighting on D-Day,[†] but by the end of the day – and despite suffering 2,000 casualties – the US forces had overrun the enemy coastal defences and over 34,000 men had been landed.

Gold Beach

By comparison with the defences of Utah and Omaha beaches, which had large numbers of tank turrets, the British and Canadian beaches had relatively few. Indeed, records seem to indicate that Gold Beach,

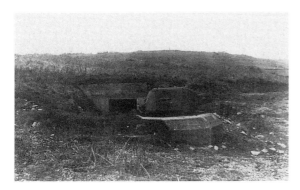

A French APXR turret mounted at Colleville-Est, near Omaha Beach. To the rear it is possible to see the entrance to a further concrete shelter, which might have been used for the crew or to store ammunition.
(Service Historique Marine)

which ran from Port en Bessin to the mouth of the River Provence, had none at all.

Juno Beach

Juno Beach ran from Courselles in the west, where it butted on to Gold Beach, through Bernières sur Mer to St Aubin sur Mer. These coastal resorts were defended by four *Widerstandsnester*: *Widerstandsnester 29* and *31* protecting Courselles; *Widerstandsnest 28* located at Bernières sur Mer; and *Widerstandsnest 27* at St Aubin sur Mer.

The defences of *Widerstandsnest 31*, to the west of Courselles, consisted of a number of emplacements including a position mounting a 50mm gun and a Renault tank turret which was located on the front roughly in the middle of the resistance nest and to the west of the canal. This position was attacked by B Company of the Royal Winnipeg Rifles whose initial landing was met with a hail of bullets from the enemy coastal positions. In spite of this they managed to advance to the concrete fortifications and in hand-to-hand fighting cleared the position. The cost was high though with forty-eight men killed and eighty-five wounded from an original strength of 160.

Another tank turret, this time an obsolete French Renault FT17 armed with a machine gun, covered the beach at Bernières la Rive. The concrete emplace-

---

* The André family farm was located on the plateau on which *Widerstandsnest 66* was built. The son of the family, Albert, who was sixteen at the time, was conscripted to help with construction work on the defences. On 5 June he was helping to manoeuvre a tank turret loaded on a truck to its position on the lower level of *Widerstandsnest 66*. Late in the afternoon the position was strafed by American fighters and on the strength of this the work was abandoned for the day – and as it turned out – forever. The tank turret remained stranded on the truck tantalisingly close to its final position where it would no doubt have added to the American casualties on 'Bloody Omaha'. (G. Bernage, *Omaha Beach*, Editions Heimdal, Bayeux Cedex, 2002, p.76.)

† *Widerstandsnest 72* was targeted by the ten 14in guns of USS *Texas* and the defenders eventually surrendered. *Widerstandsnest 60* was captured by L Company 16th Infantry Regiment by 0900 with the help of supporting Sherman tanks and the men of 116th Infantry Regiment, despite being caught in the cross fire between *Widerstandsnester 66* and *68* and suffering heavy casualties, gradually infiltrated the German positions and advanced towards Saint Laurent.

A US soldier inspects a VK3001 turret that had been installed as part of the defences of Widerstandsnest 68 on Omaha Beach. In the foreground it is possible to see the entrance to the shelter. (US National Archives, courtesy of S. Zaloga)

An American GI examines an FT17 turret with 3.7cm KwK gun. This example was mounted at Grandcamp on the Normandy Coast. The bunker is one of the unique U-shaped designs used in the Atlantic Wall. (US National Archives)

A British sailor peering through the open hatch of an FT17 turret that formed part of the Atlantic Wall defences. Although the photograph was taken in July 1944 it is still possible to see evidence of the landings in the background. (Imperial War Museum)

ment was swathed in barbed wire to protect it against enemy infantry and over the top was stretched chicken wire to hold camouflage. Although they were not supposed to – they should have landed 200m to the west in order to avoid these defences – B Company of the Queens Own Rifles of Canada landed at Bernières. These fortifications were not particularly strong but the defenders still managed to inflict heavy casualties on the Canadians, a third of its number becoming casualties in the first few minutes. Nevertheless, *Widerstandsnest 28* was soon captured and the Canadians moved inland.

Sword Beach*

Sword Beach ran from La Brèche de Hermanville in the west, through Colleville Plage and then to Ouistreham on the Orne River. Protecting Ouistreham was *Stützpunktgruppe* Riva Bella, which was made up of a series of strong points and resistance nests. *Stützpunkt 08* was furthest east and included a fire control tower and six emplacements for 15.5cm guns. To the east of the observation tower was a French tank turret. This was mounted on a locally designed bunker and somewhat unusually had a split hatch.[†]

At Hermanville la Brèche (*Stützpunkt 18*) another tank turret was installed that covered the western end of the beach. Neither this turret, nor the turret at Riva Bella seemed to have played a part in the fighting on

6 June and by the end of the day 28,845 men of the 3rd British Infantry Division and its supporting units had landed.

To the east of Sword Beach were a series of artillery emplacements whose guns covered possible landing sites. The six 15.5cm guns at Mont Canisy were protected by mines and a number of concrete positions including an emplaced Renault R35 tank turret. The turret has been restored and can be viewed today. The Merville battery, to the west of Mont Canisy and closer to Sword Beach, also posed a threat to the landing. Although no tank turrets were placed around the battery of four 10cm guns, the coast in front of the battery was protected by two strong points at Franceville Plage. *Stützpunkt 05* included in its arsenal an emplaced tank turret.

A Renault R-35 turret located on Mont Canisy. The photograph was taken in June 2001 when the new turret was installed on the shelter. Alongside the turret are Mr Zarifian (the Mayor of Berneville-sur-Mer), Mr Frederic Verbauwhede (president of the Mont-Canisy Association) and Col Olmer (the head of the Saumur Tank Museum). (B. Paich)

The original R-35 turret at Mont Canisy as it looked in 1947. (Service Historique Marine)

---

*Between Juno and Sword beaches there was a series of *Widerstandsnester* but these were located away from the main landing beaches. No tank turrets were installed as part of these defences.

[†] Unusual because the turrets used for fortifications normally retained the original dome opening. The split hatch was fitted to those tanks absorbed into the *Panzer* arm proper, which seems to indicate that this tank may have formed part of an armoured division but for whatever reason the turret was subsequently surplus to requirements and was released for use in the Atlantic Wall.

A German photograph taken on 6 June 1944 looking towards Sword Beach (from La plage d'Houlgate). In the foreground there is an FT17 tank turret. (Imperial War Museum)

One of the APX2B tank turrets that were installed by Belgium to defend the coast and which were later integrated into the Atlantic Wall defences. (Imperial War Museum)

Belgium and The Netherlands

The thirteen turrets built by the Belgians in the interwar period (*see* Chapter 2) were retained by the Germans and additionally, the defences around the major ports (Oostend, Zeebrugge, Hook of Holland, Vlissingen and the Walcheren Islands) were strengthened with the creation of a series of

Widerstandsnester and *Stützpunkte*. These resistance nests and strong points included almost 4,000 *ringstände*, some with tank turrets, although it is unclear exactly how many.

Denmark[3]

Although not perhaps an obvious invasion target to the Allies, Denmark nevertheless was heavily fortified by the Germans. Somewhere in the region of 5,000 positions were constructed of which approximately 169 were emplaced tank turrets.* The majority of these were *F Pz DT4803* (essentially modified *Panzer* I turrets), but there were also *Panzer* IIs and *Panzer* 35(t) and 38(t)s and uniquely, certainly in terms of numbers used, turrets from the *VK901* (a prototype based on the *Panzer* II which did not see active service).[†]

Most of the turrets appear to have been located along the coast. For example eighty-nine of the *F Pz DT 4803* turrets were installed in the *1.Stellung* along the west coast of Jutland. Other turrets were used to defend roads and other key installations like the ferry

---

*Numbers vary according to different sources: F. Hahn in *Waffen und Geheimwaffen des deutschen Heeres 1933–45*. Bernard & Graefe Verlag, Koblenz, (1986), p.174 quotes 194.

† Some 16 *VK901* turrets (of the twenty-seven available) were emplaced in Denmark. Two of these were emplaced at the Börsmose village position. According to the plan of the defences they were equipped with 3.7cm main gun rather than the standard 2cm gun. This was either a modification to the turrets or a mistake on the plan – it is unclear which.

The front view of a F Pz DT4803 turret (Panzer I) that was used to defend Aalborg airfield, Denmark. The commander's hatch is missing. (A. Johansen)

crossing of the Lim Ford, which separated the Jutland peninsula, where a *Panzer* I and *Panzer* 38(t) turret were used.

The other use that tank turrets were put to was the defence of airfields. *Flugplatz* Aalborg–West had four *Panzer* II turrets as a perimeter defence. At *Flugplatz* Aalborg–Ost there were a further two turrets, both *F Pz DT 4803*s, one covering the road and the other the minefield.[4] Three turrets of the same type were installed at *Flugplatz* Fredikshaven and another three at *Flugplatz* Rom. Three *Panzer* II turrets were also installed at Grove aerodrome as was an FT17 turret. This seems to have come from a scrapped tank since the turret is not mentioned in the

A special bunker mounting an F.Pz.DT 4803 at Kærsgård Strand, Denmark. This bunker is very similar to the Bauformen 243, 244, 246, 248 and 251 but the only thing in common was the footprint. The internal layout was different and the extra room was for the crew, not an ammunition store. (Lars Bertelsen)

official building programme and nor were any FT17 turrets specifically sent to Denmark for installation as fixed fortifications. However, in 1941 some one hundred FT17s were sent to *Luftwaffe* units in Denmark for airfield defence. For whatever reason one of these turrets was fitted to a *Bauform* 58c shelter using the tank's turret race. The original frontispiece was replaced and a new plate fitted with a locally improvised gun mount.

The majority of the tank turrets were mounted on standard structures or slight derivatives thereof. There were three basic structures: the *Bauform* 67; a slight variation on this design, but with a flat rather than a sloping roof over a slightly larger anteroom; and a more substantial structure with three rooms. This larger structure was based on the *Bauform* 67, and was very similar to the shelter for the T34, T70, VK3001 and KV1 tank turrets.* but there the similarities ended. The dimensions were quite different as were the locations of doors and, most importantly, the extra room in this type of shelter was used for crew accommodation rather than ammunition storage. This perhaps reflected the fact that, because of the extended coastline in Denmark, many of the shelters were constructed in isolated locations and therefore needed to be self-contained.

The larger bunker was principally used to mount the *F Pz DT 4803* but also *Panzer* 38(t) and *Panzer* II turrets. It may be that the structure was originally designed for the *F Pz DT 4803* turret since this design was the only one on the *Baufortschrittsplan* (building progress plan) that was designated as a *Bauform* 67. The *Panzer* 38(t) turrets did not have a *Bauform* number and the *Panzer* II turrets at Aalborg West were designated as 'S' or *Sonder Konstruktion* (special construction) and not a standard design.

The long stretches of isolated coastline also led to the development of another type of unique defensive structure. Every 400m or so from the border with Germany to the top of Jutland were constructed special groups of bunkers. Two *Flankierungsstände* or *F Stände* were located next to each other in such a way that they provided enfilade fire along the length of the beach. In the middle and to the rear of the two shelters was a tank turret, often a *F Pz DT 4803*, which protected the vulnerable area in between.

---

*Bauformen 243, 244, 246, 248 and 251.

The unique designs were also seemingly often constructed in a fashion peculiar to the area using 60cm (2ft) rather than 40cm (1.5ft) thick walls and, where this was the case, they dispensed with the steel reinforcing rods. It is not clear whether this expedient was restricted to Denmark and *Festungspionierstab 31* (Fortress Pioneer Staff) or whether it was common throughout the Atlantic Wall. What is clear, however, is that these structures tended to be built in the latter stages of the war so it is conceivable that this approach was dictated by either a lack of reinforcing rods, or may simply have been quicker and cheaper.

Norway

The very real possibility of Britain disrupting vital iron ore shipments from Sweden meant that Hitler made the defence of Norway a top priority and the vulnerability of this strategically important northern outpost was underlined following the battle for Narvik of April 1940 and the Vaagso raid of December 1941. However, poor communications and the unpredictable weather meant that a standing army was unsuitable for defending such a remote area and in December 1941 construction work began on a series of fortifications. These were concentrated around the fjord entrances and strategically important islands. In total some 225 batteries were constructed mounting over 1,000 medium and heavy pieces of ordnance.

As well as these larger fortifications, tank turrets mounted on concrete shelters were utilized.

A rear view of a Panzer 38(t) turret installed by the Germans to cover the beach at Solastranda, Stavanger, Norway. The turret is still visible today.
(Svein Wiiger Olsen)

According to German sources 151 tank turrets were installed in Norway. Mostly they were *Panzer* 38(t) turrets, but there were also some *Panzer* II turrets (of various types) and also seemingly a number of *Panzer* 35(t) turrets. These are not shown in the official sources but a number are still there today! As was the case in Denmark, FT17s were also used in a fixed role often with whole tanks buried in the ground so that just the turret was visible. The majority of these turrets were positioned along the coast but they were also used to defend airfields. On the island of Lista the Germans constructed an airfield that was protected by at least three *Panzer* II Flamingo turrets. Further turrets were installed at Stavanger Sola and Forus, and also Herdla (north of Bergen) and Kjevik (in Kristiansand).

Sudwall

In November 1942 the Germans occupied Vichy France, and soon after, work began to fortify the Mediterranean coast and the border with Spain. By the summer of 1943 some 500 positions had been constructed. After the Allied invasion of Sicily in July 1943 and the surrender of Italy this work was given added urgency. The coast was divided into seven coast defence sectors or *Küsten Verteidigung Abschnitt*. These were allocated letters A to G with A on the border with Spain and G on the border with Italy. In addition, special defensive zones were created around Marseilles and Toulon, which were considered to be of strategic importance. The Organization Todt (OT)* began work on submarine pens in Marseilles in the spring of 1943 and a number of tank turrets were installed to defend key locations around the city. A *Panzer* II turret was installed in the shadow of Fort St Nicolas which guarded the entrance to the harbour. In the city itself an APXR turret was installed on the Boulevard Ledru-Rollin and a *Panzer* II at Place des Abattoirs.

Further turrets were also installed at vulnerable points along the Mediterranean coast. At Collioure an APXR turret was installed together with a casemate

---

*A semi-military organization created before the war that performed all kinds of constructional work that was deemed of importance to the outcome of the war. The officers were Germans but the labourers were generally foreign volunteers, conscripts or prisoners of war.

An APX R turret captured by the Americans in August 1944. It was installed on the dockside in the shadow of La Cathédrale de la Major, Marseille. (US National Archives courtesy of S. Zaloga)

for a 5cm KwK39/1. The emplacement was transformed into a restaurant after the war and although this work obscured the turret it is still accessible. Another French turret, this time from a Somua S35 tank, was located to cover the beach at Leucate. At Pla-d'en-Guirand a strong point was constructed which included an artillery battery that was protected by a *Panzer* II turret and another *Panzer* II turret was built into the sea wall at La Franqui. At Redoute St Pierre an APXR turret was installed which is now on display on the beach of St Pierre. Along the coast of the Camargue were four Somua turrets; fifteen APXR turrets and twenty-six *Panzer* II turrets. Of these, eight were deployed to defend the port of Grau du Roi including three that provided protection for the main casemates and a further four *Panzer* II turrets that covered the beach to the south of this position. At Port de Bouc, which lay on the opposite side of the mouth of the Rhône river, a Char B1 bis turret was installed on the sea wall. Another APXR turret was installed at Carry le Rouet (and is still there).

Between Marseilles and Toulon, at La Ciotat, an APXR turret was installed to cover the entrance to the port and other turrets, including *Panzer* II turrets, were also installed in the vicinity. At Cap Saint-Jean, to protect the casemates mounting 7.5cm guns, a *Panzer* II turret was installed. Finally, along Les Lecques bay were further APXR and *Panzer* II turrets.

Spanish Border

Although nominally an ally of Germany, Spain did not formally join the triple alliance (Germany, Italy and Japan). Franco's reluctance to enter the war* caused something of a schism between the two leaders and prompted Hitler to extend his fortifications along the French border with Spain. The War Diary of *Armeepionierführer* AOK1 dated 5 July 1944 detailed the exact make up of these defences, which included a number of Panzer turrets:[†]

Panzer 38(t) – two completed.
Panzer II – eight planned of which one was ready for use, two were under construction and a further five assigned.
Panzer I – ten planned of which seven were ready for use, one was under construction and a further two assigned.

Today it is still possible to see the remains of some of these turrets. Around the strategically important town

---

* Spain continued to supply vital raw materials and some troops did volunteer to fight, but this was not officially sanctioned.
[†] The note also included a status report on a number of Panther turrets, which are detailed in Chapter 3 Part 3.

A Panzer 38(t) turret that formed part of the Sudwall defences at Cerbère on the French border with Spain. The base plate, which was formed from part of the tanks upper hull is clearly visible. Sadly the mantlet and main armament have been removed. (E Ritterbach)

A further view of the Panzer 38(t) at Cerbère, close to the border at Col de Balistres. This view clearly shows the entrance to the shelter under the turret. Hooks above the door would have been used to secure camouflage. (E Ritterbach)

of Le Perthus, which is dominated by Fort de Bellgarde built by Vauban, it is possible to see a *Ringstand* for a *Panzer* II, which stands below the road leading to the site of the Roman monument known as the *Trophée de Pompée.* A second is in front of the hornwork, below the southeast glacis. A few kilometres away at Saint-Martin de l'Albère, a *Panzer* I on a *ringstand* is also still visible. This turret, overlooking a small valley, was located to cover a route that was used by people fleeing the German occupation in France. At Cerbère, close to the border at Col de Balistres, were constructed a *Panzer* II turret, a Czech *Panzer* 38 (t) turret and also an *MG-Panzernest.* Further along the coast road towards Port-Vendres, at Banyuls – Les Elmes beach, another *Panzer* II turret was installed. This covered the sea wall and is still in position today.[5]

EASTERN FRONT

In June 1941 Hitler invaded the Soviet Union. Despite a slight delay to the operation, the three-pronged attack made substantial inroads and by the end of the year Moscow was within artillery range and Leningrad was almost surrounded. When the offensive was resumed the following year the main focus was in the south and again good progress was made. However, the defeat at Stalingrad in January 1943 proved a watershed and despite a few minor victories, the German army was in full retreat from then on. To stem the tide Hitler ordered the construction of a series of defensive lines. These consisted mainly of field works rather than permanent fortifications, but did include large numbers of emplaced tank turrets. Indeed, according to German sources, the Eastern Front was where most tank turrets were emplaced – 694 in total – although physical evidence to support this is rare. These turrets were mostly taken from obsolete German tanks, primarily *Panzer* IIs (217), but not surprisingly captured Soviet turrets were also used.* Often they were emplaced as part of the so-called 'hedgehog' (*igel*) pattern of defence. These positions were all mutually supporting, providing fire for their own defence and cover for the flanks and rear of the adjacent units. The turrets were also used to protect key strategic targets like bridges, supply dumps and rail installations.

Soviet Union

In 1943 some 183 turrets were delivered to the Eastern Front for installation as fixed fortifications. The majority of these (143) were sent to Army Group North and the rest to Army Group Middle.[†] The majority of these turrets were *Panzer* II turrets (110 normal *Panzer* II turrets, twenty *Flamingo* turrets and a further thirteen with the main armament removed and adapted to take either an MG34 or MG42 machine gun). The balance included twenty-five *Panzer* I turrets, ten *Panzer* 38(t) turrets and five Soviet T70 turrets from the *Panzer* Repair Works at Riga.[6]

Little more is known about the use of these turrets. A number were installed on concrete bunkers along the Dnieper River and further turrets were located on one of its tributaries, the Berezina River. A *Panzer* II turret was emplaced at Borisov (modern day Boriszow) in Belarus[7] and was one of a series of fortifications constructed to defend this strategically important town.[‡]

Poland

The majority of the tank turrets were emplaced by the Germans in the southern part of the country in the so-called B1 line that broadly speaking ran from the Carpathian Mountains to Czestochowa. To the west of Krakow, in the Rudawa Valley, concrete shelters for mounting tank turrets were installed. One of these shelters that formed part of the Hill 280 defences may have been fitted with a T34 turret. Large stockpiles of Soviet T34 turrets were found at both Rudawa and

A F Pz DT 4804 (up-gunned Panzer II turret) installed to the north-west of Krakow, Poland. The turret hatch has been removed and replaced with a vent. There are additionally four lifting lugs, which have been welded to the turret top. The larger hole in the roof was where the periscope was fitted. (Waldemar Broskwinia)

Krzeszowice railway stations and it is assumed that they were destined for this and similar positions. However, the Soviet 59th Army captured these positions in January 1945 before the Germans had time to install them.[8] Further north of Krakow a *Panzer* II turret armed with 37mm gun was emplaced[¶] and another *Panzer* II turret was installed at Sulejow on the Pilica River. These turrets formed part of the defensive line that ran from Krakow to the Vistula, the so-called 'Gouverment General' Line'. It is also believed that turrets were used in Breslau, modern day Wroclaw.

Germany

By January 1945 the Red Army had already reached Prussia and was nearing the borders of Germany proper. The Oder Warthe Bogen line, which had been

---

* At least twenty turrets from Soviet T34, T70 and KV1 tanks were installed.
† No turrets were sent to either Army Group South or Army Group A.
‡ Napoleon Bonaparte's army suffered heavy losses when crossing the Berezina near Borisov in November 1812 when retreating from Russia. Since then *Berezina* has been used in French as a synonym for any form of catastrophe.
¶ Until relatively recently this turret could still be visited but sadly it has now been removed. One turret does seemingly still exist in Poland near Tomaszow Mazowiecki in central Poland. It formed part of an isolated *Stützpunkt* of the A2 Line.

As the Germans became increasingly desperate, tanks – minus their running gear – were used as improvised fixed fortifications. In Berlin a Panzer IV has been used in this way. (Imperial War Museum)

built before the war to protect Germany's eastern frontier, had, like the West Wall, been abandoned in the intervening period. Now work to strengthen the defences was begun with the addition of tobruks and field works. Included in the building programme was a plan to install a number of dug-in tanks and in a section of the line running north from Starpel (modern day Staropole) to Kainscht, twelve such positions were to be constructed, although it is unclear whether they were completed.[9]

As the Germans became increasingly desperate, major cities were turned into fortresses. In the spring of 1945 Frankfurt an der Oder was afforded this status and work started on a number of emplacements on the ridge running parallel to the River Oder on the Kliestower Road. One of the positions constructed was a *Panzer 38(t)* turret mounted on a wooden pedestal. This was one of two that arrived in the city by the beginning of April 1945* and was installed by *Panzerturm Kompanie* 1312. According to witnesses who lived near the Kliestower Road at the time this turret engaged enemy troops on the eastern bank of the Oder. In response, the besieging Soviet units attempted to silence the position but without success. Eventually the crew of the turret and the rest of the

city's garrison were forced to withdraw, but the turret survived.[†]

In addition to the tank turrets mounted on specially designed shelters, disabled tanks with their running gear removed were used as improvised strongpoints.[‡] They tended to be placed at road intersections to cover all approaches and to provide the position with some added protection cobbles and masonry were heaped around the structure.

MEDITERRANEAN

Italy

Following the defeat of the *Afrika Korps* in May 1943 the Allies decided to launch an attack on Italy with a view to eliminating Mussolini's Fascist state from the war and maintaining pressure on German forces in order to create the conditions required for 'Overlord' and an invasion of southern France. Less than two months later the Allies landed on Sicily and advanced towards Messina. The German and Italian defenders had had little time to construct extensive fortifications but they did manage to dig in a company of Fiat 3000 tanks (similar to the French Renault FT17) to counter the expected invasion.[10] However, this improvisation did little to stem the Allied advance and eventually the Anglo-American armies captured the island. The Allies now prepared for the invasion of the Italian mainland with a view to advancing rapidly up the peninsula. Hitler, however, had other ideas and already in June 1943 construction units of the Organization Todt had been sent to Italy to work on coastal fortifications.* Hitler was determined that the symbolically important city of Rome should not fall

---

*It is not clear where the other turret was installed.
† After the war the weight of the turret caused the roof of the wooden shelter to collapse and this probably saved it from experiencing the same fate reserved for most of these weapons. The timber that had been used to build the wooden pedestal was subsequently removed by the landowner for firewood and a section of the turret was also cut away in an unsuccessful attempt to turn the turret into scrap metal. But apart from that, the position was in tact and was later recovered and can be visited today at Castle Königstein, Dresden.
‡ There is evidence to suggest that Panzer IV tanks and Panther tanks were used in this way, but it is conceivable that other tanks were also used.

to the Allies without a fight. Nor was he prepared to see the creation of Allied air bases in Italy capable of attacking industrial targets in southern Germany, or, more importantly, the Ploesti oilfields in Romania. Consequently, German forces were rushed south and began a series of delaying actions as more elaborate defences were constructed further north.

The topography of Italy was ideally suited to the German defensive strategy. The Apennines, which form the backbone of the Italian peninsula, ensured that the Allies could only advance along the narrow coastal plains or through mountain passes that were not suited to a modern mechanized army. These potential avenues of attack were protected by a series of defensive lines that were constructed in considerable depth. An integral part of these defences were emplaced tank turrets. In all 191 turrets were installed, mostly *F Pz DT4803* (*Panzer* I) turrets (ninety-one in number) but also a significant number of Panther turrets (*see* Chapter 3, Part 3, *below*).

The first major defensive line that the Allies encountered was the Bernhardt Line, which broadly followed the Sangro and Garigliano Rivers from Fossacesia on the Adriatic to Minturno on the Tyrrhenian Sea. The western end of this line was particularly strong, especially around the town of Cassino where a switch position known as the Gustav Line was constructed. This consisted of a thick and continuous network of wire and minefields together with carefully sited weapon positions and deep shelters to protect the defenders against air and artillery bombardment. A number of Italian P40 tanks were also used here (and at Anzio) as static fortifications.[11] Behind this position was the Hitler Line, that was also anchored on Monte Cassino. Located across the floor of the Liri Valley it relied on man-made fortifications for its strength and included in its arsenal were a number of Panther turrets, which are covered in more detail later in the book. No other turrets are detailed as being used in the Line,[†] but they were further north in the Gothic or Green Line.

Work had continued intermittently on the Gothic Line since late 1943 but it was not until June 1944 that a concerted effort was made to complete the defences. The *Organization Todt* and army engineers, supplemented by civilian labourers worked on the defences, mostly during the night to avoid the threat from Allied aircraft. The defences stretched from La Spezia in the west to Pesaro in the east, a distance of some 300km (190 miles) and in places were 30km (18 miles) deep. Particular emphasis was placed on strategically important points, like mountain passes and the coastal plains, which were heavily fortified.

Already by early July some progress had been made on the defences. In 10th Army's (AOK 10) zone eight *Panzer* II turrets had been completed and a further twelve were under construction.[12] During the rest of the summer the work continued apace. In addition to the emplaced Panther turrets, eighteen *Panzer* I[‡] and *Panzer* II turrets had been completed by 28 August 1944 with a further fifteen under construction and thirteen more planned. Eight Italian tanks had also been installed in the Gothic Line, although the type is not stated.[13] Lemelsen, the commander of 14th Army (AOK 14), was also

A Panzer II turret which formed part of the Gothic Line defences. Although the weaponry was obsolete by the standards of the day the armour provided valuable protection for the crew. This example was captured by Allied forces in September 1944. (National Archives)

*Interestingly, before the war the Italians had fortified the coast around Genoa, which was most exposed to a possible French attack. These defences ultimately included a number of concrete shelters that were built to mount obsolete Renault FT17 turrets. One FT17 was emplaced to protect the harbour entrance. C. Clerici and E. Vajna de Pava, 'Coastal Defences of Genoa During the Second World War', *Fort*, Vol. 23 (1995), pp.111–126.

† Although one photograph from the Alexander Turnbull Library, NZ depicts a Panzer II, which is quoted as having been taken in the Hitler Line.

‡ One source talks about *Panzer* I turrets but other records state that no *Panzer* I turrets were used in Italy and it is assumed that reference is being made to the *F Pz DT4803* which was simply a modified *Panzer* I turret.

promised, at some indeterminate future date, a number of obsolete 3.7cm tank gun turrets which were to be installed at the rear of the more vulnerable sectors of the line.[14] These were undoubtedly *Panzer* 38(t) turrets, twenty-five of which were later stated as having been installed in Italy, although it seems unlikely that they were ever installed in the Gothic Line.

Behind the Gothic Line, the last defensive position was the *Voralpenstellung*, which ran along Italy's northern border. As well as emplacing Panther turrets in this position, it was planned to install 30 tank turrets mounting machine guns (turret type unknown), 100 Italian M42 and 100 P40 turrets, although it is unclear whether this work was completed.

The Balkans

Like Italy, the Balkans offered the Allies an opportunity to strike at the 'soft underbelly' of the Third Reich. To counter this threat Hitler issued Directive Number 40 in March 1942, which called for the construction of defences in the Balkans and the Aegean. Plans were established to fortify the Greek mainland, Peloponnese, Crete and the Aegean Islands. However, only the defences on the island of Crete, which had been designated a fortress, were completed.

Because of the extensive coastline, the poor communications and the remoteness of many of the positions, tank turrets, which were largely self-contained fighting positions, were ideally suited and were extensively used. In total 409 turrets were installed in the Balkans. These were mostly *Panzer* I, *Panzer* II (including forty specially designed *F Pz DT 4804* which were derivatives of the *Panzer* II) and *Panzer* 38(t) turrets. A number of the latter were used on Crete[15] and were installed on the mainland along the Athens – Thessaloniki railroad line and other turrets were also used to protect strategically important installations like airfields – for example Hazani airfield, Athens (now called Helinikon).

North Africa

The arrival of Rommel and his *Afrika Korps* had reversed the tide of the war in North Africa and Churchill was keen to regain the initiative. In May 1941 Operation *Brevity* was launched. This was not a success and the British lost a number tanks including nine Matildas. After the battle the Germans began to construct a line of strongly fortified posts, particularly at the Halfaya Pass, but this work was not complete when the British launched their next attack in June.[16] Operation *Battleaxe* was an even greater failure than *Brevity* and the British lost sixty-four Matildas. The Germans were able to recover many of these and some were used against their former owners in later battles. The position was successfully held against a further offensive in November 1941 when more Matilda tanks were captured, before the position finally fell to British and Commonwealth forces in January 1942.

At some point during the second half of 1941 it seems that the Germans dug in some of the captured

A Panzer I turret installed in Greece. The twin MGs have been removed and the main hatch is missing. The entrance is just visible in the background with hooks inserted in the concrete to attach camouflage nets.
(T. Tsiplakos)

A Panzer 38(t) turret that is still in situ in Greece. The main and coaxial armament have been removed. Just discernible on the side of the turret is its original number.
(T. Tsiplakos)

Matilda tanks and used them as strong points in the defensive line around the Halfaya Pass and Capuzzo. Undoubtedly some of the *Beutepanzer* ('booty tanks') might have been damaged beyond repair and therefore only fit for this purpose, but there is another factor that might have persuaded the Germans to use the tanks in this way. British tanks were fitted with diesel engines whereas the German tanks used petrol and it would have been difficult for them to keep so many tanks running without a guaranteed supply of fuel.[17]

Note: It has been suggested that the British might have been responsible for employing the Matildas as a fixed fortifications. Certainly the British used them to provide added strength to the so-called Gazala Line, but this was the exception rather than the rule; tanks were normally held in reserve for any possible counter-attack.[18]

WEST WALL

Construction work on the West Wall began in 1936 and continued through until 1940 when work was suspended following the German invasion of France and the Low Countries. The successful conclusion of the campaign in the west meant that the border defences had seemingly served their purpose; the West Wall was abandoned and the weapons and fittings were removed and either placed in store or later used in the Atlantic Wall. But the decision to abandon the West Wall proved premature. In June 1944 the Allies landed in France and by August they had reached Paris. In that same month a study was carried out to establish the state of Germany's border defences. This concluded that urgent remedial action was needed if the line was to slow let alone stop the Allied advance. Where possible the existing structures were to be renovated and elsewhere, new fortifications were to be built with particular emphasis on anti-tank defence.

Not surprisingly, considering the widespread use of tank turrets across the Third Reich, it was decided that this expedient would be adopted to strengthen the West Wall. However, although the onus was to be placed on anti-tank defence the tank turrets ready for use were not always suitable for this role. According to an inventory produced in early October 1944 the most widely available turret was the *F Pz DT4803*, based on the *Panzer* I and armed with a single machine gun. Notwithstanding this, it was planned to install fifty-five of these turrets in the Eifel and forty in the Niederrhein (Lower Rhine). Work on the turrets in the Eifel, under the auspices of *Fest Pi Kdr* XIX, was disrupted by the enemy and only forty-four of the turrets had been emplaced by the end of February 1945.[19] As in the Eifel, work in the zone of

A Valentine tank passes a British Matilda tank turret that was captured by the Germans in the fighting in North Africa and emplaced at the Halfaya Pass. The picture was taken after the position had been recaptured by the Eighth Army in February 1942.
(Imperial War Museum)

An F.Pz.DT 4803 (Panzer I) turret that was hastily employed as part of the West Wall defences. The turret appears to be mounted on its steel base plate, which in turn appears to be mounted on a wooden framework. This turret is armed with the older MG34. The position was captured by men of the 30th US Infantry Division near Niederzier, Germany in February 1945. (US National Archives courtesy of S. Zaloga)

Fest Pi Kdr XXI to the north fell some way short of the target with only thirty-two of the forty turrets completed by the beginning of March.[20] It was also planned to install nineteen *F PzDT* 4010 turrets, a specially designed armoured hood for a machine gun, and by the end of 1944 work had begun on eleven of these positions.[21]

Because the *F Pz DT4803* and *4010* were only armed with machine guns these positions did nothing to alleviate the desperate need for anti-tank weapons. This deficiency was partially satisfied with the plan to install *F Pz DT4804* turrets, which were essentially *Panzer* II turrets fitted with a 3.7cm KwK gun. It was hoped to install sixty of these turrets, but initial progress was slow and between October and December work had only begun on ten of them. In the New Year, galvanized by the grave situation, work on the turrets was accelerated and by the beginning of March, *Fest Pi Kdr* XIX, which was tasked with installing twenty turrets,[22] had installed thirteen, and *Fest Pi Kdr* XXI a further eleven.[23]

Together with the Panther turrets the VK3001 turret with its 7.5cm gun provided the defences with much needed anti-tank firepower. However, because the VK3001 was only a prototype the turrets were only available in very small numbers. Indeed only two VK3001 turrets, that had initially been earmarked for the Atlantic Wall, and which had been stored at

the Fortifications HQ Homburg, were available for use and only at the beginning of March 1945 were they emplaced in the Niederrhein (*Fest Pi Kdr* XXI).[24]

After the war much of the West Wall ended up in the French occupation zone and in October 1946 an agreement was signed with Mitalfer of Paris to dismantle the defences. Under the terms of the contract the company was tasked with the removal and destruction of all the armoured turrets. Some defences did survive, however, including a Panther turret that can be seen at the West Wall Museum, Niedersimten.

FINLAND

The Nazi-Soviet Pact of August 1939 left Finland in Stalin's sphere of influence and in the following November a contrived border incident sparked the outbreak of hostilities between the two nations in what became known as the Winter War. The fighting continued until March 1940 and despite inflicting a number of embarrassing defeats on her much larger neighbour, Finland was forced to accept punitive peace terms. The loss of territory and the demands of the war weakened an already fragile economy, but the national will to survive enabled the country to overcome these difficulties and Finland even began to rebuild her armed forces, aided by the Germans. At the same time the Finns began the construction of a new series of border defences* called the Salpa Line. This ran from the Gulf of Finland to Lapland[†] and when work was suspended in September 1944 some 800 permanent concrete defences had been constructed including a number of emplaced Soviet tank turrets.[25] [‡]

In June 1941 hostilities began again in the so called 'Continuation War'. This fighting saw the Finns capture a number of the forward positions of the Karelian UR (near Leningrad), which included T18

---

* The Mannerheim Line, named after the commander of Finnish forces, had been constructed on the Karelian peninsula and was instrumental in slowing the Soviet advance in the Winter War.

† Most of the permanent fortifications were located between the Gulf of Finland and Lake Kivijärvi.

‡ In 1939 Finland had used dug-in Renault FT17s as static defensive positions to blunt the Soviet attack.

A BT-5 tank, or early BT-7 turret that formed part of the Salpa Line defences. The turrets were not mounted on concrete shelters, rather the tank hull was cut just after the drivers compartment and before the engine compartment and was dug in. The turrets were positioned behind bunkers, as here, so that they were never exposed to direct fire. This example is located at Luumäki, near the town of Lappeenranta in eastern Finland. (Markku Airila)

tank turrets used as fixed fortifications. Although the Finns held this position for over two years they did not attempt to destroy these emplacements* and this may have been the inspiration for using the idea in the Salpa Line.

During this fighting the Finns also captured a number of Soviet tanks and it was planned to modify them and integrate them into the Finnish Army. The Fortifications Division hoped that this might result in a number of surplus turrets that it planned to use as fixed fortifications. However, this did not prove to be the case and a request to the Ordnance Division in September 1942 for the provision of turrets was not fulfilled. It was not until June 1944 when the decision was taken to scrap the Soviet BT tanks that the turrets were released for use in the Salpa Line. In July fifty-eight turrets were made available and, according to the statistics of the Fortifications Planning Staff, by September 1944 thirty-eight turrets armed with 45mm guns and twenty turrets armed with 37mm guns had been installed.

Most of the positions were constructed using turrets taken from Soviet BT-5 (1933 and 1934 models) and BT-7 1935 model tanks. Turrets from earlier models in the BT series were also used including the BT-2 fitted with a 37mm Bofors gun. The turrets were mainly taken from obsolete BT tanks rather than the T26 because this model was used to equip Finnish Tank Divisions. Turrets taken from T-37 and T-38 amphibious tanks armed with 7.62mm DT machine guns were also used as fixed fortifications and it is possible that turrets from captured FAI, FAI-M and BA-20M armoured cars were used in this way too.

To install the BT-5 and BT-7 turrets the main body of the tank was cut away leaving little more than the section mounting the turret race. Of the original fittings of the turret and the main body, only the periscopes, sights and the ammunition racks were retained. The body of the BT2 tank was similarly cut away but additional changes needed to be made to the turret to accommodate the 37mm Bofors gun. A steel front plate was fitted to take the new main armament and the original ball-mounted machine gun was removed. When mounting the BT2 turret the section of the main body of the tank on which the turret sat was affixed to a timber framework so that only the turret was visible above the ground. A trench was dug leading to the rear of the emplacement, which obviated the need for using the turret hatches. The preparation of the T-37 and T-38 positions was slightly different with the turrets being removed completely. Four lugs were then welded onto their sides as a means for attaching them to their shelter. Because the machine gun was fitted in a ball mounting that gave it a 90-degree arc of fire it was not deemed necessary for the turret to turn.

Generally speaking the tank turrets were positioned so that they were not exposed to direct enemy fire. In some cases a wall was built to provide flank protection for the turret or alternatively, they were often set behind a concrete dugout.

The inability of the Fortifications Division to secure the release of the BT turrets until the summer of 1944 and the fact that Finland sued for peace in September 1944 meant that the turrets were seemingly never used in action and as such many of them have survived. As many as fifty turrets have been identified and are still visible today in Finland, some emplaced and others that were transported to

---

*And at least one of these turrets can still be seen today.

their final location but which were not installed when work was suspended after the cessation of hostilities. The main weaponry and other fittings were removed from the turrets at the end of the war.

FAR EAST

In the second half of the 1930s Japanese forces swept all before them on the Asian mainland and on the islands of the Pacific. The European powers, who had for so long held sway in the region, now found their interests in the Far East threatened at the very same time as they were fighting for survival at home against Nazi Germany. Unable to conduct operations in two theatres, their dependencies were lost one after the other. However, one obstacle threatened Japanese ambitions and that was the might of the United States and more particularly its Pacific Fleet. In December 1941 the Japanese attacked Pearl Harbour in a calculated gamble that they hoped would destroy America's capital ships and carriers. But the operation was only partially successful and once this sleeping giant mobilized for war it was only a matter of time before the Japanese would be defeated. Determined not to relinquish its Far-Eastern empire the Japanese turned each island into a fortress and fought fanatically, defending every position literally to the last man.

By this stage of the war much of the equipment that had been superior or at least comparable to the enemy's at the outbreak of war, was now outdated and this was certainly true of much of Japan's armoured force. The Type 95 (1935) Ha Go was the army's principal light tank and was armed with a 37mm gun, while the Type 97 (1937) Chi Ha the main medium tank was only armed with a 57mm gun. They both had very thin armour and were only available in very small numbers. To use these precious resources in open combat was suicidal as was found on Saipan and Peleliu where the obsolete Japanese tanks were used in uncoordinated counter attacks in a desperate attempt to repel the US invasion force. They were targeted by everything from Sherman tanks to hand-held bazookas and were decimated.

A better use of the tanks was to employ them in a hull-down position in open pits that were supported by rifle and light machine gun positions. By installing them in this way it ensured that the tank survived longer and inflicted more casualties on the enemy. Furthermore, because they were simply positioned in shell holes and were not 'dug in' in the strictest sense of the phrase, they retained the ability to manoeuvre out of the position if necessary. Both the Type 95 Ha Go tank and the Type 97 Chi Ha tank were used in this way.

In the defence of San Manuel village on Luzon the Japanese used more than forty tanks – some were used in their traditional role but most were dug in.[26] Dug-in tanks were also used on Guam and on the Marshall Islands. Three Type 95 (1935) Ha Go tanks were emplaced on each of the main islands: Parry Island; Eniwetok Island and Engebi Island. However, they were easily knocked out by the US Shermans.[27]

ADDENDUM

Sockellafetten

As well as tank turrets used as fixed fortifications, the Germans also employed surplus tank guns fitted on pivot mounts, or *sockellafetten*. A series of mountings were developed to take 5cm, 7.5cm and 8.8cm guns produced in the main by Rheinmetal Borsig (see Table 1 *below*). The guns were often fitted with shields of varying designs to provide the crew with a modicum of protection, but later in the war, as the situation became more desperate, these were dispensed with completely. The shortages at the end of the war were also reflected in the mounting to which the gun was fitted. At the outset the guns were mounted on pedestals or cruciform platforms,* but later a simple extemporized framework was developed. The *sockellafetten* were sometimes mounted in specially designed bunkers but were more often located in open pits. Initially, and particularly in the Atlantic Wall, these tended to be constructed from reinforced concrete but later, simple field works were used and this was especially true of their use in the West Wall in late 1944 and 1945.

---

*The 8.8cm KwK 43 was mounted on a four-legged framework, or *kreuzbettung,* that was not dissimilar to that of the Flak '88'.

Table 1 *Sockellafetten*

Designation	Weapon
Sockellafette Ia	5cm KwK 39/1
Sockellafette Ib	5cm KwK 39
Sockellafette Ic	5cm KwK 39, 39/1, 40 7.5cm KwK 51, 67, 68
Sockellafette Id	7.5cm KwK 67
Sockellafette IIa	8.8cm KwK43 (and PaK 43)
Sockellafette III	7.5cm KwK42

Atlantic Wall

The 5cm *Sockellafetten* were used extensively along the length of the Atlantic Wall. They were mounted in a series of positions including a specially designed *ringstand* and in various *Regelbau* or standard constructions. The *ringstand* (the old designation was *Bauform* 65a and was later changed to *Bauform* 221) consisted of an open pit constructed from reinforced concrete. The gun was mounted centrally and the

position additionally incorporated a munitions room and a shelter for the crew, however, the crew's living quarters were in a separate concrete bunker.

A standard construction (*Regelbau* 600) to mount a 5cm KwK in an open position was also designed with accommodation underneath for the crew and ammunition. Numerous variants of this shelter were built including one where the fighting position was fitted with a concrete roof. The *Regelbau* 653 was an embrasured emplacement with a fighting compartment and separate crew and ammunition rooms. It also had a close defence position covering the main entrance and an observation post. The *Regelbau* 654 was the same but the stand to area was omitted and the *Regelbau* 667 was a much simplified shelter with an embrasure but no ammunition store or guardroom.

Two *Doppelschartenstände* (double loophole shelters) were also developed to mount the 5cm KwK. The Casemate SK was not a standard construction per se (or *Regelbau*) but was a *Sonder Konstruktion*' (special construction). Access to the shelter was from the rear via a staggered passageway

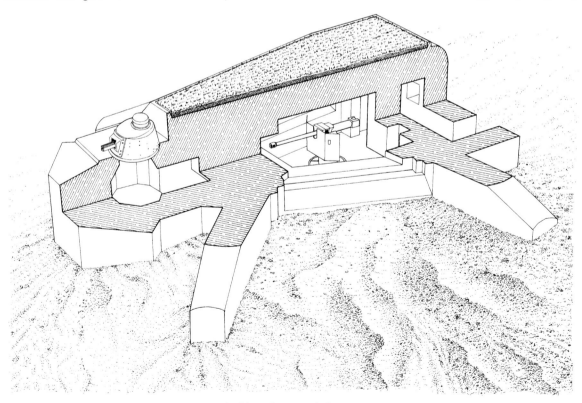

Casemate SK – FT17 turret with 5cm KwK in double embrasure shelter.

A 5cm KwK 39 L/60 in a Type 600 open shelter with reinforced roof. This example is located at St Aubin sur Mer and formed part of the defences of Juno Beach. (Author)

that led into the main fighting compartment, which housed the 5cm KwK. This could be brought to bear on either flank through embrasures on both sides. A passageway led from here to a tank turret mounted at the front, which could cover the entire beach. The turret could be traversed through 360 degrees but could not fire to the rear because of the main structure of the bunker. An example of this type of structure was constructed at Anse de Vauville and another at Biville (on the Cotentin peninsula). An alternative *Doppelschartenstand* design had the turret positioned

The rectagonal base plate (now capped) for a tank turret that was positioned to the rear of a 5cm KwK Doppelschartenstand on Omaha Beach. The concrete wall facing the sea would have protected the turret from direct fire, but meant the turret was only able to enfilade the beach. (Author)

at the rear of the shelter. On the seaward side a low concrete wall was constructed. This meant that the crew of the turret was only able to enfilade the beach, but it did protect the turret from direct enemy fire. An example of this type of structure can be seen at Vierville (part of Omaha Beach).

Eastern Front

Tank guns used in this way were also employed on the Eastern Front. At the beginning of April 1945 Frankfurt an der Oder was defended by a hotchpotch of units including *Festungs PaK Verband* 26 (Fortification anti-tank gun unit 26) and *Panzerturm-Kompanie* 1312 (Tank turret company 1312). These units were equipped with an assortment of makeshift fixed weapons including a number of Panther and *Panzer* 38(t) tank turrets but also twenty-four 7.5cm KwK 51 L/24 guns and ten 5cm 39/1 L/60 guns.

The 7.5cm gun had previously been mounted on a wide range of armoured vehicles including the *Schützenpanzerwagen* Sdkfz 250/8 and Sdkfz 251/9 and the *Panzerspähwagen* Sdkfz 234/3. Now the weapon was mounted on a makeshift Y-shaped carriage that was secured in place by piles rammed into the ground. The weapon was comparatively heavy (2 tonnes) and had no wheels, which made the piece difficult to transport even with a crew of ten (one non-commissioned officer and nine members of crew).

The value of using of these slightly outdated weapons in the latter stages of the war was question-able because the 7.5 cm 38 HL/C shell could only penetrate 100mm (4in) of armour at a distance of 500m (1,640ft), while the 38 HL/B, which was supplied to units defending the city, could only penetrate 75mm (3in) of armour. However, by the latter stages of the war the Germans were so desperate that even obsolete guns were pressed into action and it did have the advantage of a low profile, rising to less than a metre off the ground, which made it difficult for the enemy to see let alone hit.

A 7.5cm KwK 51 L/24 on this type of makeshift platform has been on permanent exhibition at the *Militärhistorischen Museum*, Dresden since December 1990. The example on display was constructed from a gun found at Usedom and another example found at much the same time and that had formed part of the Frankfurt an der Oder defences in the spring of 1945.[28]

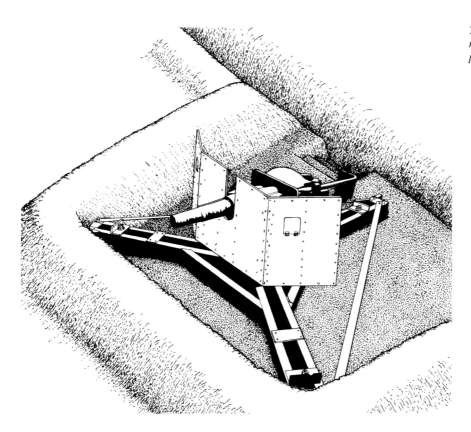

7.5cm KwK 51 L/24 mounted on special platform.

West Wall

On the western front plans were drawn up to use *sockellafetten* as part of the renovated defences of the West Wall. These were to be installed either in open pits, which were often little more than fieldworks, or in concrete bunkers. Many of the existing structures were unsuitable for the more powerful weapons so a series of new standard constructions were designed. One, the *Regelbau* 703, was developed to mount the 8.8cm KwK with crucible platform. This measured 9.3m × 7.5m (30ft 5in × 24ft 6in) and used some 370m³ (1,214ft³) of concrete. As well as the main fighting compartment there was a small munitions room capable of storing 180 rounds of ammunition.[29]* The lack of time and materials and the proximity of the enemy meant that the construction of new positions, like the *Regelbau* 703, was extremely difficult and so further consideration was given to the possibility of using existing structures. Two standard constructions – *Regelbauten* 18 and 22 – offered genuine potential and with some minor adjustments,

including new concrete foundations, these shelters were suitable for mounting the 8.8cm KwK 43 and KwK 43/3.

In spite of the desperate position on the western front in the autumn of 1944 work on the defences pressed ahead. On 27 November 1944 it was reported that some 350 *Sockellafette* IIa with 8.8cm KwK43/3 were available for use and of these sixty-five were en-route to the front, 185 had arrived, sixty were being installed and thirty-six were ready for action.[†] These were to be reinforced with PaK 40 anti-tank guns and, as will be seen later, emplaced Panther tank turrets.[30]

---

*It was planned to build thirty-three of these bunkers in the *Rurstellung*, but only four were actually constructed in NordRheinWestphalia. By 25 February 1945 a further thirteen had been constructed in the zone of *Fest Pi Kdr XVIII* Niederrhein (Lower Rhine). M. Gross, *Der Westwall zwischen Niederrhein und Schnee-Eifel* (Rheinland-Verlag GmbH, Colognes 1989), pp.364 and 374.

[†] The remaining four are unaccounted for.

A GI inspects a hastily installed 8.8cm gun (probably a Sockellafette IIa). This emplacement formed part of the Vogesenstellung and was captured by US forces in November 1944. (US National Archives)

At the express order of Hitler on 28 November these anti-tank defences were to be further strengthened. In total some 450 *Sockellafetten* IIa with 8.8cm KwK43/3 were to be installed along the length of the West Wall together with 300 *Sockellafette Ic* with 7.5cm KwK 67 and 150 *Sockellafette Ia* with 5cm KwK 39/1.[31] But in spite of Hitler's direct intervention, progress was painfully slow and even in January 1945 relatively few of the positions were ready for action (*see* Table 2 *below*).

Tanks

Even before the idea of using tank turrets as fixed fortifications had been widely adopted, the Germans had developed a number of tanks with turrets that could be removed from the chassis and used independently. In 1941 Krupp designed a self-propelled gun based on the *Panzer IV* chassis to mount the 10.5cm leFH18/1 L/28. A number of test units were produced, but it did not enter full production. Instead, attention was turned to weapons with all round traverse (the original design could only traverse through 70 degrees) with the possibility of

Table 2 West Wall Dispositions as at 18 January 1945[32]

Designation	Weapon	Assigned	Arrived	Ready for action
Sockellafette IIa	8.8cm KwK43/3 (*Jagdpanther*)	418*	309[†]	153
Sockellafette IIa	8.8cm KwK43 (*Tiger II*)	50	–	–
Sockellafette Ic	7.5cm KwK 67	132	–	–
Sockellafette Ia	5cm KwK 39/1	200	150[‡]	20
Sockellafette Ic	7.5cm KwK 51	168	–	–

*Plus a further 32 not assigned to fortifications command.
[†] 19 had been destroyed by enemy action.
[‡] 50 were missing or defective.

A Heuschrecke 10 or 10.5cm leFH18/1 L/28 auf Waffenträger GWIVb at the Krupp factory. The gantry is in place to lower the turret to the ground. (Imperial War Museum)

dismounting the weapon. The *Heuschrecke* 10* was developed by Krupp in 1942 again using the *Panzer III/IV* chassis developed for the Hummel self-propelled gun. Externally the *Heuschrecke* 10 looked like a typical tank, but to dismount the turret the chassis was fitted with a folding gantry with a block and tackle assembly. Once the gantry had been assembled the crew could lift the turret from the superstructure and emplace it on the ground. The tank also carried a set of wheels and a carriage, which could be used to tow the turret to a new location without the need to reinstall it on its normal mounting. Internally, the turret could not be fitted with a power traverse, but instead was rotated by hand. The weapon could also not be depressed below the horizontal but could be elevated to +68 degrees.

This innovative design overcame one of the major drawbacks of emplaced tank turrets, which was their lack of mobility; the turret could be deployed, used, recovered and installed elsewhere. However, although the idea was good in principle, in practice the actual installation and recovery of the turret was a long and convoluted process, exposing the crew to enemy fire. This meant that the operation either had to be carried out under the cover of darkness or covered by supporting fire. This was not a major problem because although an armoured pillbox, the turret mounted a light field howitzer and was

primarily designed for indirect rather than direct fire support. The turret also had an open top making it unsuitable for close engagements with the enemy. However, these difficulties were clearly considered to be a sufficient handicap that none of the designs entered full production.† Only three prototypes of the *Heuschrecke* 10 were built in 1943.

Armoured Trains‡

Before the First World War the Germans had used Grüson turrets, or *Fahrpanzer*, to provide additional

---

* More correctly called the *10.5cm leFH18/1 L/28 auf Waffenträger GWIVb*.

† A further design, the *Heuschrecke* 15, based on the unsuccessful Leopard chassis was also developed. In early 1944 a further weapons carrier, the *Geschützwagen Panther für sFH18/4(Sf)*, based on a shortened Panther chassis was ordered. Like the *Heuschrecke* it was fitted with a lifting beam for emplacing the turret. Daimler Benz built a prototype, but the end of the war prevented any further work. P. Chamberlain, H. L. Doyle and T. L. Jentz, *Encyclopedia of German Tanks of World War Two* (Arms and Armour Press, London, 1978), p.132.

‡ Germany was not alone in using tanks and tank turrets to provide added firepower to armoured trains. In the interwar period Poland had invested heavily in armoured trains and constructed a number of reconnaissance versions that mounted FT17 and Polish TK and TKS Tankettes. These could be unloaded for use in the field.

Heuschrecke 10

Turret statistics:[33]
Manufacturer: Krupp
Crew: 5

Armour (thickness/angle):

	Front	Side	Rear	Roof
Turret	30mm 30°	16mm 20°	16mm 25°	Open
Superstructure	30mm 20°	16mm 0°	16mm 20°	10mm 90°
Hull	30mm 20°	16mm 0°	16mm 20°	10mm 90°
Gun mantlet	30mm round			

Weight:	23 tons	Length:	6m
Height:	3m	Width:	3m

Weapon statistics:
Armament: 1 × 10.5cm leFH18/1 L/28
Traverse: 360°
Elevation: +68° −0°

firepower for German fortifications. These turrets with their 53mm gun proved highly versatile and during the war they were used on armoured trains. The turret sat on a wagon with armoured sides so that just the revolving hood was visible. Double doors in the centre of the wagon enabled the turret to be removed from the vehicle as and when necessary. Two of the larger 77mm guns, each fitted in a rotating armoured box mounted on a flatbed wagon, provided the main firepower of the armoured train which was ideally suited for use on the eastern front.[34]

After the First World War, Germany was ordered by the victorious Allies to dismantle the armoured trains it possessed.* The German High Command did not mourn the demise of the armoured train. They were expensive to build and maintain and offered little to the fluid, expansive type of warfare that they now favoured, bound, as they were, to the railway network. Moreover, they presented a large target not only to ground forces but also the new menace of ground attack aircraft. Yet, despite these reservations a number of armoured trains were retained. These trains were given further protection and more heavily armed and played minor roles in the Polish campaign and the fighting in the Low Countries.

The German successes saw further armoured trains fall into their hands, notably from Czechoslovakia and Poland, and these were absorbed into the German armoury. These and other German trains were seen as being of some use in the forthcoming Russian campaign (despite the difference in rail gauge) because of the vast distances involved. The decision to use armoured trains, however, came very late in the day and necessitated a series of improvisations to increase the train's firepower. This included mounting two, sometimes three, French Somua S35 tanks on open wagons with added side armour to protect the tanks' exposed running gear. This improvisation provided the added advantage of mobility, although unloading the tank from the wagon was slow and difficult and exposed the crew to enemy fire.†

These trains were not widely used in the early stages of Operation *Barbarossa*, largely being kept in

---

* However, unrest in the new republic meant that the authorities were allowed to establish 'railway protection trains' which were to prevent disruption to rail services.
† Armoured trains were also deployed in occupied France, Greece and Yugoslavia. These mounted obsolete French FT17 and Hotchkiss H39 tanks on flat bed wagons in much the same way as the Somua S35 was employed.

reserve. This was in marked contrast to the Soviets whose armoured trains inflicted some notable reverses on German forces. However, such successes were never likely to stem the German advance and as the Soviets retreated many of their armoured trains were captured and put to use against their former owner. Some of these, like the 'Stettin', or 'A', renamed by the Germans as *Eisenbahn Panzerzug Nr 51* or Armoured Train 51, were fitted with four BT7 tank turrets which mounted 4.5cm guns. These were fitted to wagons in a stepped formation so that the turrets could be deployed to the front at the same time.*

Later the more powerfully armed BP42 train was introduced. This included two specially designed flat wagons to accommodate a *Panzer* 38(t) tank. The tank sat in a lowered area that provided protection to the tank's running gear. The tanks bow gun was removed and the opening covered by an armoured plate. Loading ramps enabled the tank to be quickly deployed against partisans.† Previously bicycle mounted infantry had been the only means of taking the fight to the enemy. These trains with their thin armour (limited because no further weight could be added to the axles) and their lack of weapons that could fire armour-piercing rounds meant that they were susceptible to attack by enemy armour. As a consequence the trains were later provided with flat wagons mounting *Panzer* IV (*Ausf* F or H) turrets with 7.5cm KwK L/48 guns‡ and were renamed Type BP44.

In 1943 a completely new concept was introduced: the *Panzerdraisinen* (or armoured trolley), which was constructed by Steyr of Austria. These were self-contained armoured vehicles with their own crew (eight men – two non-commissioned officers and six ranks), weaponry and an air-cooled 76-hp Steyr motor which could propel the unit at a top speed of 70km/h (43mph).¶ These armoured railcars could be used individually or as part of longer trains. Of special note were the armoured cars mounted with a tank turret. These were fitted with either a *Panzer* III *Ausf* N or *Panzer* IV turret with the short KwK L/24 gun, although a number were also constructed using captured Soviet T34 turrets. Only a few of these units reached the front before the war ended.

In the spring of 1944 the Italian firm Ansaldo received an order from Germany for nine ALn56

armoured railcars, similar to the five built for the Italian army.§ These were fitted with two Italian M13/40 tank turrets mounting 4.7cm guns. They were used in the final months of 1944 in the Balkans to escort larger armoured trains. Not all of the units were finished by the time the war came to an end. A similar German version of this train was built by Steyr at the very end of the war. It mounted two *Panzer* IV Ausf H turrets with 7.5cm KwK L/48 guns. Only one of the three planned was actually built and was captured by the Americans at the end of the war in the Steyr works

In addition to the specially designed and produced armoured rail vehicles, improvised vehicles were also constructed. *Panzer Zeppelin*, a self-propelled armoured railcar, was constructed from scrap material from destroyed tanks and was armed with a Soviet BA10 turret with 37mm gun. The track protection train 'Michael', which was deployed in the Crimea from November 1943 until it was destroyed the following May, had an armoured wagon fitted with a T34/76 turret.[35]

Patrol Boats

Another less widely known use for tank turrets was as the main armament for patrol boats or river monitors. Again, as with the use of tank turrets as fixed fortifications, the lead was taken by the Soviets. The Russian landscape is criss-crossed with mighty rivers and studded with great lakes. With few roads, these waterways provided a vital communication link and as such were of great strategic importance. Before the First World War, Tsarist units patrolled these inland waterways and during the Civil War the Red Army continued the tradition.

In the years before the German invasion of the Soviet Union the naval forces were strengthened but

---

*A number of captured Soviet armoured trains were also supplied with additional flatbed wagons to accommodate Somua S35 tanks.
† French Panhard armoured cars were also used as reconnaissance vehicles. They had their road wheels replaced with flanged steel wheels so that they could run on tracks. With a quick wheel change they could revert to their original role.
‡ Captured T34/76 Model 43 turrets were also used.
¶ Although this was reduced for the turreted model.
§ Known as *Littorina Blindate* or *Eisenbahn Panzerwagen Littorina Modell 43*.

much of its fighting strength was lost in the early part of the war as the Germans captured huge tracts of land. To make up for these losses a new vessel was designed. It was to have a shallow draft and a flat bottom which meant that the boat could be transported from one river system or lake to another and was to be capable of mounting more than machine guns. This led to the development of the Type 1124 and 1125 Armoured Motor Gun Boats. These vessels were armed with one or two tank turrets. Initially they were fitted with T35 turrets but its main armament proved less than satisfactory and as spare T34 turrets became available they were used. Where a single turret was fitted this was located at the prow and where two were mounted one was fore and one aft. Sometimes the aft turret was dispensed with and replaced with a multiple rocket launcher. Machine guns, varying from two to six in number, were used as secondary armament and were also often enclosed in armoured turrets.*

Table 3 Soviet patrol boats

	Type 1124	**Type 1125**
Length	25m	22.6m
Width	3.8m	3.5m
Draft	0.8m	0.5m
Weight	50t	30t
Top speed	28km/h	20km/h
Crew	17	10
Armament	2 3 T34 76.2mm	1 3 T34 76.2mm
	2 3 MG 12.7mm	3 3 MG

In 1942 the Germans began work on a similar gunboat, the *Pionier Sicherungsboot*, or *PiSi-boot*. The boat was initially to be armed with a *Panzer* III turret fitted with a 5cm Kwk L/42 gun mounted forward but concerns over weight necessitated the replacement of the main armament with a 3.7cm U-boat gun mounting. At the stern there was to be either a 2cm quadruple flak mount or a *Drilling* MG151. A specially designed hull, which had removable sections, meant that the boat could be moved by rail.

Initial development and construction work was carried out in Hamburg before the boat was moved to the Elbe for trials in May 1944. Later it was moved

once again, this time to Lake Constance, where the tests were completed before finally being transported to Denmark where it was handed over to the Amphibious Engineers Regiment. The gunboat still had a number of teething problems which had not seemingly been resolved when the boat was destroyed in an Allied air raid.[†][36]

Part 3 – Panther Turrets

ORIGINS

By 1943 the idea of using tank turrets as fixed fortifications was accepted practice. Turrets from captured tanks or obsolete German models were emplaced in all the major theatres. However, they tended to have thin armour and because the guns mounted were small by the standards of the day, these turrets posed little threat to Allied tanks. That was all to change in October of that year with the idea of using Panther tank turrets in this way. This was a major departure for the Germans because the Panther was the main German medium battle tank, it was still in production and it was well armed with the powerful 75mm KwK42 L/70 gun.

Initially it was planned to mount Panther turrets on one of the steel shelters designed by the *Organization Todt* that had been specially adapted for the purpose. This, it was hoped, would take significantly less time to install than a typical concrete structure and as such would 'reduce [the] time of exposure to enemy fire during their emplacement'.[1] Nevertheless, only a year later (October 1944) plans were drawn up to mount a Panther turret on a standard reinforced concrete bunker – the *Regelbau* 687. However, by this stage in

---

*After the war the *Schmel* Class boats, which were built from 1965 to 1970, were fitted with PT76 turrets.
† Another PiSi boat was built but lacked any armament. This was captured by the Czechs and after the war the Defence Ministry decided to make the boat operational. It was fitted with a *Panzer* IV turret mounting a 7.5cm KwK 40 gun both of which were in plentiful supply after the war. It was sent for trials in 1948 before becoming part of the Danube Flotilla and served with this unit until it was decommissioned.

the war it was clear that Germany had neither the time, the manpower nor the materials needed to construct such elaborate fortifications and plans were hastily drawn up for a wooden framework that was capable of mounting the Panther turret and its base plate. This led to the development of the third and final shelter, the *Holzunterstand*.

OT STEEL SHELTER

OT Stahlunterstand mit aufgesetztem Pantherturm

Other Designations: *Pantherturm* I *Stahluntersatz*
By 1943 Hitler's dreams of a Third Reich were in tatters with his armies in retreat on all fronts. Thinking now turned from the offensive to the defensive and how to consolidate the gains that had been made. In the west, work began on the Atlantic Wall. Concrete bunkers were time consuming to build and consumed valuable resources and it was clearly not feasible to build such defences in Italy or on the Eastern Front so the *Organization Todt* developed a series of prefabricated steel shelters, one of which was adapted to mount a Panther turret. This idea was of great interest to Hitler and he was in regular communication with Speer* about its progress and it

is even reported that the Führer was intimately involved in the design of the shelter. In October 1943 Technical Directive No. 3 for Construction Work in Accordance with *Führerbefehl* 10 (Führer Order 10) was issued.[2] This included detailed drawings of the shelter and how it was to be installed in the ground.

The OT Shelter was constructed in two parts from electrically welded steel plates. The *oberteil* or upper box was roughly 3m (10ft) square and 1m (3ft) high and essentially formed the fighting compartment. It held the ammunition for the main weapon and was sufficiently deep to accommodate the turret basket. The roof, which was 100mm (4in) thick, incorporated the turret ball-race onto which the turret was mounted. The walls were 80mm (3in) thick and were fitted with bins that were capable of holding 175 rounds of 75mm ammunition. The ammunition for the machine gun (4,500 rounds) was stored in the turret itself.

The *uberteil* or lower box was substantially higher than the upper box, at two metres (6ft) with enough room for a man to stand upright comfortably. Because it was lower in the ground it was less well armoured; the exterior walls being only 70mm (3in) thick, the interior walls 50mm (2in) and the base plate 40mm

*Minister for armaments and munitions.

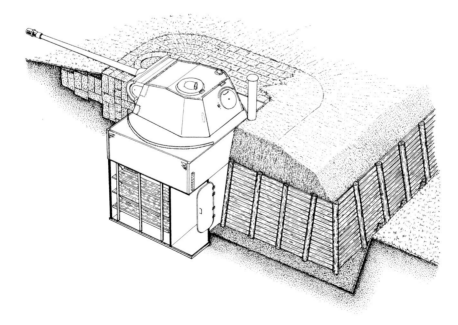

OT Stahlunterstand mit aufgesetztem Pantherturm – OT Steel Shelter.

The top box of an OT steel shelter that has been destroyed and flipped upside down giving a rare view of the inside and the ammunition storage. The photograph was taken in September 1944 near Rimini.
(QE II Army Memorial Museum)

One of the Panther turrets that was to be installed in the Gothic Line near Rimini in September 1944. The lower box has been tipped on its side, which gives a clear view of the inside and in particular the ladder that linked the two boxes. (QE II Army Memorial Museum)

(1½in). It was divided into three compartments. The largest, which was lined with board, formed the living accommodation. It was fitted with fold down bunk beds* and a pressure-proof Wt 80K stove to heat the room. The stove was fitted with a flue which also served as an exhaust pipe for the machinery in the passageway.† In the right hand rear corner of the compartment there was an escape hatch. This led to a vertical shaft clad with wood and fitted with climbing rungs. Where no escape tunnel was provided the hatch could be sealed with a plate that was bolted in place. It was possible to fit a radio set in the shelter and a hole in the wall near the main entrance was provided for the aerial. However, if a radio was fitted then three of the bunks had to be removed.

An opening led from the crew's quarters to a further compartment that acted as either a general store or as home to various pieces of equipment. These included a 2hp DKW motor with 600-watt dynamo, a 150-amp storage battery and a 20-litre compressed air tank. These powered the lights and the electric fan in the turret and a compressor to flush out the barrel. Initially it was planned to dispense with the compressed air but it was soon realized that without it, conditions in the turret became intolerable when the main armament was being used (unless the hatches were left open which compromised the operation of the turret) and the decision was reversed.[3] The turret, however, was not gas proof, but the shelter was. It was

A very rare photograph of the inside of the lower box. It shows the escape hatch and two of the three bunk beds on that wall. The wooden cladding is also clearly visible. (Tank Museum)

fitted with a gas lock and a ventilator (located in the crew's quarters), which was manually operated and was capable of producing 1.2m³ of fresh air per minute.

A hinged door with pistol port led from here to the final compartment. This was fitted with a steel ladder

---

*The official drawings depict the shelter being fitted with nine, but in practice, three to six was more normal.
†When the turret was in use the chimney could be collapsed to allow free turning of the turret through 360 degrees.

that linked the upper and lower boxes and was also where the main entrance was located. From here a trench, which sloped fairly steeply upward, led away from the shelter and linked it to the main trench system at the rear. The trench was revetted with brush or cast building blocks and near the shelter was covered with timber cross members and spoil. Immediately outside the entrance was a soakaway to prevent flooding of the shelter. According to a captured German file the entrance had caused some debate, but in practice it had proved to be satisfactory.[4]

Table 1 Steel shelter weight

Turret	8.8 tonnes
Upper box	13.5 tonnes
Lower box	18.5 tonnes
Equipment	1 tonne
Total weight	41.8 tonnes

The initial turrets supplied for use on steel shelters were not fitted with power traverse and *Inspektion der Festungen* (Fortress Inspectorate) enquired of the *Waffenamt* whether it was possible to add this facility. Their response made it quite clear that shortages of parts meant that it was not possible to meet demand for *Panzerkampfwagen V* Panther production let alone meet this additional requirement and as such the modification was rejected. With no traversing gear the crew had to rotate the turret by hand.* This, as a captured German document stated, 'was both slow and difficult and generally unsatisfactory'.[5] The weight of the turret was such that the hand traverse had to be highly geared and meant that the turret could only be traversed at approximately 2 degrees per second.[†] To alleviate the problem an auxiliary drive was installed. This enabled the loader to support the gunner by hand and resulted in a marginally increased speed.[6] Traversing of the turret also suffered from other teething problems. On early models the turret became jammed by splinters entering the turret ring. To overcome this problem, the area was covered by a plate, and sandbags provided additional protection.[7]

The shelter was to be installed by the *Organization Todt* and its personnel were responsible for ensuring that the position was ready for immediate occupancy by the crew, although in reality the crew was often required to help. A hole was excavated that was to be big enough to accommodate both the steel boxes and a collar of reinforced concrete blocks. These were to provide added protection to the steel boxes and were positioned so that they sloped away from the turret base at a gradient of 1:10. Approximately 55m³ of blocks each 20 × 25 × 50cm were needed and were secured with wire and pointed with cement. The whole was to be covered with turf and channels cut into the apron to direct rain away from the shelter at the front and on both sides.

OT Stahlunterstand mit Betonummantelung für Pantherturm

A year after Technical Directive No. 3 was promulgated Detailed Instructions No. 2 for the 'Improvement of the Western Fortifications and the West Wall' was issued. This included an annex detailing a slightly different method of installation for the Panther turret, the *OT Stahlunterstand mit Betonummantelung*. Instead of concrete blocks the boxes were to be encased in concrete 1–1.5m (3–5ft) thick and an inclined concrete apron, or *sogplatte*, was to be constructed that gave the shelter added protection and also served to counter blast damage to the loose soil around the turret when the gun fired.

This formalized a practice that had already been adopted in Italy in the Hitler Line and which, in the opinion of *Waffenamt Prüf Festung* (Fortification design office), was at variance with the original concept of this type of shelter. In a report sent to *General der Pioniere und Festung* (General in Charge of Engineering Works and Fortifications) and *Chef des Generalstabs des Heeres)* Chief of General Staff (Army)) in May 1944 it questioned the logic of encasing the shelters in concrete. The OT Steel Shelter, it contested, had been developed for use where rapid installation was necessary or when poor

---

*The power for the turret traverse was normally drawn from the main drive shaft of the tank.
[†]Even then a full rotation would take three minutes, which compared with seventeen seconds when the hydraulic traverse was used on the tank.

OT Stahlunterstand mit Betonummantelung für Pantherturm – Panther turret on OT Steel Shelter with concrete surround.

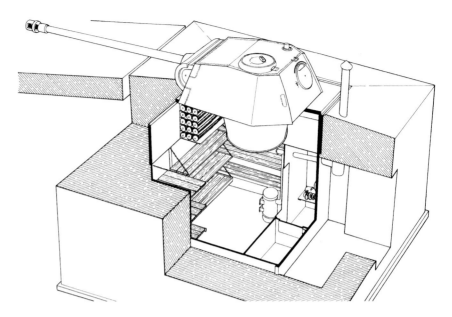

A Panther Ausf D turret mounted on a steel shelter. The concrete jacket that provided further protection for the base units is still under construction with only the steel reinforcing rods in place. The turret was located on the approaches to Rimini, Italy. (J. Plowman)

weather precluded the use of concrete. If this was not the case then a reinforced concrete shelter was preferable because it provided better protection and did not waste valuable steel that could be used more profitably elsewhere. Because of this the *Waffenamt* could not support the further mass production of Panther turrets on steel shelters.[8]

The concerns raised by the *Waffenamt* were not the only problems with the OT Steel Shelter. There were also more general difficulties with transportation and installation. The steel shelters were dispatched in two parts: the upper box with turret and the lower box. For the first part of their journey the sections were transported from the assembly plant on flatbed rail wagons. These were widely used to transport both war materials to and from the front and for the movement of supplies inside the Reich. As war production escalated demands on the railways increased

A good view of one of the twelve-wheeled trailers that were used to transport the Panther turret and lower box from the railhead to its final destination. This example was abandoned somewhere along the Gothic Line and was captured by Canadian forces.
(Canadian National Archives)

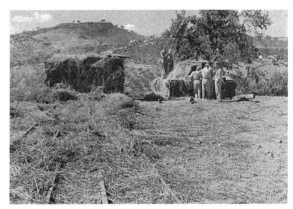

A Panther turret and steel shelter ready for installation. In the foreground are the rails on which the lower box, which formed the crew's living quarters, was moved into place. The two sections have been covered in hay in an effort to camouflage them. (Imperial War Museum)

A further view of the special trailer showing four of the six internal wheels. The large number of wheels dissipated the tremendous weight of the turret and box.
(Canadian National Archives)

being only slightly longer than the box they carried, and were fitted with twelve wheels with solid rubber tyres, six on the outside and six on the inside. These trailers were then towed by tractors to the final site for installation. The OT, which was responsible for transporting the Panther turrets, had very few tractors, which meant that they could not guarantee delivery and even if they could provide a vehicle to tow the trailer there was often insufficient fuel for the journey. A captured German document provided an insight into the transport difficulties of the OT Shelter. 'A handicap is that they are heavy to transport and at present their use is limited to the vicinity of roads capable of taking the heavy trailer which carries them.'[9]

To ease the transport problems the turrets were to be installed as near as possible to the railway or at least near good roads a short distance from the railway station,* and increasingly the OT had to rely on Army Groups to provide help.† But even these expedients did not completely eliminate the

and this, together with the impact of Allied air raids, meant that these wagons were in short supply and not always available to transport the steel shelters.

Matters did not improve at the rail terminus. Here the upper and lower boxes were loaded onto trailers. These were specially designed and were immensely strong since they were required to carry loads in excess of 20 tonnes. As such they were compact,

---

* The difficulty of transporting the turrets in Italy was such that, according to Italian civilians, the Germans were seemingly forced to use oxen to tow the trailer. E. Thomas (12 RTR) letter to author dated 19 November 1992.
† In the construction of the Gothic Line in AOK14's zone in August 1944 *Pz.Berge-Kp.*9 (9th Panzer Recovery Company) was responsible for transporting the Panther turrets from the railway station to their final destination. BA, RH20-14/48.

An excavation ready to accommodate the upper and lower boxes for a Panther turret. The base section would have been manoeuvred down the inclined plane, a technique used when no lifting gear was available.
(J. Plowman)

problems. At the site itself the upper and lower boxes needed to be unloaded and lowered into place by means of a mobile crane, the two sections being assembled in the excavation. As the war progressed heavy lifting gear was increasingly difficult to find and instead the individual sections had to be manoeuvred along 'rail tracks' to their final resting place. It was then necessary to dig an incline down which the boxes were lowered. The soil was then backfilled.

REGELBAU 687 (STANDARD CONSTRUCTION)

Other Designations: *Pantherturm* II *Betonsockel*
The difficulties of transportation and the concerns expressed by the *Waffenamt* about the value of using valuable steel in the production the OT Shelter prompted consideration of alternative structures to accommodate Panther turrets and in May 1944 Hitler agreed that surplus Panther turrets could be mounted on a concrete shelter. A design and technical note were drawn up and were issued in October 1944, along with the *OT Stahlunterstand mit Betonummantelung*, in Detailed Instructions No. 2 for the Improvement of the Western Fortifications and the West Wall.

The shelter on which the turret was mounted was installed below ground, so that when it was finished only the turret was visible. It was constructed from reinforced concrete with exterior walls 1.5m (5ft) thick and interior walls and the floor half as thick at 80cm (31in). Somewhat surprisingly the roof only measured 1.2m (4ft) at its thickest which may have been in recognition of the fact that the turret was more likely to be engaged by enemy armour and anti-tank guns that would have a flat trajectory rather than artillery fire. An apron of concrete that ran away from the leading edge of the bunker was also added, much like that constructed around the later OT Steel

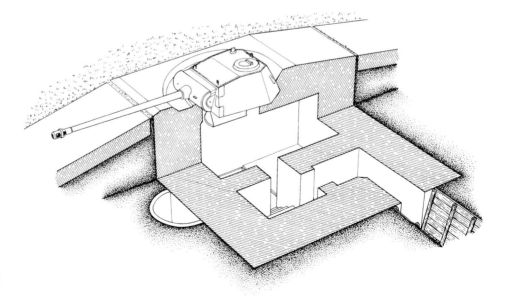

Regelbau 687 – A Panther turret mounted on a reinforced concrete shelter.

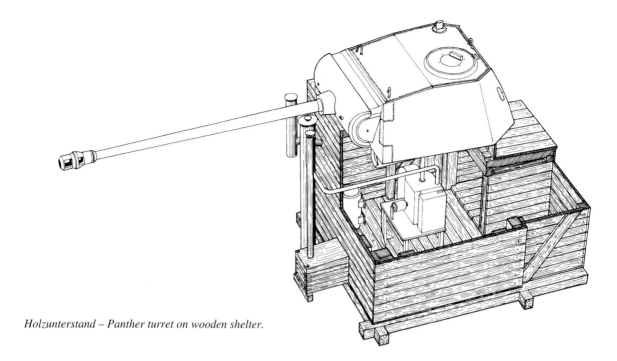

Holzunterstand – Panther turret on wooden shelter.

Shelter, with the same aim of providing added protection and to counter blast damage.

The bunker itself had three rooms, which were accessed via the entrance at the side of the shelter. A steel door led from here to the crew's quarters. This measured 2m × 1.5m (6ft × 5ft) and housed a stove that provided heat for the crew and a means of warming food. The smoke from the stove was vented outside through a chimney. There were few other concessions to comfort. There was no room for bunk beds, but an escape hatch was fitted which led to a vertical shaft at the front of the shelter.

From the crew's quarters wooden steps led to the fighting compartment below the turret. The room directly below the turret housed an 8.7hp DKW motor that was positioned on a concrete plinth in the middle of the shelter. A vertical shaft linked the motor with the hydraulic rotation mechanism in the turret. This enabled the gunner to turn the turret mechanically. Using this the turret could be traversed at 6 degrees per second. A V-belt from the motor ran a compressor that provided the compressed air to flush out the barrel. The motor also powered a dynamo that provided electricity for lighting, to operate the turret fan and for the electrical discharge. A coupling between the motor and the gears enabled the crew to

disengage the motor when it was being started up. Exhaust from the motor was vented outside via the chimney. Metal rungs set in the wall linked the fighting compartment to the turret itself. Adjacent to the fighting compartment was a 1.64m- (5ft) high recess measuring 2.3m × 2.0m (7ft × 6ft) that could accommodate 450 rounds of 7.5cm KwK ammunition.*

HOLZUNTERSTAND

Other Designations: *Schnelleinbau* or *Pantherturm* II or A

As the war entered its final months it became clear that the ambitious plans for mounting Panther turrets on reinforced concrete shelters would not be possible so urgent consideration was given to the possibility of designing a quicker, simpler and cheaper alternative. This led, in November 1944, to the development of a wooden framework that was capable of mounting the Panther turret and its base plate. However, it was made very clear that the *Holzunterstand* was only a

---

* 4,500 rounds of machine gun ammunition could be stored in the turret.

stopgap measure and was only to be used where it was not feasible to construct a reinforced concrete shelter.[10]

Construction of the shelter was very simple. Four wooden props, 20cm (7in) square, supported an upper and lower framework constructed from squared off timber (20 × 16cm, 7 × 6in), which was bolted together. Two sets of cross members (16 × 8cm, 6 × 3in) at the top and at the bottom provided added strength. The outside of the box-like framework was then lined with 25–30mm (1–1¼in) thick baffle boards before being installed in the ground. On top of this framework the turret and its base plate – which weighed 11 tons – were affixed with 14¾in (37cm) bolts.

It was essential that the upper and lower frameworks were absolutely horizontal and true if the turret was to operate effectively because, like the concrete shelter, the *Holzunterstand* was fitted with an 8.7hp DKW EL462 motor to rotate the turret. The motor sat on a welded steel *grundplatte* that was positioned at the base of the structure. A vertical shaft led from here to engage with the transmission gear in the turret. The motor simultaneously drove a dynamo and compressor. The dynamo provided electricity for lighting, the turret fan and the electrical discharge system. The compressor for the production of compressed air to automatically flush out the barrel was driven via a V-belt.[11]

Regardless of whether the framework had been constructed perfectly level, the motor, gears and coupling arrangement were not without their problems. Even when running for relatively short periods (thirty minutes) the gears became very hot. Some cursory investigations found no evidence of the shafts jamming or sticking and the bearings had enough oil, so it was concluded that the heat was simply the result of the number of revolutions (2,000–3,000rpm). With no time for design changes the crews were advised to uncouple the gears on the motor and only to activate them when turning the turret, so as to reduce the possibility of damaging the gears.[12]

Understandably, given the desperate situation for the Germans at this time, the shelter was functional with few concessions to the crew's comfort. There was no room in the shelter for any bunk beds, but a Wt 80k stove was installed, which provided heat and somewhere to cook. A chimney and flue for the motor were fitted to vent fumes outside. A two-part recess was let into the side of the shelter that provided storage room for 162 rounds (eighty-one rounds in each) of 75mm ammunition, while a recess on the opposite side of the shelter accommodated a battery. The entrance to the structure was located at the side. It consisted of a simple board door, which ultimately led to the approach trenches.[13]

Despite the seemingly flimsy nature of the structure, test firing of the main weapon in the zone of *Fest Pi Kdr* I on the West Wall proved the framework was stable and did not move. Nevertheless, the shelters did suffer a number of teething problems. After installing the Panther turret on the wooden framework a number of the base plates on which the turret was mounted developed noticeable sags of approximately 6–10mm (under an inch). This was particularly evident along the diagonals and caused the turret to jam. The problem was exacerbated by irregularities in the plate surface, which had to be removed by rubbing down. Various solutions to overcome these problems were developed. One alternative developed by *Fest Pi Kdr* I in March 1945 was to use two timber props to support the base plate and this seemed to solve the problem. Another solution was the addition of 10mm thick steel ring between the turret and the base plate, which raised the turret just enough to allow it to rotate (although it was not clear whether there might be further sagging that might again jam the turret). The long-term solution it was suggested was increasing the thickness of the base plate, but by that time (21 March 1945) major modifications were not feasible.[14]

PANTHER TURRET

The Germans used three separate turret types on the different shelters. Initially, because of the critical nature of the situation, Panther *Ausf* A turrets were used. These were taken directly from the main Panther production line and were used largely unaltered on steel shelters in the Hitler Line, in Italy. Later refurbished *Ausf* D turrets were used. Somewhat confusingly this was an earlier design than the *Ausf* A but was easily distinguishable by the drum cupola. The *Ausf* D turrets used included the original version with a circular communications hatch in the

'*Nahverteidigungswaffe*', or close defence weapon, which could fire grenades, smoke or flares. The roof armour was also increased in thickness from 16mm to 65mm. This was simply because of the greater threat to the turret from artillery fire and tests showed that the thicker roof could withstand a direct hit from a 15cm artillery shell.

The turrets mounted on the concrete and wooden shelters, in common with the standard production tank, had power traverse and used a slip ring transfer to connect the communications cable and the lighting circuit to the shelter.[15] In stark contrast the turrets mounted on OT steel shelters had to be rotated by hand and rather than a slip ring were fitted with a drag cable. This prevented the turret from rotating more than three times either clockwise or anti-clockwise, although trials had shown that the cable would withstand 4–5 rotations. To avoid twisting off the cable completely an indicator was provided in the turret that showed the number of revolutions out of the zero position. The commander was also advised to turn the turret back to the zero position after every exercise and following any engagement with the enemy.[16]

An emplaced Panther turret mounted on a steel shelter that formed part of the Gothic Line. The turret is an old Panther Ausf D model that is clear from the commander's cupola and the side pistol port. The turret was captured by American forces in September 1944.
(US National Archives, courtesy of S. Zaloga)

PRODUCTION

Initially the *Heereswaffenamt Amtsgruppe für Industrielle Rüstung* (Industrial Armaments Department of the Army Ordnance Branch) had ambitious plans for Panther turret production. After the initial

left turret wall and later versions where the hatch had been removed. Similarly, early *Ausf* A turrets were employed which retained the pistol ports in the side and rear turret walls and also later modified examples where these had been dispensed with.

Later a specially designed turret was developed. The *Ostwallturm,* or *Ostbefestigung,* as it was known, differed from the standard turret in a number of ways. The mantlet was slightly narrower than the *Ausf* A, but it retained the two openings for the TZF12 gun sight (one of the apertures was sealed with a plug if the monocular TZF12a sight was fitted). The cupola was removed and was replaced by a simplified hatch with rotating periscope. A simple turret support was also fitted for when the turret hatch was open. Though simplified the turret did have

A close-up of the Ostwallturm with its thicker roof plate and turret hatch with swivelling periscope. This turret is on display at the Westwall Museum, Niedersimten, Germany.
(Author)

Panther Turret

Turret statistics:[17]

Armour (thickness/angle):
Ostwallturm or Ostbefestigung*

Gun mantlet	Front	Side	Rear	Roof
100mm/round	100mm/12°	45mm/25°	45mm/25°	65mm
Panther *Ausf A* and *Ausf D*				16mm

Weapon statistics:

Armament: 1 × 7.5cm KwK42 L/70
    1 × 7.92mm MG34
Traverse: 360°
Elevation: +18° −8°
Maximum range: Approx. 9,400m (with HE shell)
Effective range: Up to 1,500m
Muzzle velocity: Pz.Gr 325m/sec
    Sprg.Gr 420m/sec
Rate of fire: 6–8 rounds a minute
Penetration performance: (mm at an angle of 60°)

Ammunition	V°	100m	500m	1,000m	1,500m	2,000m
Pzgr.Patr.39/42	925m/sec	138	124	111	99	88
Pzgr.Patr.40/42	1,120m/sec	194	174	150	127	106

*These dimensions are taken from an actual turret and are at variance to official sources that quote the following:

Gun mantlet	Front	Side	Rear	Roof
100mm*	80mm/78°	45mm/60°	45mm/60°	–
–	120mm†	45mm	–	60mm

*RH11 III/105.
†RH11 III/150.

ramp up in production in late 1943 it was hoped to produce one hundred *Ostwallturm* per month. However, shortages of steel meant that this was not achievable unless other more important areas of war production (U-boats and tanks) were sacrificed and that was patently unacceptable. Consequently a more realistic target was set, at first thirty per month and then finally fifteen per month.

The basic Panther turrets were to be manufactured by Dortmund Hoerder Hüttenverein (DHHV) and Ruhrstahl. DHHV began work on the armoured components in November 1943 and by the middle of May 1944 the two companies had completed 104 of the 259 turrets that were now planned. The unfinished turrets were sent to Demag Falkensee for final assembly. By the end of May 1944 the company had completed ninety-eight of the turrets but because of the need to increase Bergepanther production (a recovery tank), the last of the 130 turrets were not finished until the end of October. The remaining 129 turrets were to be mounted on concrete shelters. The majority of these turrets were completed before the

A Panther turret at the Rheinmetall proving ground, Hillersleben. The turret appears to have been taken from a standard production Ausf A tank because it still has its zimmerit and camouflage paint scheme. The tracks on either side would appear to be for the mobile crane to lower the turret onto the bunker. (G. B. Jarrett collection, US Army MHI, courtesy of S. Zaloga)

end of 1944, but an Allied air raid damaged ten turrets beyond repair. These had to be replaced and were not finished by Demag until the first week in February 1945.* [18]

The steel upper and lower boxes for the OT shelter were also assembled by Demag of Berlin. Once completed they were dispatched to the *Heimat Festungspionierpark* (Home Fortifications Engineering Depot) Pardubitz where they were fitted out with additional equipment including bunk beds, stove, motor, compressor, dynamo and battery as well as having the walls of the lower box lined with board. The *Heimat Festungspionierpark* at Pardubitz was also where minor modifications were carried out, like the alterations to the motor support. Other problems, like the sagging and poorly finished base plates, had to be rectified on site.

The concrete and wooden structures were constructed at the front with the work overseen by the Organization Todt, but they in turn relied on industry to produce some of the key components. Alkett, the tank manufacturer, built some of the foundation plates[19] and Daimler Benz designed the motor support and the arrangement for transferring power to the turret for these shelters. DKW produced the motor, the Osthoff Company supplied the ventilation piping and Boehringer the hydraulic power traverse.[20]

CREW

The Panther turrets were manned by a specially trained crew of three – a *Kommandant* (commander), a *Richtshütze* (gunner) and a *Ladeschütze* (loader) – who were assigned to a *Festungs (Panther-Turm) Kompanie* made up of twelve turrets. In April 1944 Tenth Army in Italy established a Panther turret company to man the positions on the Hitler Line. This was attached to 15th *Panzer Grenadier* Division that initially held the Liri valley.[21] When this division was relieved the Panther turret company was absorbed by the Straffner Battle Group, a group of miscellaneous units, which formed part of 44th Infantry Division and later 90th *Panzer Grenadier* Division.[22] Other turrets along the line, in the zone of 1st *Fallschirmjäger* Division, around Monte Cassino, were manned by *Fallschirmjäger Pz Jäger Abt* 1. After the battle for the Hitler Line *Gefreiter* Fries of 2/*Fallschirmjäger Pz Jäger Abt.* 1 was awarded the Knight's Cross for his part in the battle.[23] The turrets manned by crews from 15th *Panzer Grenadier* Division were similarly successful, but were not as fortunate as their comrades and 'In the absence of any definite evidence, the telephone conversations of the

*And of these, six were ultimately used on steel shelters.

period permit the conclusion that many crews of the armoured turrets perished in the Senger line . . .'[24]

The Panther turret company that manned the turrets on the Hitler Line was later reformed under AOK10 and given the designation *Festungs (Panther-Turm) Kp.*1. This unit manned the Panther turrets at the eastern end of the Gothic Line. A sister unit, *Festungs (Panther-Turm) Kp.*2, was established by AOK14 in July 1944 to man positions in the west and to cover the central passes.[25] In December a platoon of the company was ordered to man Tiger and P40 turrets in the Massa Line while the rest of the company was ordered to remain ready to transfer to the *Voralpenstellung.*[26] At the end of September, with the Gothic Line unhinged, *Festungs (Panther-Turm) Kp.*1 was ordered to prepare for Operation *Herbstnebel*, the evacuation of the Po Plain, and by April both Panther turret companies were stationed at Vittorio Veneto in north eastern Italy.

Later in the war the organization of Panther turret crews became more ordered so that in addition to *Festungs (Panther-Turm) Kp.*1 and 2 *Festungs Pantherturm Kp.* 1209 and 1210 were formed as part of *Heeresgruppe* C. The companies had been established at the end of December 1944 and in mid-January 1945 were sent to Vittorio Veneto. At the beginning of April the two companies were located around Görz (Gorizia).

This numbering system was adopted on all fronts following an order from *General-Inspekteur der Panzertruppen* (Inspector General Armoured Troops) in November 1944 that called for the creation of thirteen companies. Thus in addition to the two companies in Italy, *Festungs Pantherturm Kp.* 1201–1208, which were to be ready for employment by the beginning of December 1944, were to serve with *Der Oberbefehlshaber West* (Commander in Chief West) and *Festungs Pantherturm Kp.* 1211–1213, which were to be ready by the end of December, were to serve on the Eastern Front. These companies were sent east during January 1945 and were stationed in Küstrin (Kostrzyn), Frankfurt an der Oder and Stettin (Szczecin) respectively.

Note: The numbering of the Panther turret companies has caused a little confusion since numbers adopted by the German army were not repeated and in the official lists[27] some of these numbers (for example, 1204, 1205, 1206, 1209 and 1210) were used by other units. However, the Panther turret companies are quoted in official documents and as such the author has retained these numbers.

The dire straits in which the German army found itself in the closing months of the war meant that the Panther turret companies did not simply man their respective positions, they were also called on to undertake other duties. In Italy one of the Panther turret companies stationed on the Gothic Line was given guard duties and also ordered to undertake night patrols to counter partisan activity in and around Monte Cimone, near the strategically important Poretta pass (on route 64 Pistoia to Bologna).[29] In the West Wall the crews were also required to help install the turrets.[30]

Table 2 Panther turret companies west wall

Fest Pi	*Fest Pi*	Date	Fest.Pantherturm Kp.							
			1201	1202	1203	1204*	1205*	1206*	1207	1208
Kdr I	*Stab* 1	03/01/45							X	
	Stab 11	03/01/45								X
Kdr IV	*Stab* 9	27/12/44					X			
	Stab 17	27/12/44				X				
Kdr XIX	*Stab* 13	09/12/44	X	X	X					

**Festungs Pantherturm Kp.*1204 formed part of *Festungs* PAK Verband 17 in Wehrkreis XVII and *Festungs Pantherturm Kp.*1205 and 1206 formed part of *Festungs* PAK Verband 18 in Wehrkreis XVIII.[28]

EMPLACEMENT

The positioning of the turret was dictated by tactical considerations and by ground conditions. The former was very much the domain of the army while the latter was the concern of the *Fest Pi Stab* (Fortification Engineer Staff) that oversaw the installation work. Not surprisingly this caused some friction. When considering possible sites to install Panther turrets the engineers had to take into account a number of factors. Firstly, the underground water level had to be considered, because any flooding would seriously jeopardise the operation of the turret – the motor and electrical equipment were below ground level. Secondly, it was important that the turret was positioned on slightly rising ground so that the turret did not stand out against the horizon. Finally, it was considered desirable to avoid prominent landmarks, like road junctions, even if this meant that in some cases the turret did not have all round operation. Clearly such a constraint was difficult for the army to accept, because Panther turrets were ideally suited to cover mountain passes and road intersections and not being able to traverse through 360 degrees meant the turret was vulnerable to attack from the rear.

Once the location of the turret had been decided, the actual installation work was to be carried out by the *Organization Todt* and its army of foreign labourers and locally employed workers. However,

One of the two Panther turrets that were built to protect the Futa Pass. This turret was carefully positioned to cover a blind bend in the road. (US National Archives)

often men co-opted to help absconded, so the crews of the turrets were frequently forced to help.

Each of the three designs required a different installation technique. Typically, a hole was dug large enough to fit the sub-structure whether it was concrete, steel or wood. For the concrete shelter a lattice of reinforcing rods was fabricated in the excavation. Once this was complete and the shuttering in place the concrete was poured. For the steel shelter a level concrete base was laid at the bottom of the hole onto which the first of the steel boxes was lowered. The upper box was then attached to this. Sufficient soil had to be removed to accommodate the concrete blocks, or concrete jacket, which provided the shelter with added protection. For the wooden shelter, care had to be taken when excavating the earth to remember to allow for both the battery and ammunition recesses which protruded from the base of the structure. Once this was done the framework could be installed and the turret mounted. The spoil could then be backfilled and the approach to the entrance could be completed which included a soakaway to prevent flooding.

Because the turret sat so close to the ground it was essential that nothing prevented the turret from rotating and that it had a clear field of fire. The crew was therefore required to clear plants and trees (and in the winter – snow), which might otherwise impair the effective operation of the turret.

CAMOUFLAGE

The Allies' air supremacy meant that the Germans had to go to great lengths to camouflage the structure when it was under construction and when the work was complete. Much of the building work was carried out at night when the threat from Allied air and artillery bombardment was much reduced. During the day construction work was suspended and the area covered with camouflage nets and mats. Some positions in Italy were even constructed within or near to buildings. When the turret was ready for action these structures were demolished. To eliminate the telltale shadow of the gun-barrel it was depressed into a channel between two rows of sandbags and painted to blend in with the surroundings.

A Panther turret with the three-colour camouflage scheme clearly visible. The position was captured by Polish troops during the battle for the Gothic Line in September 1944. (Polish Institute and Sikorski Museum)

The barrel of the Panther turret cast a long shadow, which could be seen by Allied air reconnaissance planes. To conceal it, a sandbagged line trench was dug in which to depress the barrel. (Imperial War Museum)

The turrets also received a camouflage paint scheme that was much the same as that given to standard production models. Photographic evidence suggests that the normal three colour camouflage pattern was used and the only two colour images in

existence that depict Panther turrets* do not suggest any different. This would imply that the turrets (and upper and lower boxes of the OT Steel Shelter) received a base coat of *Dunkelgelb* (dark yellow) which was applied in the factory. The field units were then able to apply *Olivgrün* (olive green or drab) and *Rotbraun* (reddish brown) in a variety of camouflage patterns. Those turrets taken from older *Ausf* D and *Ausf* A tanks and the dug in Panthers seem to have been left largely unaltered with at least one example retaining its turret identification number.

HULL DOWN

In the final months of the war Panther tanks were also used in hull down positions. In Italy, in the Gothic Line, disabled tanks were manoeuvred into specially dug pits and the soil back-filled around the tank to produce a very simple fortified position. On the eastern front Panther tanks, often minus their running gear, were used as improvised strong points. They were often positioned at street intersections in major cities and towns to cover the main avenues of attack.

*A painting by Maj C. F. Comfort of a destroyed Panther turret in the Hitler Line, May 1944 and another by Capt G. C. Tinning of a turret in the Gothic Line in September 1944.

One of the Panther tanks buried in the ground and used as improvised fixed fortifications. The driver and machine gunner's hatches of the Ausf A are clearly visible in the foreground. It is also possible to see the tank's original zimmerit paste covering. This example was captured by Polish forces in the fighting for the Gothic Line. (Polish Institute and Sikorski Museum)

A Panther Ausf G, minus its running gear, being used as a fixed fortification. Paving slabs and spoil have been heaped around the structure to provide added protection. Tanks of all types were used like this in the latter stages of the war as the Germans became increasingly desperate. This picture was taken late in the war, probably in Berlin. (Sergei Netrebenko)

No effort was made to dig the tanks in, although cobbles and masonry were often heaped around the structure to provide the position with a little more protection.

DEPLOYMENT

Emplaced Panther turrets were encountered by the Allies on all fronts in the European campaign. In Italy they were used to strengthen the various defensive lines that were constructed. On the western front they were installed in the West Wall and in the east they were employed in a last desperate attempt to stem the advance of the Red Army. A number of turrets were also used in the so-called *Sudwall*, on the border with Franco's Spain. (*See* Table 3 *below*.)

Italy

The Allies' decision to invade Sicily and the landings on the Italian mainland in 1943 in many ways helped the Germans to crystallize their thinking on the strategy to be adopted in Italy. Once the Allies had a secured a foothold on the toe of Italy and the prospect of dislodging them had disappeared, it was decided to fight a series of delaying actions with the aim of keeping the Allies as far from Germany as possible. The topography of Italy was ideally suited to this type of warfare and by constructing defensive lines across the most likely routes of any advance it was hoped to entangle the Allies in a protracted and bloody battle of attrition. The first real opportunity to put this strategy into practice was along the so-called Gustav Line which was dominated by Monte Cassino. The Allies

Table 3 Locations[31]

	Atlantic Wall/ West Wall	Italy	East	Schools/ Experimental	Total
Panther – Stahluntersatz	119	18	6	0	143
Panther – Betonsockel	63	30	30	2	125

*This source quotes the number of turrets as being installed in the Atlantic Wall/West Wall, but aside from the six turrets used on the Spanish border, no Panther turrets were used in the Atlantic Wall proper.

launched four large-scale assaults against this position over a period of four months before it was finally captured. This delay gave the Germans valuable time to construct a further defensive line to the rear which was initially called the *Fuhrerriegel* or Hitler Line, although this was quickly changed to the *Sengerriegel** after the Anzio landings in January 1944, because the collapse of a line bearing the Führer's name, it was believed, would be used for Allied propaganda.[†]

Hitler Line

The Hitler Line straddled the Liri Valley through which ran Route 6, the most direct route to Rome.[‡] It was vital that this potential avenue of advance be blocked and all the more so now that the Allies attempted outflanking manoeuvre at Anzio had been contained. As such great efforts were made to fortify this line and included in its arsenal for the first time were a number of Panther turrets that had been delivered at the end of 1943. In total eleven turrets[¶] were installed in the valley and were positioned in a single defensive line in such a way that they were able to cover the line throughout its length of approximately 3km (2 miles). They were deployed in a series of spearheads. At the tip of each spear there was a Panther turret and echeloned back on either side were two or three towed 75mm or 50mm anti-tank guns. The turrets were located so that they commanded the approaches to the line with particularly long fields of fire to their front where

A Polish soldier inspects the damage to a Panther turret that formed part of the Hitler Line defences. It was positioned just below the town of Piedimonte and was destroyed in the fighting of May 1944. (Polish Institute and Sikorski Museum)

trees had been cut down to approximately 45cm (18in) from the ground. The turrets, however, had more restricted fields of fire to the flank and particularly the rear, and these weak spots were covered by the towed anti-tank guns, which at the same time supplemented the turrets' firepower. The towed guns were generally employed in pairs approximately 150/200m behind or to the flank of the turrets and were often hidden behind houses, in sunken roads or in thick cover. Some twenty-five self-propelled guns also took up fire positions along this same line with some in position further to the rear to give depth to the defences (or provide the punch for any counter-attack). In all there were some sixty-two anti-tank guns.

Gothic Line

With the defeat of the Hitler Line and later the Caesar Line, which protected Rome, the Germans now fell back to their next prepared position, the Gothic or Green Line. Work on these defences had begun in late 1943, but had been suspended to concentrate resources on the construction work further south. Now, in the summer of 1944, work was resumed. As with the Hitler Line, the main anti-tank defence was to be provided by emplaced Panther turrets, which were extensively used on the eastern coastal plain and to protect the passes through the Apennines.

The eastern end of the Gothic Line was the responsibility of von Vietinghoff's 10th Army (AOK 10). At the beginning of July there were plans to install sixteen Panther turrets and to use disabled Panther tanks as improvised strong points. One of these had been dug in and three more were under

---

*After Fridolin von Senger und Etterlin, the commander of 14th Panzer Corps, who was responsible for the defence of the Liri Valley at that time.
[†] However, the Allies continued to use its original name in an anglicized form and it is this widely accepted, if not wholly accurate, title that is used in this book.
[‡] The Line actually ran from Monte Cairo in the north to Terracina on the coast, but the main defences were constructed in the Liri Valley.
[¶] Maj Gen Erich Rothe in his interrogation after the war on the defences of the Senger Riegel states that 18 *PaK Panzertürme* were installed, but this may have included other turret types like the Panzer II. CNA, RG24, Vol. 20513 *The Senger Riegel,* Maj Gen Erich Rothe.

Map 4

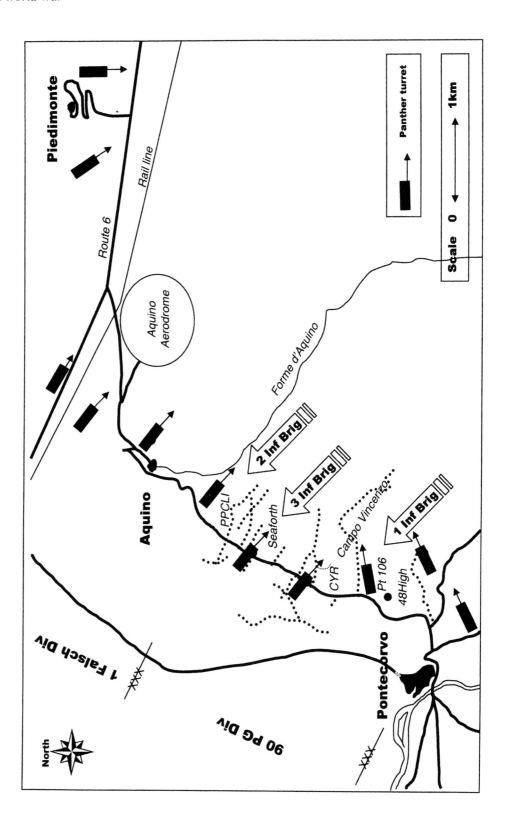

Hitler Lane

A Panther turret mounted on a concrete shelter, which was positioned in the Gothic Line to protect the strategically important Futa Pass. This was one of the main passes through the Apennines and led directly to Bologna. The turret was destroyed by a direct hit from US artillery in September 1944. (US National Archives)

A Panther turret under construction on the west coast of Italy. Barbed wire entanglements are visible in the background along the length of the beach. The roof section was erected in an attempt to prevent observation by Allied aircraft. (US National Archives)

construction, but work had only been started on four of the Panther turrets.[32] The pace increased through July and August so that by 28 August it was reported that four Panther turrets had been completed, eighteen were under construction with a further seven planned.[33] Further headway was also made digging in disabled Panther tanks with seven ready for action and another one being installed.

The Panther turrets (both mounted on shelters and dug in) were heavily concentrated along Green I* in the section of the line that ran along the River Foglia from Pesaro on the east coast to Montécchio. Turrets were also installed further to the rear to provide depth to the defences. Two Panther turrets were installed at Miramare airport near Rimini, another was positioned near Bellaria and another at Celle.[34] A veteran responsible for scrapping these turrets also recollects one turret located just north of Rimini at the fork in the road where the main road from Rimini to Forli branches off from the Rimini to Ravenna road and another at the junction south of Forli on the high ground north of the Forli to Ravenna road.[35] A number of veterans of the campaign also recounted seeing turrets installed much further north in the breakout from the River Senio to the Po Valley. Two in particular were located north of Ferrara on the high

ground covering the approaches to the bridge over the River Po.[36]

The western section of the Gothic Line was dominated by the Apennine Mountains and as such offered fewer opportunities for an Allied breakthrough. Nevertheless, Lemelsen, who commanded 14th Army (AOK14), which was responsible for this portion of the line, was not complacent. Between 8–19 August, possible sites for the emplacement of Panther turrets were reconnoitred with particular emphasis placed on the strategically important mountain passes. At the Futa pass, through which passed Route 65, which linked Florence and Bologna, two turrets were installed, one close to the village of Santa Lucia, guarding the long anti-tank ditch dug a few kilometres south of the pass, and another on the pass itself. To the west, a Panther turret installed at the Poretta pass protected Route 64, which also led to Bologna.[37] † At this time there were also discussions with *SS Pz Abt* 16 about the possible installation of Panther turrets on the Magra estuary near La Spezia and on 25 August

---

*Green I ran from Pesaro in the east to La Spezia in the west. Green II was approximately ten miles to the rear.
†After the war the turret at Pistoia was destroyed and the metal taken for scrap.

possible locations were assessed.[38] However, it is unclear how far this work progressed.*

Voralpenstellung

Determined resistance and poor weather meant that the Allies were not able to exploit the breach of the Gothic Line and the German engineers were again given time to prepare further defensive lines. The last of these was the *Voralpenstellung*, which was to be constructed in north-eastern Italy and across the so-called 'Ljubljana Gap'. In January 1945 the *Der Oberbefehlshaber Südwest* (Commander in Chief South West) wrote to the *Kommandostab Voralpen* (Command Staff of the *Voralpenstellung*) concerning anti-tank defences and particularly plans to install thirty-seven Panther turrets in the *Voralpenstellung*. At that time, work to install the Panther turrets had begun but was hampered by Allied air attacks.[39] At the beginning of March 1945 nineteen Panther II turrets destined for Laibach (Ljubljana) (twelve) and Görz (Gorizia) (seven) were damaged in an air raid on the marshalling yard at Wörgl. These turrets were to be recovered and returned to Pardubitz for repair, but snow and the bomb damage made this difficult. In early April there were still plans to send a crane to Wörgl to rescue those turrets that had only suffered minor damage, but it is doubtful whether this salvage operation was ever successfully completed. A further eleven turrets to be mounted on wooden shelters, seven destined for Asiago and four for Ospedaletto, were dispatched at the beginning of January 1945 and were delivered, but it is unclear whether they were installed before the Allies overran the position at the beginning of May.

Sudwall

Somewhat surprisingly given the situation in Italy and on the Eastern Front in early 1944 a decision was taken by the German High Command to send six Panther turrets to France. This might have been comprehensible had the turrets been destined for use in the Atlantic Wall to counter any invasion threat, but bewilderingly they were to be sent to southern France to be installed along the border with Spain. The requirement for the Panther turrets on OT shelters had initially been made in a note from the *Chef Heeresrüstung und Befehlshaber des*

Ersatzheeres (Chief of Military Armaments and Commander of the Reserve Army) to *O.T Zentrale* (OT Headquarters) in Berlin on 22 February 1944.[40] This detailed destinations for the Panther turrets and for eighty OT steel shelters. The Panther turrets were to be sent to:

> Bayonne railway station (three in number);
> Bouluo railway station (one in number);
> Oloron St Marie railway station (one in number);
> and
> Latou de Carol railway station (one in number).

By June the turrets had been supplied and some progress had been made to install them: two were useable and another was in the process of being completed.[41] Today it is still possible to see the remains of one of these turrets. It is located close to border marker 570, below the south-west point of the hornwork of Fort Bellgarde near the strategically important town of Le Perthus.

West Wall

After the fall of France in June 1940 much of the West Wall was abandoned or dismantled, its job seemingly done. However, with the Allied invasion of occupied Europe in June 1944 and the subsequent breakout from the beachhead it was realized that these outmoded defences were all that stood between the Allies and the German homeland. On 24 August, the day before the fall of Paris, Hitler issued an order that called for the renovation of the defences with particular emphasis on anti-tank defences. The bunkers built in the late 1930s were incapable of accommodating the new generation of anti-tank weapons, so new, larger shelters were to be built and a series of improvised positions were also to be constructed to mount the so-called *Sockellafetten* (*see* Chapter 3, Part 2). Various tank turrets were also to be installed. These tended to be fitted with smaller

---

*According to one source a number of Panther turrets were installed along the Tyrrhenian Sea coast. These did not see action and a number were destroyed by their crews as the American forces approached. The others were destroyed by the Allies at the end of the war. D. Guglielmi, 'Linee fortificate tedesche in Italia 1943–1945', *Storia & Battaglie*, pp.21–32.

Table 4 West Wall Panther turrets by *Festungspionierkommandeur*[42]

	Planned	In build	Ready	Date
I	30		23*	10/03/45
IV	33	12	11	06/03/45
XIX	33	7	7	04/03/45
XXI	–	–	–	
XVIII	–	–	–	

*Originally planned to be installed on concrete shelters, but eventually mounted on *Holzunterstände*.

calibre weapons or machine guns, but there were also ambitious plans to emplace large numbers of Panther turrets.

By the beginning of September, US forces had already crossed the German border and were threatening the historic city of Aachen. To meet the threat, plans were instituted at the beginning of October to install the first of the Panther turrets in the Eifel (*Fest Pi Kdr* XIX). And by 27 November, thirty-three turrets to be mounted on steel shelters had been dispatched and were under construction. Further south Free French forces were advancing towards the Vosges and similarly excavation work was started and even some concrete poured for the planned shelters (*Regelbau* 687). However, by the beginning of December it was clear that this was not practical

A Panther Ausf A turret with its application of zimmerit paste still evident. The turret is atop a steel and wooden framework prior to being buried in the ground. This turret was captured in the Vosges in 1944.
(US National Archives)

and the sixteen turrets destined for the region were redirected to the West Wall proper.[43]

These turrets were now to be mounted on reinforced concrete shelters in the section of the West Wall from Saarbrücken to the Swiss border. In total it was planned to install sixty-three turrets here, thirty in the area of the Upper Rhine and thirty-three in the Saarpfalz. On paper the figures looked impressive, but there was little progress on the ground and at the express order of Hitler on 28 November 1944 work to install these turrets was expedited. With the clarion call of the Führer ringing in their ears the commanders responsible for the construction of defences in these zones (*Fest Pi Kdr* I and *Fest Pi Kdr* IV) redoubled their efforts. They, together with *Fest Pi Kdr* XIX (Eifel) were responsible for the portion of the West Wall that was most vulnerable to attack and, accordingly, were where most of the Panther turrets were to be situated. The two remaining zones under the commands of *Fest Pi Kdr* XXI and *Fest Pi Kdr* XVIII that covered the Lower Rhine were considered of less consequence and little effort was made to fortify this section of the line.*

Fest Pi Kdr I

In the Oberrhein (Upper Rhine), which was the responsibility of *Fest Pi Kdr* I, there were initially plans to install thirty Panther turrets, all of which were to be mounted on reinforced concrete shelters (*Regelbau* 687). By early January 1945 all of the turrets had reached their respective rail terminus: ten

*In the zone of *Fest Pi Kdr* XXI (Niederrhein) no Panther turrets were planned to be used, but in a paper dated 3rd March 1945 there was a request to transport two steel shelters for Panther turrets to Rommerskirchen railway station. BA, RH12-20/44, p.241.

at Offenburg; ten at Rastatt and ten at Freiburg and by the end of the month work had begun to install three of these turrets.[44] However, no further progress was made on these positions and in February the decision was taken to mount the turrets on the new *Holzunterstand*. By 10 March all the turrets had been delivered to their final destination and most of the turrets were installed. In *Fest Pi Stab* 4, despite the fact that the turrets had had to be transported to their respective construction sites without the benefit of a crane, all ten turrets were ready for action in Sector Oa. A further five were ready in Sector Ob with five more in various stages of assembly. In *Fest Pi Stab* 11, progress was similarly advanced and in spite of enemy pressure on the bridgehead west of Breisach, eight of the turrets were ready for action and two more had been mounted but could not be rotated.[45]

Fest Pi Kdr IV

As was the case in *Fest Pi Kdr* I's zone, the thirty-three turrets to be installed in the Saarpfalz (*Fest Pi Kdr* IV) were all to be mounted on concrete shelters. From the middle through to the end of November the turrets were dispatched from the *Schwerslastengerätepark West* (Heavy Equipment Depot West) at Aschaffenburg and, despite the effects of Allied bombing which necessitated a number being taken by road,[46] by the New Year all of them had

reached their designated railway station: twenty at Einsiedlerhof and thirteen at Rinnthal.[47]

The turrets were now transported to their installation sites, but the proximity of the enemy meant that it was not feasible to mount the turrets as planned on concrete shelters and instead it was decided to use the new *Holzunterstand*. A number of these had been pre-assembled in the zone of *Fest Pi Stab* 9 but were destroyed by enemy aircraft and had to be rebuilt. This work was hampered by enemy artillery fire and further air attacks and meant that installation work had to be completed under the cover of darkness. This severely delayed progress and by the beginning of March only five of the twenty turrets allocated had been completed, with a further seven under construction.

And progress was little better in the sector of *Fest Pi Stab* 17. By the beginning of March 1945 six of the thirteen turrets planned were ready for action with a further five still under construction. By the middle of the month the turrets that were being installed had been completed, as indeed was the case with *Fest Pi Stab* 9, so that in total twenty-three turrets were operational. Of the remainder, two units that were damaged in transit were returned to the Seibert Company in Homburg for repair, the rest were not installed.[48]

A Panther turret mounted on a Holzunterstand. Chicken wire on the barrel would have been used for camouflage. This example was installed near Püttlingen in the Saarland and was photographed in the summer of 1945. (Alfred Schmidt, courtesy of Dieter Bettinger)

Fest Pi Kdr XIX

Further north in the Eifel, under the auspices of *Fest Pi Kdr* XIX, there were plans to install thirty-three turrets on OT steel shelters. Of these two were transported to Jülich, three to Kall and twenty-eight were destined for the *Rurstellung*; one of the forward defences of the West Wall. However, by December 1944, US troops had already reached the River Rur at Bergstein (near Nideggen), which meant that work on this defensive line had to be carried out under the cover of darkness. This provided the construction workers with some respite, but the heavy lifting gear required to manoeuvre the components into place created such a noise that it drew heavy enemy fire and it was therefore decided to suspend work on these defences. Only two of the turrets were installed and the rest were taken back to the *Erftstellung* for employment. This position protected Cologne and was the last defensive line before the Rhine. By Christmas 1944, 500 men from the *Organization Todt* and 150 men from the three Panther turret companies assigned to man the turrets, were set to work transporting the turrets back from the *Rurstellung*, or, when suitable sites to locate the turrets had been identified in the middle of January, were employed installing them.[49]

At about the same time, Christmas 1944, *Fest Pi Kdr* XIX drew up plans for two improvised structures to mount the Panther turret and upper box. Drawing No. 104 *Panthertürme mit Oberteil des OT Stahl-unterstandes auf Holz-Unterbau* was a design for a wooden structure and Drawing No. 105 *Panther-türme mit Oberteil des OT Stahlunterstandes (Stahlbetonunterteil)* was a design for shelter constructed from concrete. The catalyst for the development of these blueprints is not clear but it may have been prompted by the loss of twenty *Stahlunterstände für Pantherturm* earlier in December. Regardless of the motive, the two designs were sent to *Inspekteur für die Landesbefestigung West* (Inspector of Fortifications West) for approval. Both designs were eventually accepted in the second half of January, albeit that the concrete alternative was only approved by exception after it was explained to *Insp.d.L.West* that a lack of wood meant that the *Stahlbetonunterteil* could be built more quickly. Soon after consent had been given for their use (and it is not clear if the two events were linked)

Fest Pi Kdr XIX reported that twenty-five *Stahlunterteile* were so close to the front that in the opinion of the *Organization Todt* they could not safely be retrieved and would have to be abandoned.[50]

The difficulties of constructing defences almost literally on the front line, which were exacerbated by a lack of fuel for transport and poor weather, meant that work to install the turrets in this section of the line was severely delayed. It was not until the New Year that construction work began in earnest and even then little headway was made. By 4 March 1945, of the thirty-three turrets supplied to *Fest Pi Stab* 21, only seven were ready for action.[51] And progress was not helped by sabotage. A note written at the end of February stated that the turrets were not being guarded during their installation and one shelter (P17), which had been completed, was damaged by persons unknown to such an extent that it had to be dismantled and new spare parts sourced.[52]

On 7 March 1945 the Allies finally crossed the Rhine and as such the West Wall became an irrelevance. Accordingly, the *Festungspionier-kommandeurs* were set to work on the east bank of the river. One turret stored at the *Heimat-Festungs-Pionierpark* (Home Fortifications Engineering Depot) at Siegburg, and probably the last Panther turret on the Western Front, was to be installed near the depot itself some time on or after 18 March 1945 as a shortage of petrol meant that it was impossible to transport it elsewhere.[53]

A Panther turret and top box captured by American forces near Bonn, 1945. The serial numbers are clearly visible. The letters may have been applied by the manufacturer to ensure that the upper and lower boxes were correctly aligned. (Tank Museum)

A rare photograph of a Panther turret installed on the Eastern Front. The turret is from an Ausf A and just distinguishable on the side is the turret number, suggesting it has been taken from a disabled tank. (Soviet National Archives)

Eastern Front

At much the same time that there were plans to install Panther turrets in the Hitler Line in Italy and along the border with Spain, plans were developed for the employment of sixteen Panther turrets on steel shelters on the Eastern Front. In April 1944 these turrets were sent to the OT-*Lager* at Brest Litovsk. From here the turrets were to be sent to their final destinations at the rear of 56th *Panzer Korps* front.[54]

Soviet offensives in the summer and autumn of 1944 saw the German forces pressed back into Poland and Panther turrets were hurriedly rushed to the east for defence of the *die Heimat* (homeland). German records state that as at 27 November 1944, thirty-six Panther turrets were available to be sent to the eastern front for installation on concrete shelters (*Regelbau* 687).[*] On 30 December the turrets were dispatched to Thorn (Torun) and Graudenz (Grudziadz) on the River Vistula (Wisla) in what was then East Prussia.[55] This neatly corresponds with a report written in March 1945 that lists thirty-six turrets as having been installed on the eastern front, albeit that six were subsequently installed on OT steel shelters.[56]

However, in the middle of January the Soviets launched the largest single offensive of the Second World War and the 2nd Belorussian Front, under Marshal Rokossovsky, smashed through the German lines towards Thorn and Graudenz. The plans for the Panther turrets were now changed and they were allocated for homeland defence with turrets sent to

Stettin (Szczecin), Küstrin (Kostrzyn) and Frankfurt an der Oder.

The first two of the turrets for Stettin were dispatched at the beginning of February and, despite damage to one, one had been installed and the other was under assembly by the beginning of March. Soon after, four more turrets arrived, which were also to be mounted on wooden shelters. Three of these were installed to the east of the Oder River, but did not fulfil the role for which they had been designed. One was demolished without firing a shot when the area was evacuated; another provided some indirect fire support before being ordered to cease fire for fear of drawing enemy fire on troops retreating across a nearby bridge and was blown up when the withdrawal was complete; the other turret was damaged by enemy fire, but was repaired before finally being destroyed by enemy action. The three other turrets were installed to the west of the Oder, although it was realized that one of these had been incorrectly sited and needed to be moved. However, it was recognized that such action would be futile because of inevitable enemy interdiction. The city fell to enemy forces on 26 April 1945.[†]

The six remaining turrets that were to be mounted on steel shelters, were dispatched to Stettin on 11 March, but circumstances now dictated that they would have to be mounted on wooden shelters like the rest of the turrets in the city. This caused a problem because the carpenters and joiners had since been released. The problem was soon resolved, however, albeit unconventionally, with the turrets being redirected to Dresden. Delays meant that they did not arrive in the devastated city, that was now classified as a *Verteidigungsbereich*, or defensive area, until 5 April.[‡] The men and equipment to install the turrets were available, but there was no fuel for the tractor and it seems that the turrets were not installed by the time the Soviets entered the city on 8 May 1945.

---

*Originally sixty-six were to have been sent, but in the event only thirty-six were. BA, RH 12-20/44, p.198.
† One of the turrets mounted on a wooden shelter was recently discovered in Stettin (Szczecin), and is being restored.
‡ On 16 April Dresden was made a 'fortress' although this was more of 'a propaganda device rather than [making] a practical difference'. F. Taylor, *Dresden – Tuesday 13 February 1945* (Bloomsbury Publishing plc, London, 2004), p.437.

A dug-in Panther turret at a road intersection somewhere on the Eastern Front. Masonry has been stacked around the base of the turret to provide further protection. There are at least fifty spent shell cases littering the floor, which indicates the ferocity of the fighting. (Unknown)

Küstrin lay in a direct line between the Soviets and Berlin. Because of its strategic importance it was declared a fortress and allocated twelve Panther turrets for its defence. The high water table complicated the installation of the turrets and so it was decided to mount them on a foreshortened wooden shelter measuring 1.10m (3½ft) high compared to 2.84m (9ft) normally. This overcame the problem of flooding, but meant that it was not possible to fit power traverse and nor was there room for the loader to pass ammunition. However, it was a compromise that had to be made to get the turrets installed as quickly as possible.

By the beginning of March, eight of the turrets had been destroyed by enemy action. Three further turrets were readied for action by the end of the March and another was under construction on a concrete shelter. The fate of these turrets is uncertain following the fall of the city on 29 March 1945.

Further to the south, Frankfurt an der Oder was another strategically important city and was also given fortress status. By the beginning of February the first of the twelve turrets were being installed and, as in Küstrin, there were similar problems with flooding. In addition, installation was hampered by difficulties with the tractor and trailer, exacerbated by poor ground conditions, and a lack of timber. Nevertheless, work continued on the wooden shelters and considerable progress was made, but because the OT did not follow the instructions issued by the *Wa Prüf Fest* (Fortification Design Office) for the construc-

tion of the *Holzunterstand,* additional strengthening work had to be undertaken. Problems with the power traverse meant that it was temporarily dispensed with. It was to be installed later if circumstances permitted, but in the meantime the turret would be traversed by hand. In spite of all this, and the impact of enemy action which necessitated the abandonment of the work at the eleventh site (Dammvorstadt) and the installation of the turret elsewhere, all the turrets were ready by the beginning of March.

In addition to the turrets mounted on specially designed shelters, improvised positions were constructed using disabled tanks with their running gear removed. The parlous situation meant that there was no time to dig the tanks in, but cobbles and masonry were heaped around the structure to give some added protection. The turrets tended to be placed on road intersections of larger German towns and cities and it is believed that in Berlin alone as many as twenty-five of these extemporized strong points might have been constructed.

Panther Turrets in Action

Hitler Line

During the winter of 1943/4 the British Eighth and American Fifth Armies had been involved in a bloody battle of attrition to break the German Gustav Line

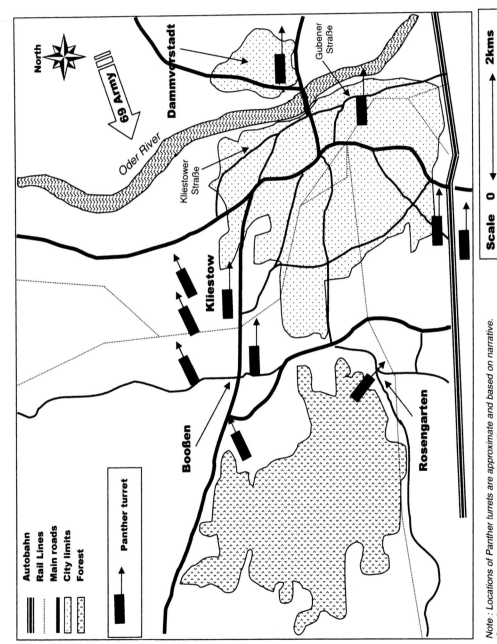

Frankfurt an der Oder

Map 5

Note : Locations of Panther turrets are approximate and based on narrative.
One further turret was located near the Poultry Farm but could not be found.

A disabled Panther tank used as a strong point. This is the same Panther Ausf G as as shown on p. 159, but this time a view from the rear, showing how the crew entered the tank. (Sergei Netrebenko)

This Panther turret was positioned in front of the Aquino-Pontecorvo road. It was credited with knocking out two enemy tanks, which can be seen in the distance. The Germans cut the trees in front of the turret to give a better field of fire. (Imperial War Museum)

south of Rome. But despite three major assaults on the German defences, which were constructed around the Cairo massif and in particular the Monastery above the town of Cassino, the Allies failed to break through, and suffered heavy casualties. The failure of the Allies to breach the defences of the Gustav Line had given Kesselring and the German High Command time to reappraise their strategy in Italy and it was decided to reinforce the defences south of Rome with the construction of the Hitler and Caesar Lines, rather than fall back to the prepared positions on the Apennines. Work on the defences continued apace through the winter and by the spring of 1944, work on the Hitler Line, which straddled the Liri Valley to the rear of the Gustav Line, was well advanced. At the same time, Eighth Army, which was tasked with capturing Monte Cassino and advancing along the Liri Valley, had taken the opportunity to rest and refit and stockpile ammunition and stores and by May was in a position to launch what was hoped would be a decisive blow.

The first attack on the Hitler Line was launched on the morning of 19 May 1944 and was, in terms of casualties, to set an unwanted precedent for future attacks. At first light, two battalions of infantry supported by tanks of 17th/21st Lancers and the Ontario Regiment of Canada moved off. Screened by the early morning mist they advanced to within 300m of the town of Aquino, destroying an enemy anti-tank gun in the process. But as the sun rose the mist began to clear and the tanks found themselves in the open, almost literally looking down the barrels of the enemy's anti-tank guns, which included a number of emplaced Panther turrets. Despite strenuous efforts by air-photo interpreters to identify certain patches of camouflage it had not been possible to determine the exact nature of the structure they covered. The mystery was soon solved. 'At that moment a well camouflaged high velocity anti-tank gun, in a steel and concrete pillbox, opened fire at point blank range from the right, holed all three tanks at least twice and set them on fire.'[57] The supporting infantry also came under heavy fire and were forced to retire. The tanks of the Ontario Regiment, however, were ordered to hold their ground and await a renewed infantry attack. This they did, but as the battle unfolded it became clear that there was little hope of breaking the enemy line and it was decided not to renew the assault. Under the cover of darkness the remnants of the Regiment withdrew. The Ontarios had lost thirteen tanks in this costly attack – twelve to anti-tank fire – and of those tanks of the two leading squadrons that withdrew, not one escaped at least one direct hit.[58]

By the evening of 19 May it was clear that the attempt to 'bounce' the Hitler Line had failed and that in order to breach the formidable German defences it would be necessary to launch a concerted attack. This was planned for 23rd May and was to be led by 1st Canadian Division, in what was to be the first major operation by a Canadian Corps in the Second World War. However, the success of the French on the Canadian left suggested that the German resistance around Pontecorvo might be weakening and Gen Vokes, the commander of 1st Canadian Infantry Division, ordered his 1st Infantry Brigade to attack the town on 22nd May with a view to turning the line from the left. A small detachment of tanks from 142nd Royal Armoured Corps (the Suffolks) was ordered forward prior to the main attack to reconnoitre the enemy positions. This was met with a firm rebuff and an emplaced Panther turret knocked out three of the Suffolks' tanks. Unperturbed, the main assault was launched with 48th Highlanders supported by 'C' Squadron of 142nd RAC, but the tanks were held up by an anti-tank ditch and eventually the attack was suspended and all efforts

were concentrated on the main assault, Operation *Chesterfield*.[59]

Mindful of previous failures, Gen Vokes planned to attack with two battalions of 2nd Infantry Brigade – the Seaforth Highlanders on the left supported by two squadrons of tanks of the North Irish Horse (B Squadron with C in reserve); and the Princess Patricia's Canadian Light Infantry on the right supported by A squadron. At 0600 hours the offensive began.

The Patricias, despite suffering heavy casualties, reached the enemy wire. However, their supporting tanks were stopped by an undetected minefield and as they struggled to find a way through came under heavy anti-tank fire, which knocked out four tanks. The remainder fell back and attempted to find an alternative route forward. The Seaforth Highlanders made better progress but their armoured support, when only 100m from the first objective, came under intense anti-tank fire which accounted for five of its number, including the squadron leader. His tank was later found to be no more than 30m from a Panther turret emplacement.* The remaining tanks withdrew and, together with tanks from C squadron, advanced on a new axis. They had not progressed far when they came under heavy artillery fire and were ordered to withdraw. Unfortunately, in trying to carry out this order the composite force was caught in a fusillade of enemy anti-tank fire, which resulted in seven tanks being destroyed, while the defenders lost one emplaced turret and a 75mm anti-tank gun.[60]

In accordance with Vokes' plan, and knowing nothing of their countrymen's plight, the Loyal Edmontons, together with a squadron of 51st Royal Tank Regiment (RTR), advanced according to the second phase of the attack. The tanks, however, were soon halted by mines, just as those of the North Irish Horse had been previously, and provided the enemy anti-tank gunners with yet more inviting targets. With the reserves committed the commander of 2nd Infantry Brigade, Brig Gibson, had nothing with which to exploit the success of the Seaforth Highlanders and so the battle on this portion of the front reached deadlock.

In front of Pontecorvo, 1st Canadian Infantry

---

*The bombardment that preceded the attack, which was designed to neutralize the enemy's defences, did little more than knock the camouflage away from the Panther turrets.

Brigade maintained the pressure on the German defenders. On the morning of 23rd May, 'B' Squadron 142nd RAC moved forward in support of 48th Highlanders and in the ensuing engagement accounted for another of the emplaced Panther turrets protecting the town.[61] On their right, a feint by 3rd Infantry Brigade, supported by two squadrons of 51st RTR, enjoyed rather more success. Indeed, the tanks, after a fierce battle with enemy anti-tank and self-propelled guns, fought their way forward to the Aquino-Pontecorvo road – the first objective of the main thrust. During this advance another Panther turret was spectacularly put out of action and is described here by G. Birdsall, troop sergeant of 5th Troop 'A' Squadron 51st RTR:

'We kept moving forward (A squadron) and eventually came within sight of the objective, the Aquino-Pontecorvo road. In front of me was a Churchill tank, which I later identified as the Colonel's (Lieutenant Colonel Holden) that was engaging a Panther turret, which was the only one in our immediate front as far as I could see. As I came up behind the COs tank I saw the gun barrel on the Panther turret suddenly shoot up in the air to an almost perpendicular position followed by a message on the wireless exhorting the battalion to "stand fast" and to "look what Father's done." Lieutenant Colonel Holden had advanced to approximately 300–400yd of the turret before engaging the target.'

This, as another veteran of the battle recounted, was the sole method of destroying these fortifications. As he stated, 'The only way to knock the turrets out was to get in close, which was feasible, although extremely dangerous, and fire a round under the gun mantlet and above the base plate which stopped the turret traversing,' or, as in the example above, exploded the ammunition stored immediately below.[62] By the end of 23 May the Hitler Line in the south had been broken and the enemy began to fall back in some disarray. Accordingly, on the morning of 24 May, a probing attack was launched against the northern part of the line around the town of Aquino. In light of the enemy's heavy defeat the previous day, it was hoped that they might have withdrawn during the night. But soon after moving off the Lancashire

Canadian soldiers pose beside the Panther turret knocked out by Col Holden of 51st Royal Tank Regiment during the battle for the Hitler Line, May 1944.
(Canadian National Archives)

Fusiliers were pinned down and to assist them two troops of tanks of 14th Canadian Armoured Regiment pushed forward and began to bring fire to bear on the enemy. When they were within 400m of the town, however, they were engaged by two Panther turrets.* Four of the six tanks were instantly holed and set on fire resulting in seventeen casualties. The remaining two tanks beat a hasty retreat as it was clear that the enemy, despite being outflanked, still held the defences in strength. Only on 25 May did the enemy

---

*The original unit diary states that four turrets were present but this is undoubtedly an error.
† Post-battle reports talk about the MarkI emplacement destroying seven Allied tanks on 24 May at a distance ranging between 1,400 and 1,700m and the Schmittsberger emplacement destroying a further seven tanks on the same day at a distance of between 200 and 400m but the numbers are probably exaggerated. W. Trojca, *PzKpfw. V Panther*, Vol. 6, (A. J. Press, Gdansk, Poland, 2003), p.73.

A Panther Ausf D turret mounted on an OT shelter. This turret was located near Aquino and was destroyed by its crew before being captured by the Allies.
(National Archives)

Another view of the same Panther turret. This view clearly shows the revetted trench leading to the main entrance and the reinforced concrete that encased the lower boxes.
(National Archives)

finally withdraw having first demolished the two Panther turrets.[63] [†]

The two turrets protecting Aquino were the last of the eleven turrets to be destroyed – the nine others having been accounted for by the Shermans and Churchills of 25 Tank Brigade. The price, however, was high. An intelligence report written after the battle noted: 'In front of each position there was a graveyard of Churchills and some Shermans . . . This is, at present, the price of reducing a Panther turret and it would seem to be an excellent investment for Hitler.' Indeed it was, the Panther turrets inflicted on the Eighth Army its heaviest tank losses of the Italian campaign.[64] In all 25 Tank Brigade lost forty-four tanks (although some were later recovered).*

And it could have been a lot worse. As another report stated, 'If the enemy had been able to complete his preparations and received better (and more) infantry support, the attack would have been much more costly.'

Gothic Line

As the Allies approached the Gothic Line it was generally believed that the Germans would again use emplaced Panther tank turrets. Well aware of the damage inflicted on the Eighth Army in the Liri Valley, Clark, the commander of the US Fifth Army, decided to bypass the defences of the Futa Pass,[†] that guarded Route 65 to Bologna, and instead attacked the less well defended Il Giogo pass with great success. However, bypassing the enemy's defences was not an option for Gen Leese, the commander of Eighth Army, on Clark's right flank who was tasked with advancing up the east coast. The beaches had been fortified to prevent another sea-borne invasion (as happened at Anzio) and further defences had been constructed inland as far as the foothills of the Apennines in an effort to block the most promising avenue of attack for a mechanised army. These positions had been constructed in depth with Panther turrets situated at key strategic locations. One such strategic location was Miramare airfield, near Rimini,

---

*A post-battle report of 15 *Panzer Grenadier* Division dated 29 May 1944 stated that fifty-three enemy tanks were destroyed during the battle for the Hitler Line including twenty-two that were accounted for by the *Panther-Turm Kompanie*, but again this is probably an exaggeration.
[†] Two Panther tank turrets were later found emplaced here.

The Panther turret located in the south-west corner of Rimini airfield that barred the way of Greek and New Zealand forces in the battle for the Gothic Line in September 1944. (Alexander Turnbull Library)

which was attacked by the Greeks and New Zealanders in September 1944. Reconnaissance of the area had identified 'suspicious bumps' on two corners of the airfield.[65] These could not be identified immediately, but the truth soon emerged.

On 15 September 1944, the 3rd Greek Mountain Brigade began to advance towards the airfield but the lead elements were soon pinned down by enemy fire and the tanks of C Squadron, 18th NZ Armoured Regiment were ordered forward: 9 Troop on the right; 10 Troop in the middle towards the airport; and 11 Troop on the left. As the tanks of 10 Troop under Lieutenant Collins approached, the 'suspicious bump' at the southern end of the airfield opened fire; it was a Panther turret that had been sited to cover Route 16 (the coast road). One of Collins' tanks was hit [Sgt Wood's], not by the Panther turret though, but by a self-propelled gun on the left edge of the airfield which set the tank on fire. Collins reacted immediately laying down a smoke screen to obscure the view of the enemy gunners and advanced to the crippled tank and together with Cpl White attempted to rescue the crew. Collins now engaged the enemy infantry with his machine gun and with the support of the Greek infantry killed thirty-eight of the defenders and took twelve prisoners; the remnants beating a hasty retreat. Darkness prevented a concerted assault on the Panther turret, which continued firing until after dark. However, in the course of the night,

abandoned by the infantry and no doubt unnerved by the 'noisy demonstration' put on by 10 Troop, the crew blew up the turret and withdrew. This came as an enormous relief to 9 Troop, commanded by Lt Barber, which had been ordered to attack the turret the following morning.

The following day was quiet, as was the start of 17 September, but this was all to change. On that day the Seaforths of Canada supported by a squadron of 145th Regiment RAC put in an attack on San Martino. The attack started well, but soon six of the supporting tanks (out of two troops of Churchills and two troops of Shermans) were knocked out and infantry casualties began to rise forcing the Seaforths to withdraw. The tank losses were believed to be due in part to the Panther turret located at the northern end of the airfield. Aircraft of the 250th Kittyhawk Squadron were dispatched to silence the turret and although near misses were scored, it still kept firing. The 25-pounders of 4th Field Regiment were also directed to target the turret but were similarly unsuccessful.

The only alternative was a direct attack by the tanks of 18th NZ Armoured Regiment. This presented something of dilemma for the new commanding officer, Maj Allen, because 9 and 10 Troops were in no position to engage the turret without exposing themselves to potentially deadly enemy fire. The other alternative, 11 Troop, on the left flank, seemed

The Panther turret located at the northern end of Miramare airfield, near Rimini. The turret was knocked out by Lt Collins of 18th NZ Armoured Regiment in the fighting for the Gothic Line in September 1944 and he is pictured next to it with the shell holes visible in the side. (J. Plowman)

to offer the best chance of success but even this was deemed too dangerous. The turret had been shrewdly sited with a perfect field of fire in all directions.

Lt Collins solved Allen's dilemma, although he took some convincing that the proposed plan would work. Collins initially suggested advancing towards the turret under the cover of a smoke screen with sappers in the fore to clear any mines. He would engage the turret and then withdraw covered by another smoke screen. Allen was not persuaded that the risks were worth it and denied Collins' request. In the meantime Collins had identified a less hazardous alternative that involved moving up the western fringe of the airfield. Then, covered by a smoke screen, move to a predetermined point near a house some 100m from the target which offered a little cover and engage the turret. Once destroyed he would withdraw again protected by a smokescreen. Collins' confidence in his new plan convinced Allen and he was given permission to go ahead.[66]

Collins' tank had a damaged radiator so a replacement was brought forward. This was stripped of all unnecessary equipment and loaded to capacity with armour piercing shells. It was also heavily camouflaged to make it less of a target. Then, under cover of a smoke-screen provided by 4th Field Regiment, Collins led his tank on foot through machine gun and mortar fire out to the west of the turret before striking north to the perimeter of the airfield. Meantime another tank advanced around the

southern end of the airfield to create a diversion. Jim Sloan, the lap gunner of Collins' tank, vividly describes the attack, 'As we stalked the gun it came into view through the gaps in the scrub from time to time and we watched anxiously to see if that big 75mm traversed in our direction. It didn't. We finally got within range and poked the gun around the corner of a *casa* [house] and then let drive. Maurie [Sergeant M. Woolley] got it with his fourth shot* and then we just kept blazing away at it, putting the gun out of action and knocking hunks of the emplacement while Joe [Collins] and I sprayed the area and the escaping gun crew with our Brownings. Altogether we fired off 14 AP [armour piercing] and two HE [high explosive] plus three smoke shells to cover our getaway.'[67] Collins' tank now came under mortar and small arms fire but, obscured by the smoke, it was able to withdraw safely. For his bravery in the battle for Rimini airfield Collins was awarded the Military Cross.[68]

Allen's unit was relieved at first light on 18 September by C Squadron of 19th NZ Armoured Regiment, but any ideas they had that the threat from Panther turrets had been extinguished were soon dispelled, because, 'The area of Celle and Route 16 bristled with dug-in Panther turrets ... formidably manned by paratroops [of 1st *Fallschirmjäger*

---

*The official history and other sources state the second shot.

Division, elements of which had manned similar positions in the Hitler Line] . . .'[69] On the night of 21 September the tanks attempted to cross the Marecchia. Their progress was slowed by mud and mines and whilst bogged down came under fire from what was later discovered to be another Panther turret situated near Celle, a small village half a mile west of Rimini. Once again, come the moment, come the man. Corporal Reeve, the section commander of 7 Platoon of 1 Company, 22 (Motor) Battalion, disposed his men in positions from which they could bring covering fire to bear. He then charged across the open ground in front of the turret and engaged the defenders with hand grenades. The defenders responded in kind, but Reeve got the better of the exchange and the defenders were forced to withdraw from their positions. Unable to spare any troops to secure the position, Reeve and his platoon pressed on to their ultimate objective, the Fossa Turchetta. In the meantime, the paratroopers, finding the emplacement empty, reoccupied the position and opened fire. Reeve was again given the job of capturing the position which he did, capturing six paratroopers in the process.[70]

POSTSCRIPT

After the war all traces of the emplaced Panther turrets were systematically removed as governments attempted to remove all reminders of this unhappy chapter in twentieth-century history, and, more

A Panther tank turret that was mounted on a Holzunterstand in the West Wall. It was originally installed near the village of Niederwürzbach in the Saarland but it is now on display at the Westwall Museum, Niedersimten, Germany. (Author)

pragmatically, these turrets presented a valuable source of scrap metal which was in short supply in the post-war world. By sheer chance two examples survived. One is on display at the West Wall Museum, Niedersimten, Germany. It was originally installed on a wooden superstructure near the village of Niederwürzbach in the Saarland and it seems that over the years the wooden supports rotted away and, unable to support the weight, the turret collapsed into the hole where it lay for some fifty years until it was recovered and restored. Another turret has recently been discovered near Szczecin (Stettin) in Poland and is currently being renovated.

Table 5 Dimensions

	Earth excavation (m³)	Concrete (m³)	Formed steel (tonnes)	Round steel (tonnes)	Length (m)	Width (m)	Height (m)	Walls (cm)		Roof (cm)	Base (cm)
								Exterior	Interior		
OT Stahlunterstand	170	70	–	3.5	3.32	2.90	2.96	8 (upper box) 7 (lower box)	5	10	4
OT Stahlunterstand mit Betonummantelung	–	–	–	–	5.84	5.26	3.25	As above			
Regelbau 687	230	175	1.4	9	7.30	7.30	4.40	150	80–100	120	80
Holzunterstand	Varied	–	–	–	3.64	3.06	2.70	–	–	–	–

4 Post War

In the immediate aftermath of the Second World War, alliances that had been forged in the fight against a common foe were quickly forgotten as the world descended into a Cold War where the two diametrically opposed ideologies of capitalism and communism vied for dominance. In Europe, despite the availability of nuclear weapons, the two superpowers invested heavily in conventional forces to deter possible aggression by the other. This included fleets of ships and submarines and countless bomber and fighter squadrons that played a dangerous game of cat and mouse in the seas and skies. On the plains of Western Europe, large standing armies were massed which were regularly and menacingly on manoeuvres. To counter the threat posed by these ground forces nations on both sides of the ideological divide, and neutral countries caught in the middle of the sabre rattling, installed tank turrets along their respective borders. This improvisation not only provided a powerful deterrent but was also cost effective in a world where post-war austerity meant that countries had limited funds to devote to their defence budgets and where significant stockpiles of war material were widely available.

Outside of Europe the ideological struggle was played out on a small scale in regional conflicts, as Moscow and Washington sought to gain the upper hand. From the bitter fighting in the Middle East as Arab fought Jew to the Far East where guerrillas sought to throw off the imperial yolk, the involvement of the superpowers was often all too evident. Here too the combatants on both sides saw emplaced tank turrets as a cost effective way of protecting their strategic interests.

In the post-war world then the use of tank turrets as fixed fortifications was if anything more widespread than during the war, with examples found on almost every continent. However, with the collapse of communism and the rise of global terrorism, countries reappraised their defensive strategies and almost without exception the tank turrets that had played a pivotal role in safeguarding the national security of some countries for almost half a century, were either mothballed or removed altogether.

AUSTRIA

In the immediate aftermath of the Second World War Austria was prohibited from having an army. This remained the case until May 1955 when Austrian sovereignty was restored. Still, though restrictions remained in place. Austria was not allowed to have nuclear weapons, submarines or artillery with a range greater than 30km (18 miles). Moreover, the victorious allies retained the right to outlaw any new weapons that they deemed unsuitable.

The new Austrian army was, however, permitted to have tanks, which were all sourced from the country's former adversaries. From the Soviet Union came the T34/85, from America the M47 and from Great Britain the Charioteer, and later the Centurion.[1] As these tanks were replaced, the turrets were often removed and were mounted on specially built concrete shelters or prefabricated constructions. These varied according to ground conditions and were sometimes installed as individual positions or formed part of larger, interconnecting bunker systems. Many were disguised as barns typical of the area. These could be removed to give the turret a full field of fire.[2]

Generally these shelters could accommodate eight men, all of them reservists, and were emplaced to cover the main avenues of a possible attack from the Warsaw Pact, principally on the low lying plains to the south and east of Vienna. The turrets provided the focal point of the anti-tank defences and as such were positioned at strategically important locations like the Wurzenpass and at Bruck an der Leitha.*

With the end of the Cold War the turrets have been gradually deactivated and no longer play a part in the country's defence plan. One of the turrets has been retained and can be visited, but others have been sold and now serve as garages or wine cellars.[3]

Charioteer[†]

After the Charioteer was withdrawn from service by the Austrian army the turrets were mounted on concrete shelters or were installed in casemates. These gave the turret additional protection, but did restrict its field of fire. The Charioteer was initially armed with an 8,34cm gun that had a maximum range of 5,500m although its effective range, depending on the ammunition used, was 1,500–3,000m. The weapon was fitted with an electrical discharge system that would eject the shell case when the gun barrel recuperator opened. Later some Charioteer turrets were rearmed with the 10.5cm Panzerkanone M.68.[‡]

It is not clear exactly how many Charioteer turrets were used in this way, but it was no more than fifty-six, because this was the maximum number that were in service with the Austrian Army. This broadly corresponds with figures quoted in unofficial sources which state that sixty turrets armed with 20 pdr guns were installed.[4] The Charioteer turrets were still in use up until the late 1980s but appear to have been removed soon thereafter.

Charioteer

Turret statistics:
Armour (thickness/angle):

Gun mantlet	Front	Side	Rear	Roof
–	30mm	20mm	20mm	–

Weapon statistics:
Armament: 1 × 8,34cm Panzerkanone L/70 M.2
Traverse: 360°
Elevation: +10° to −5°

T34/85

The T34/85 was originally constructed by the Soviet Union and was instrumental in the defeat of Germany. Its powerful 85mm gun could be fired at six rounds per minute and had a maximum range of 13,600m, although its effective range was in the region 1,000–4,000m depending on the type of ammunition used. It was fitted with either a manual or electrical discharge system that would eject the shell case with the gun recoil. The coaxial machine gun was capable of firing 100–120 rounds per minute but was prone to jamming. The turret could be rotated by hand at 1.5–2 degrees per second but with power traverse this increased to 12 degrees per second.

After the war the Austrians acquired twenty-six of these tanks which served with the army until the early 1960s when they were withdrawn and replaced with the US M47. The obsolete T34s were transferred to the *Sperrtruppe*, or Barricade Force of the Austrian Army, and a number were used as fixed fortifications along the border with Czechoslovakia. Somewhat unusually the whole of the tank was simply buried in the ground so that just the turret was showing, rather than removing the turret and mounting it on some form of concrete structure.[5]

M47

The American M47 replaced the obsolete T34/85. It was armed with a 90mm gun, which was capable of penetrating 1,500mm (59in) of armour at a range of 1,800m and could fire a high explosive shell more than twice as far. The weapon was fitted with an electro-mechanical discharge system, which would automatically eject the shell case when the gun barrel recuperator opened.

Eventually the M47 was replaced by the British Centurion and 147 of the turrets were used as fixed fortifications.[6] One of these was installed near Fort Nauders[‡] and was fitted with appliqué armour to

*Interestingly a number of Panzer III turrets were dispatched to Bruck an der Leitha in March 1945 to protect Vienna, but the city fell before the turrets had arrived. *See* Chapter 3, Part 1.
† The Charioteer was a post war conversion of the Cromwell chasis with a new turret and a 20pdr gun.
‡ Fort Nauders was built between 1834 and 1840 to defend the narrow gorge south of Resia in the Tyrol on the border with Italy.

T34/85				

Turret statistics:
Armour (thickness/angle):

Gun mantlet	Front	Side	Rear	Roof
–	75mm	75mm	75mm	–

Weapon statistics:
Armament: 1 × 8,5cm Model 44 (ZIS-S53)
                    1 × 7.62mm MG 41/45 type DTM
Sight: TS16 direction finding telescope
Traverse: 360°
Elevation: +25° to −5°

M47				

Turret statistics:
Armour (thickness/angle):

Gun mantlet	Front	Side	Rear	Roof
–	110mm	64mm	76mm	–

Weapon statistics:
Armament: 9cm Panzerkanone M36 L/48
Traverse: 360°
Elevation: +19° to −10°

provide added protection.[7] By 1998 with the thaw in East–West relations, all of the M47 turrets had been deactivated.[8]

Centurion

During 1953 and 1954 the Dutch Army procured 591 Centurion Mk 3s under the Mutual Defence Assistance Programme.* In 1967/68, 343 of these were rearmed with the L7 105mm gun and reclassified as Mark 5/2. A year later the Dutch decided to buy the new German Leopard I and sold 122 Mk 5 Centurions to a Middle-Eastern country. The Dutch Army considered a proposal from Krauss-Maffei Wegmann of Germany to modernize the remainder, but this option was dropped in favour of an order for Leopard 2 tanks that was signed in 1979. In the mid-1980s the Dutch sold 120 of the remaining Mark 5s to Austria. A

Centurion				

Turret statistics:
Armour (thickness/angle):

Gun mantlet	Front	Side	Rear	Roof
152mm	152mm	89mm	89mm	29–51mm

Weapon statistics:
Armament: 10.5cm Panzerkanone L.7A1
Traverse: 360°
Elevation: +20° to −10°

further 107 tanks came from Canada (via Kruass-Maffei) when they replaced the Centurion with the Leopard 1.

By this time the Centurion was beginning to show its age and the upkeep of the chassis became increasingly expensive. A modernization programme was considered, but was rejected as impractical and not cost effective, so in the early 1990s a decision was taken to use the turrets as fixed fortifications. The bulk, if not all, of the Centurion turrets were used in this way and protected the Austrian border for a decade until the turn of the millennium when the turrets were taken out of service.[9]

BULGARIA

Having fought with the Axis powers in the Second World War Bulgaria found itself in 1945 in the Soviet sphere of influence. As one of Moscow's satellite states it was equipped with T34/85 tanks. At its peak the Bulgarian Army fielded nearly 600 of these tanks and as late as 1988 it still had 200 in service. Unconfirmed sources state that a number of the scrapped turrets were installed along the border with Turkey.[10]

CUBA

In common with Cuba's ideological mentor and her main supplier of military materiel, the Soviet Union,

*A US sponsored initiative to rebuild the military strength of NATO countries during the Cold War.

A Centurion tank turret that formed part of the Neu Bruck defences on the Austrian border. It was housed inside a wooden hut to provide camouflage. The turrets have now been withdrawn from service but this example has been retained and can be visited by the public.
(Charles Blackwood)

Cuba used tanks in a static defence role. In the late 1980s it is reported that some of the 150 T34/85 tanks described as being in store were used in this way as were a number of SU100 self-propelled guns. In addition, fifteen 122mm IS2 tanks were used in fixed emplacements.[11]

CYPRUS

Following the Turkish invasion of Cyprus, Yugoslavia supplied the Greek Cypriots with T34/85 tanks. In the 1980s, twenty-four of these tanks were still in service and according to unofficial sources the Republic of Cyprus installed eight of these tanks in a static defence role in the early 1990s.[12]

CZECHOSLOVAKIA*

Following the defeat of Germany and the start of the Cold War, Europe was split into two blocs which were later to crystallize into NATO and the Warsaw Pact. Czechoslovakia, which had been annexed by Germany in 1938, now fell under the influence of the Soviet Union and formed one of the buffer states between the powers of the capitalist west and the communist east. As such steps were taken fortify the western border against any possible enemy incursion. These defences included the use of emplaced tank turrets that had been used by the Soviets before, during and after the war.

Panzer IV

Although a Soviet satellite state, Czechoslovakia had after the war acquired some eighty German Panzer IV tanks which the *Velitelstv' tankomechanizovaného vojska* (VTMV) or Command of the Mechanised Armoured Corps absorbed into its ranks as the T40/75N and T42/74N which reflected the two different variants acquired.[†]

In 1955 the majority of these (forty-five) were sold to Syria. The remaining tanks (and wear and tear would have reduced the number still further) were deemed to be too few in number to retain as frontline vehicles and so, on the recommendation of Maj Gen Derzicky, the Soviet Advisor to the Czech Engineering Corps (VZV), it was decided to undertake tests to assess their suitability for deployment as fixed defences.[‡] In December 1954 the Chief of the General Staff, Lt Gen Václav Kratochvil ordered that three turrets be made available for tests at the Milovice training centre. However, the training centre was found to be unsuitable so the tests were moved to the anti-tank firing range at Jince-Padrt.

It was planned that the construction of the experimental structure should commence in the middle of March 1955 and was to be finished by May. Thereafter trials were to be undertaken to understand the tactical use of the turret in an anti-tank defence. It was also hoped to get a better understanding of how easy or difficult it was to construct, particularly mounting the turret and baseplate on the bunker, the materials needed, the build-up of carbon monoxide as a result of firing, and crucially the effect of the firing of the weapon on the structure.[¶]

---

* It has been suggested that the newly formed Czech Republic is planning to use emplaced turrets, but this is unconfirmed.
† It is believed that these were *Ausf* G and *Ausf* J tanks but mention is also made of the KwK40 L/43 gun which was fitted to the *Panzer* IV *Ausf* F2.
‡ Somewhat surprisingly, considering this later experiment, the Engineering Corps in May 1950 turned down the opportunity to take delivery of forty complete and twenty incomplete *Panzerkampfwagen* V Panther turrets. These, as is detailed in Chapter 3, Part 3, were most effective in a static defence role.
¶ It would seem, as with later models, that the turret would be installed only as and when needed, thus it was essential to understand how best to cover the opening where the turret would sit and how long it would take to install the turret when taken from store.

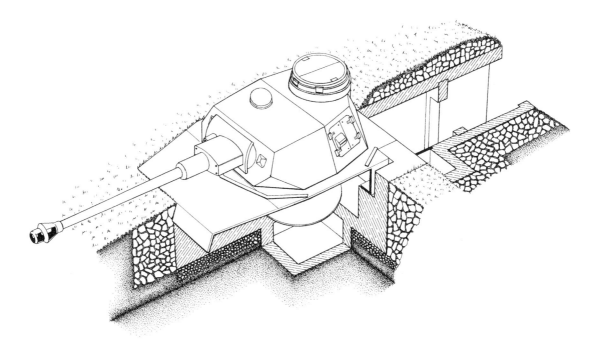

Czechoslovak Panzer IV on concrete shelter.

Structure

A revetted trench led to the walled (15cm (6in) thick walls) entrance in front of the main wooden door. Behind the door was a passageway which housed a single Model 37 ventilator that drew in clean air through a gravel filter.* The walls were constructed from concrete 25cm (9in) thick which were capable of withstanding a direct hit from an 82mm mortar.† The passageway led to the main fighting compartment which housed the turret basket and above it the turret. Below the turret was a chamber for spent cartridges. The access to this was through a sprung flap that ensured that no fumes could return to the fighting compartment. A flue led from here to the surface to ensure gases were vented safely outside. Under the chamber was a drainage channel for the dispersal of any water. The turret was mounted on the original tank superstructure, which was in turn secured to the bunker by ten 30mm (1in) diameter bolts.‡ The front wall was 1m (3ft) thick and the side walls 60cm (2ft). The whole structure was 609cm (239in) long and at its widest was 292cm (115in) across.

Construction

On 21 March, 23 men supervised by four NCOs began excavating the soil that was necessary to install the structure. This work was completed by 26 March and work on the concrete structure began. This was delayed by test firings on the range and the inexperienced workforce. By 8 April the last of the concrete was poured and the shuttering was removed ten days later. To provide added protection a metre-thick belt of hard core was packed around the walls. Meantime the last of the work preparing the turret and base was completed as the superstructure was cut to shape and the holes drilled to take the securing bolts. The superstructure was lifted into place and secured and the whole was turfed over. The work was complete by 30 April.

---

*Initially gravel 4–6mm diameter was to be used, but this proved unsatisfactory and was replaced with gravel of 10–12mm diameter.
† This protection could be increased by carefully covering the passageway with spoil, but this restricted the turrets traverse.
‡ It is assumed that the driver and radio operator hatches were retained, but could not be used because of the concrete bulwark at the front.

Panzer IV

Turret statistics: Panzer IV Ausf J
Armour (thickness/angle):

Gun mantlet	Front	Side	Rear	Roof
50mm/0°–30°	50mm/10°	30mm/25°	30mm/15°	18mm/86°–6mm/90°

Weapon statistics:
Armament: 1 × 7.5cm KwK 40 L/48
             1 × 7.92mm MG34
Sight: 1 × TZF5f/2
Traverse: 360°
Elevation: +20° −8°

Bunker statistics:

Earth excavation	Concrete	Formed steel	Round steel
70m³	13.6m³	–	–

Ventilation: Model 37   Munitions storage: N/K

However, it is not clear whether the tests were completed and, if they were, whether they were successful. The remains of the structure are inaccessible to the public, and the archive records incomplete so it is only possible to surmise as to the outcome. What is clear, however, is that the idea of using tank turrets in this way was not dismissed.[13]

T34/85

Although the tests on the Panzer IV were inconclusive, the Czechoslovak army continued to experiment with other turrets including the Soviet T34/85.* This was mounted on the so-called 'KZ-3' shelter that was in many respects markedly different to that for the Panzer IV. One of the main differences being that the base structure was constructed from prefabricated concrete sections.

Structure
At the front of the position was the turret mounting with circular track that sat on top of a concrete shaft. From here a tunnel led to the main entrance door. An inclined drainage channel under the passageway took excess water to a soakaway just beyond the door. The door, constructed from steel, led to a further section of tunnel, which was linked to the ammunition stores that were located around the main entrance shaft.

From here a ladder led to the access hatch. The crew's shelter was located to the rear and was accessible via a trench that was also linked to the main trench system. This was partially covered to afford the crew more protection. Further soakaways in these trenches prevented any flooding.

The fighting compartment itself was rudimentary. No discrete ventilation system was provided other than the turret's own and as such when the main armament was used the crew was forced to leave the main door open. This also served to enable the ammunition feeder to dispose of spent cartridges. The functional design of the shelter meant that storage was limited and no specific room was set aside for ration packs and water, or for the tools for maintaining the turret and its equipment which all had to be stowed as best as possible.

Construction
Once the location for the turret had been identified[†] the recess for the turret was excavated. This was dug

---

*And seemingly the Soviet T54, but this cannot be confirmed.
[†] The location was determined in accordance with general army regulations governing the positioning of anti-tank weapons. It was necessary to ensure that there was no dead ground in front of the position and that there was cover for the crew to enter.

An interior view of the KZ3 concrete shelter that mounted a T34/85 turret. Just visible are the prefabricated concrete sections that formed the corridor and at the end is the shaft leading to the fighting compartment. This position was located at Tri Sekery. (Jan Pavel)

A further interior view looking the other way which shows the interior door and steps leading to the entrance. Leaning against the wall is the anti-pressure door (Zdv-1). (Jan Pavel)

to a diameter of 340cm (134in) with the centre corresponding to the anticipated central point of rotation of the turret.* It was then necessary to establish the main direction of fire because this dictated the location of the shelter which was to be constructed to the rear of the turret. The excavation was to be 660cm (259in) long and 210cm (82in) wide and extended down some 245cm (6.2ft). In total some 28-35m³ (91–114ft³) of earth had to be excavated, depending on the method of excavation. Along the length of the dugout an inclined drainage channel was dug which led to the soakaway. The concrete shelter was then installed which was constructed from prefabricated sections (*see* Table 1 *below* for complete list of components).†

Directly under the turret, two precast concrete sections (squared or semi-circular) were placed on top of each other to form the shaft leading to the fighting compartment. A further seven prefabricated concrete frames were then positioned in the dugout by a crane. They were loosely joined with wire before eventually being secured together with iron tie rods. These sections formed the tunnel leading to the main door. Further concrete frames were installed after the door and led to the main access chamber, which was fitted with a hatch. Before being buried the concrete, sections were covered with plastic sheeting to waterproof the shelter and then a layer of spoil was applied to a thickness of approximately 80cm (31in).

---

*Where an excavator was used the diameter had to be increased by 50cm (19in).
† This approach limited the structure's ability to withstand enemy fire but it was considered capable of withstanding a single hit by a 105mm round or an 82mm mortar.

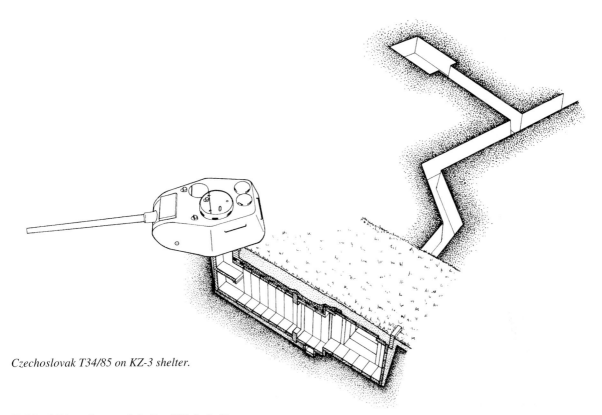

Czechoslovak T34/85 on KZ-3 shelter.

Table 1 List of materials for KZ-3 shelter

Number	Description	Identifying mark	Requirement (reserve)	Weight (kg)	Total Weight
1	Base panel of tank turret	Zpa 4	1	2300	2300
2	Cover	Zpa 6	1	938	938
3	Shafts	Zpa 5	2	837	1674
4	Passage frames 160 × 90cm	Zra 7	13(1)	495	6930
5	Passage frames 190 × 90cm	Zra 6	1	547	547
6	Door frames with opening 65 × 130cm	Zdr 2	1	975	975
7	Planks 30 × 110 × 8cm	Zde 6	26(2)		
8	Anti-pressure doors	Zdv 1	1	64	64
9	Reinforcing rods		1	42	42
10	Steel railings for shaft		1	19	19
11	Insulating sheet	Izofol B	10m²		6
12	Base planks		2	7	14

Finally the ground around the turret was levelled off and the turfs replaced. One of the more critical tasks was the installation of the base panel for the turret, which had to be perfectly horizontal. To achieve this the plate was mounted on a thin layer of damp sand. Provided all the materials and a crane were available the structure could be completed in four days.

When not in use the turret base plate was covered with a lid that was covered with soil. Similarly, the access hatch was covered with planks and soil. A marker identified where the entrance was. The turret for the structure was held in store and was transported to the site on a Tatra T111 transporter in times of tension and installed with an IT34 crane. The operation could be completed in seventy-five minutes.

Turret

The turret was a standard T34/85 turret* with 85mm main armament and 7.62mm coaxial machine gun. The only noticeable difference was the addition of openings in the side of the turret, which served as emergency firing points – the crew was equipped with automatic weapons and grenades for their own protection. The turret had three seats for the commander, gunner and loader and another member of the crew acted as feeder for the ammunition from the shelter.

The turret could be rotated manually or with power traverse.† An MB-20V electric motor powered by two batteries (with two further in reserve) provided the power. When these were fitted in the rear of the turret, however, they reduced the space available for ammunition from ten rounds to three rounds. The electric motor also provided power for the MV12 ventilator. This was fitted in such a way that it concentrated the fresh air round the loader who was at most risk from the gun exhaust fumes. Even so, the ventilation system was not considered powerful enough to prevent the build-up of carbon monoxide so the crew was provided with gas masks, which also served to protect them against other agents since the structure was not proof against chemical or biological weapons.

Postscript

Trials of the turret were carried out in 1959 and these seem to have been passed satisfactorily. Construction

T34/85			
Turret statistics: *See* Austria			
Bunker statistics:			
Earth excavation	Concrete	Formed steel	Round steel
28–35 m³	–	–	–

Ventilation: MV12 ventilator in turret.
Munitions storage: 85mm – 51 rounds (of which ten were held in the turret) 7.62mm MG – 16 magazines of 62 rounds (2,340 rounds in total)

of positions began along Czechoslovakia's western border soon after, but numbers built is unclear. In 1978 the Chief of the General Staff ordered their decommissioning.[14]

DENMARK

In 1953, as part of the Mutual Defence Aid Programme, Denmark procured 216 Centurion MK III tanks, a number of which had been used in the Korean War. These tanks formed the backbone of the Danish Army until 1976 when the first of an order for 120 Leopard I tanks was delivered. The Centurion was now gradually phased out of service and, in common with other Scandinavian countries, Denmark used 126 of these turrets as fixed fortifications.[15] In 1989 the government ordered a further 110 Leopard Is which were delivered between 1992 and 1994. This would have breached Denmark's commitment under

---

*The original type RM31T radio was replaced with an RM105 unit that was fitted to the turret wall.
† A full rotation using the hand crank took three minutes, while with the power traverse one revolution could be completed in approximately thirty seconds.
‡ The Treaty on Conventional Armed Forces in Europe, signed in Paris on 19 November 1990, by the twenty-two members of NATO and the former Warsaw Pact. It is an arms control agreement that established parity in major conventional forces/armaments between East and West.

the CFE Treaty[‡] which limited the army to 300 main battle tanks and as a result in the mid 1990s 146 Centurions were scrapped. Of these, ten found a home in museums, or on static display, while another eight were used as range targets. The remainder, including seemingly all the emplaced turrets, were disposed of leaving just seventy Centurions still on active service.

EGYPT

The Egyptians used dug-in T34, T54 and T55 tanks in Gaza during the Six-Day War of June 1967 and in the Yom Kippur War of October 1973 this tactic was used once again. In a pre-emptive strike, the Egyptians caught Israel off-guard, crossed the Suez canal, overwhelmed the unprepared garrison of the 'Bar Lev Line',* advanced 4km (2½ miles) into the Sinai and dug in. Once the Israelis had recovered from the initial shock they responded with a tank attack. This proved to be an unmitigated disaster. Advancing against the hull-down Egyptian tanks, the Israelis lost practically every tank.

FINLAND

The Finnish Army, which is responsible for the country's coastal defence, has taken numerous steps to protect its vulnerable coastline including mobile missile units and towed guns. Additionally, turret mounted guns were installed including the Patria Vammas 130mm coastal defence gun which is mounted in a bespoke steel turret.[16] Since the mid-1980s Finland has also used Soviet T54 and T55 (D10T) turrets set in concrete.

The turrets were bought from Russia and originally they were installed without any modifications except for the loading mechanism. Later the turrets were adapted for their new role with the addition of laser rangefinders, a thermal sight, a ballistic computer and were supplied with more modern ammunition.

The turrets were driven to the location on a tank, lifted off and emplaced. The tank hull was then driven away to fetch the next turret. They are extremely well camouflaged which makes them difficult to see and

they tend to be located in areas where the public normally cannot visit and certainly not take photographs. In spite of the secrecy it is believed that sixty-one such turrets have been installed.[17]

FRANCE (INDO CHINA)

In common with many European powers France had, prior to the war, held significant interests overseas. With the defeat of Germany and Japan the French government sought to re-establish this empire, and in October 1945 French troops arrived in Indo-China (modern day Vietnam). This attempt at restoring French rule was not welcomed by elements of the indigenous population and in December 1946 Vietminh forces attacked French garrisons, and during the ensuing years guerrilla activity increased in the countryside.

Having endured over four years of German occupation France was ill prepared to meet this new threat. French armoured units, for example, were equipped with American Shermans and a mixture of tanks from other nations including a number of captured German Panther tanks and a few ex-British army tanks. They also employed a number of tanks produced in France before the war including the Char B1, the Hotchkiss H39 and Somua S35. Some of these were transported to Indo-China to counter the insurgents[†] and it is also possible that a number stationed there prior to the war were still serviceable.

In addition to the use of conventional forces to counter the threat of the Vietminh, France also built a series of fortifications. These included blockhouses fitted with tank turrets, which were designed to protect key communication links like the Hanoi ring road. The turrets were taken from pre-war French tanks including the APX R armed with a 37mm gun

---

*See section on Israel for a description of the Bar Lev Line.
[†] The first H39 tank arrived in May 1947 to equip the *Regiment Etranger de Cavalerie* (Foreign Legion Cavalry Regiment), with twenty more arriving in April 1948.
[‡] An armoured enthusiast travelling in Indo China observed several very large bunkers mounting what appeared to be twin APX1 (Somua S35) turrets. D. Seguin, 'Panzerstellung – Part Two', *AFV News*, Vol. 9, No.1, January 1974, pp.4–5.

A Crusader tank turret armed with a 6-pounder gun mounted on top of a concrete position dominating Quang Yen, north of Haiphong. (Francis Jaureguy, courtesy of D O'Hara)

Another H39 turret mounted on top of a concrete blockhouse in Indo China. The design of the position is unusual in that there has been no attempt to bury the bunker and it is also had a number of apertures. (ECPA)

and the APX 1 armed with a 47mm gun.[‡] There is also evidence to suggest that turrets from British Cromwell and Crusader tanks were used.[18, 19, 20] This seems to be borne out by a French report on operations in Indo China published in 1955 after a ceasefire had been agreed. This stated that 'a tank turret (with 37mm, 47mm or 57mm gun) could be placed above and just to the rear of the forward embrasure [of a pillbox]'.[21] Certain models of both the Crusader and Cromwell tanks were fitted with 6-pounders, which broadly equates to a 57mm gun.

An H39 turret mounted on top of a French blockhouse in Indo China. Of interest is the split hatch, which could indicate that this turret was previously used by the Germans. (ECPA)

GREECE

Britain had always had a close involvement with Greek affairs, not least because of its strategic location, and supported the anti-communist forces in the Civil War that erupted in 1946. The British backed forces prevailed and a constitutional monarchy was restored.[*] The new government aligned itself with the west and although not on the Atlantic, its proximity to the Middle East and the Eastern bloc meant that the United States soon recognized the importance of the Balkan state and in 1951 Greece became a full member of NATO.

Being one of the western nations with a common border with a Soviet bloc country – in this case Yugoslavia – Greece, in a throwback to the interwar years when the Metaxas line had been built, constructed a series of fortifications along the border to deter a possible invasion. These defences included tank turrets used as fixed fortifications. The turrets were taken from old Grant and Sherman tanks and were mounted on concrete shelters. These positions were still in use up until the 1980s and many of the turrets are still in place today and in an excellent state of preservation.

*In the post war carve up of continental Europe, Stalin accepted that Greece should fall under the British sphere of influence.

The Sherman turrets were either taken from M4 or M4A1 tanks, a number of which had been left behind when the British forces departed from Greece after the war. The gun and the mantlet of the original turret was removed and replaced with welded steel plates arranged in such a way to leave a small opening at the front to take a machine gun. On the right-hand side of the turret, appliqué armour was welded on to provide extra protection. The turret was painted in a three-tone camouflage scheme; two shades of green and one of sand. The whole turret was additionally covered in chicken wire so that camouflage could be applied. The turret was mounted on a concrete shelter. To the right was an access hatch that led to the fighting compartment beneath. This was some 3m (10ft) deep and could accommodate five to eight men.[22]

The Grant tanks were similarly installed on concrete shelters. They were installed on the shore of Lake Doiran, which straddles the border with Greece and the former Yugoslavia, and were constructed during the Colonels' dictatorship (1967–74).[23]

IRAQ

There is circumstantial evidence to suggest that turrets taken from obsolete Soviet tanks that had previously been used to equip the Iraqi army and Republican Guard, have been used as improvised strong points in Baghdad.

One of the Sherman turrets that was installed at Evzoni on the Greek border with the former Yugoslavia. This view clearly shows the stepped concrete shelter on which the turret was mounted. Chicken wire covers the turret and would have been used to attach camouflage.
(T. Tsiplakos)

ISRAEL

Following the end of the Second World War in 1945 there was a huge stockpile of military materiel as the victors reduced their armed forces to peacetime levels and the Axis powers were disarmed. The surplus hardware was either scrapped or was sold to newly liberated countries or to states that had secured independence. In this scrabble a number of Sherman tanks, which had formed the mainstay of the American armoured forces during the war, were 'acquired' by the Israelis and some were used in the 1948 War of Independence, although most arrived after the hostilities had ended.

Despite this setback Israel's neighbours were determined to eliminate this Jewish homeland and began to strengthen their armed forces. The Egyptians, for example, from 1953 began to procure Soviet T34/85 tanks and SU100 tank destroyers. These were more than a match for the basic Sherman and although the Israelis were able to purchase a number of AMX13 light tanks form France it was clear that the most logical approach was to upgun the reliable Sherman. It also seemed eminently sensible to use the high velocity long-barrelled 75mm gun fitted to the AMX13 (and which had been used so successfully by the Germans in the Panther tank).

The larger breach and length of recoil meant that the turret had to be remodelled and the new tank was christened the M50 and by 1961, one hundred Shermans had been reconfigured. Advances in armour technology, however, meant that the 75mm main gun was no longer powerful enough to penetrate the armour of the tanks now fielded by Israel's enemies. Plans to mount the French 105mm gun (from the AMX30) were introduced which meant that the turret had to be remodelled again and in 1962 the first of the so-called M51s was delivered. The M50 and M51 served throughout the 1960s and were the mainstay of the Israeli armoured forces in the Six-Day War in 1967. However, by the time of the Yom Kippur War in 1973 the Sherman had been relegated to the reserve, replaced by the more powerful American M48, M60 and British Centurion tanks. Some Shermans were still in use in the 1980s and 1990s but they were gradually withdrawn from service.

The fighting that had raged on and off since the War of Independence, and in which the Sherman had

Israel
Map 6

An M50 tank that was used in a static defence role by the Israelis. This view shows the access to the shelter. To give added protection the spoil would have been built up around the sides of the tank so that only the turret was visible. This example was located on the coast at Kibbutz Hanita, just south of the Israel/Lebanon border. (Svein Wiiger Olsen)

played such an important part, had seen the state of Israel grow significantly in size with land seized from her Arab neighbours. The occupied territories were soon settled, but being so close to Israel's avowed enemies they were exposed to attack and needed defending. One solution was to use emplaced tank turrets.

As the M50 was withdrawn from service a number were modified and were used in a static role to defend the West Bank* and the border with Lebanon and Syria. The tank was emplaced whole and all variants of the Sherman hull (including M4, M4A2 and M4A4 models) were seemingly used. Before installation the more modern HVSS tracks and suspension were removed and replaced by the old VVSS bogies which enabled the tank to be unloaded from the transporter and more easily moved to its final location. The engine deck was sometimes removed and replaced with a flat plate. Access to the position was gained either through an enlarged rear door or by removing the transmission cover at the front.[†] A concrete walkway linked the entrance to the tank to a revetted communication trench that often led to further defensive positions. To provide extra protection for the hull, earth and rocks were banked around the tank so that only the turret was visible. Inside the M50, the engine was removed, as

---

*The West Bank (of the Jordan River) was captured from the Jordanians following the Six-Day War.
[†] Access via the transmission cover meant that the more heavily armoured glacis plate of the tank faced away from the enemy leaving the lightly armoured engine cover exposed to artillery and mortar fire.

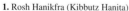

● **Tank turrets**   Scale 0 ◄———► 40km

1. Rosh Hanikfra (Kibbutz Hanita)
2. Bar'am
3. Kibbutz Yiron (1 × M48 turret)
4. Yiftach
5. Mehola × 2
6. Argaman*
7. Massau × 2
8. Peza'el × 2 (one at Kibbutz Peza'el)

*Reported to have two turrets, but no evidence remains

The Israeli Defence Force also used obsolete American M48 tank turrets as improvised fixed fortifications. (www.israeli-weapons.com)

were all other fittings save for the turret basket and ammunition stowage.[24] The tank retained its 75mm CN 75-50 main gun and coaxial 7.62mm MG. Later turrets from the more modern M48 tank were used with one being emplaced at Kibbutz Yiron.[25]

Many of the tanks fielded by Israel's neighbours in the six wars that punctuated the second half of the twentieth century were supplied by the Soviet Union or its satellite states. Many of these were captured by the Israelis and were pressed into service by the Israel Defence Forces, some as fixed fortifications. Turrets taken from ex-Soviet BTR 60 Armoured cars were used in the Golan Heights as were T34/85 turrets and there are also unconfirmed reports that IS3 turrets were used in the Bar Lev Line.[26] *

Today a number of these turrets can still be seen, but they are no longer in active service. The role of deterrent has now passed to helicopter gunships and ground-attack aircraft that are quickly able to strike at enemy insurgents.

ITALY

Italy's northern border with the rump of Continental Europe is dominated by the Alpine mountain chain. This natural feature offered the new Italian state† an excellent opportunity to defend its land border from attack. In the late nineteenth century work began on the first fortifications and these were improved during the First World War. In 1931 work began on the 'Vallo Alpino' (or 'Vallo del Littorio') which was a system of permanent fortifications designed to block all routes into Italy particularly those leading from France, Austria and Yugoslavia.‡

The Israelis also used captured tanks in a static defence role. Here a T34/85 has been installed near the southern edge of the Sea of Galilee. The tank is surrounded by a dirt berm, which originally covered everything but the turret. The position was damaged by fire – the note reads 'fire inside' – and now sits inside the fence of a construction company. (Tom Gannon)

The work continued for a decade until it was stopped in 1942 and although incomplete Italy was protected by a large semi-circle of defences stretching from the Ligurian sea to the Adriatic. The defences saw little fighting in the Second World War and after the war many of the fortifications were either destroyed or were taken over by neighbouring states

---

*The Bar Lev Line was a chain of fortifications built by Israel along the eastern bank of the Suez Canal after it captured the Sinai Peninsula from Egypt during the 1967 Six-Day War. The line was named after the Israeli Chief of Staff Haim Bar-Lev and consisted of an earthen rampart and a series of concrete observation posts positioned every 10–12km along the canal, with extra fortifications at potential crossing points.
† The modern state of Italy as it is known today was created in 1870.
‡ Little work was done on the border with neutral Switzerland where reliance was placed on defences built during the First World War.

as the peacetime borders were moved. This left Italy's land border largely undefended and this was particularly evident on the border with the newly formed communist state of Yugoslavia. Here many of the defences had been lost when part of the Venezia Giulia was ceded to Marshall Tito and most of the remainder were destroyed in accordance with the peace treaty which required a 20km (12 miles) wide demilitarized zone.

After the war, Italy aligned itself with the western powers and was one of the original signatories of the NATO alliance in 1949. With the heightened tension of the Cold War in the 1950s and 1960s there was a debate about how best to maintain Italian security and in particular the value of fortifications in the nuclear age. In the end it was decided that such defences did have a role to play. Along the border with Austria (a large part of which was occupied by Soviet forces immediately after the war) the structures of the original Vallo Alpino were used, but along the border with Yugoslavia the defences had to be built from scratch. Lacking any strong natural features it was decided to adopt a similar approach to that of the Germans in their strategic withdrawal up the Italian peninsula during the Second World War with the emphasis on small-scale field works* built in depth rather than large-scale permanent defences.

The new defences stretched from the Piz Lat mountain area to the mouth of the Natisone and as far back as the left bank of the Tagliamento River. Much of the work was financed by NATO through its Mutual Defence Aid Program. The mountain defences included some 200 permanent positions some of which were continuously manned by men of the so-called 'Arrest units' while others were simply maintained in a state of readiness. Included in these defences were emplaced tank turrets; the idea being taken from the German example which had been so successful in the defence of Italy in the latter stages of the Second World War. This expedient was used more extensively on the plains below where natural defensive features were largely absent. Here concrete pits were constructed to house unserviceable Sherman and M26 Pershing tanks (with their engines removed).[†‡] In peacetime the turrets were concealed in metal or wooden sheds, or in the mountains, trees were planted which would be cut down when the turret was needed to afford the crew a good field of fire.

A Sherman tank turret installed at Dignano, Italy. It was concealed by wooden shuttering, which would have been removed when the position was readied for action. The sign prohibits dumping! (C. Vermeulen)

M26 Pershing

During the early 1950s the American M47 was selected by the Italian Army to replace the obsolete M26 Pershing, which had until then formed the backbone of the post war Italian Tank Corps. The surplus Pershings were made available for use as fixed fortifications and were employed in a number of ways. Whole tanks with their engines removed were put in specially constructed concrete pits. These positions also included concrete shelters for the crew, munitions and a generator. Other turrets were removed from their hull and mounted on reinforced concrete emplacements. These also included accommodation for the crew and equipment, including a generator, and a facility for disposing of spent

---

*This term is used loosely because many of the defences were constructed from concrete, but were not on the scale of the original Vallo Alpino fortifications.
[†] Some sources state that M47 tank turrets were also used but it has not been possible to verify this.
[‡] Second World War vintage Fiat M15/42 tanks were also used. Plans had been drawn up by the Germans to use these turrets in the defence of Italy – *see* Chapter 3, Part 1. The engines and the other internal fittings were removed as was the main gun, replaced with a machine gun. C. Clerici, G. Muran and S. Poli, 'Le Fortificazioni di Frontiera Italiana de Secondo Dopoguerra', *Notizie Ai Soci – Gruppo di Studio Delle Fortificazioni Moderne* (Jan.–Feb. 1995), pp.13–22.

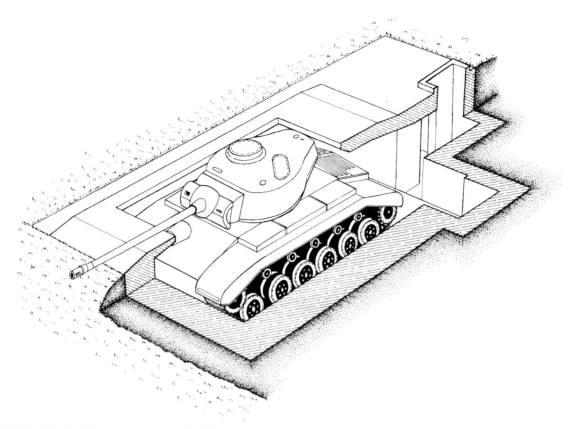

M26 Pershing hull-down in a concrete pit, Italy.

cartridges. The turrets retained their original optical equipment, electrical firing equipment and hydraulic traversing gear.[27]

These fortifications were mainly positioned to cover roads, motorways and bridges. In support of these positions were constructed command and observation posts for fire control, observation positions on higher ground to communicate details of enemy movements and dispositions and also armoured cupolas mounting machine guns to provide protection from infantry assault (generally one for each gun). These included German MG Panzernests left over after the war.[28]

Sherman Firefly

Along with the M26 Pershing, the Italian Army's obsolete Shermans were also replaced in the early 1950s. Again many of the tanks were used as fixed fortifications with a number of tanks positioned in concrete pits. Alternatively, the front of the hull and the engine deck were removed leaving just a square section of the superstructure mounting the turret, which was mounted on a concrete shelter. The turrets retained many of their original fittings and all the positions were fitted with CPRC/26 type radios and sometimes field telephones. Three Sherman Firefly turrets, along with three MG turrets, mounted on concrete shelters were installed near Dobbiaco, which had formed part of the Vallo Alpino.[29]

Sherman M4/M4A1

In a number of cases Sherman tank turrets were used but without their main and coaxial armament. Instead the MG42/59 machine gun was fitted (the NATO version of the German MG42).[30] The machine gun was mounted on a standard pedestal that had been

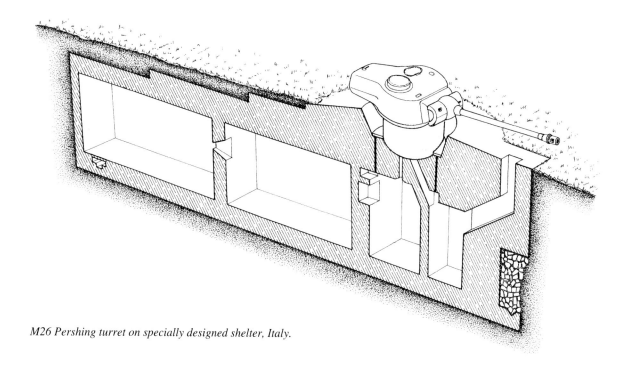

M26 Pershing turret on specially designed shelter, Italy.

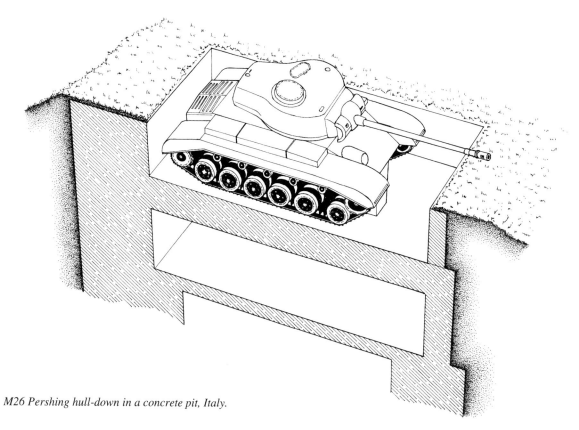

M26 Pershing hull-down in a concrete pit, Italy.

M26 Pershing

Turret statistics:
Armour (thickness/angle):

Gun mantlet	Front	Side	Rear	Roof
114mm	102mm/0°	76mm/0–8°	76mm/0–5°	12–25mm/90°

Weapon statistics:

Armament: 1 × 90 mm M3
                        1 × .30 cal (7.62mm) Browning M1919A4 coaxial
                        1 × .50 cal (12.7 mm) Browning M2 for anti-aircraft defence
Traverse: 360°
Elevation: +20° to −10°

Sherman Firefly

Turret statistics:
Armour (thickness/angle):

Gun mantlet	Front	Side	Rear	Roof
–	76.2–88.9mm	50.8mm	50.8mm	25.4mm

Weapon statistics:

Armament: 1 × 17 Pounder
                        1 × 0.30 Browning
Traverse: 360°

used in other bunkers of the Vallo Alpino built in the 1930s. The embrasure was slightly enlarged to improve the field of fire. Other openings were welded shut. A small part of the original hull was retained and this served as the base plate for the turret. Two hatches were cut in the front to allow the crew access. The tanks engine was removed and this meant that there was no power to heat the shelter and that the turret had to be traversed by hand. The lack of power and the cramped conditions were not considered a major handicap because the turrets were only intended to be used as holding positions before the Italian army could be fully mobilized. When not in use the turret was concealed with wooden shuttering.

Postscript

In 1986 plans were considered for replacing the older Sherman and Pershing turrets with more modern M60 and German Leopard Mk I turrets. However, this would have contravened the terms of the CFE Treaty that expressly stated that equipment over certain limits set in the agreement should be destroyed and not reused. The possibility of improving the turrets against NBC threats was also considered, but no further action was taken. With the demise of the Warsaw Pact the border defences were no longer of any use and from 1992 all the Italian fortifications, including the tank turrets, which were by this time obsolete, were gradually dismantled.[31]

THE NETHERLANDS

In the immediate aftermath of the Second World War, and before NATO was established, the countries of Western Europe faced the very real threat of a Soviet invasion. Emergency defence plans were quickly

Sherman M4/M4A1

Turret statistics:
Armour (thickness/angle):

Gun mantlet	Front	Side	Rear	Roof
–	76.2–88.9mm	50.8mm	50.8mm	25.4mm

Weapon statistics:
Armament: 1 × MG42/59 machine gun
Traverse: 360° (manual)

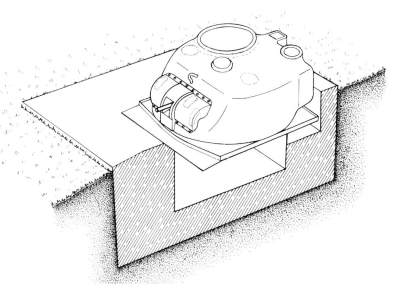

Sherman turret on a concrete shelter, Italy.

The main and coaxial armament of the Sherman were removed and replaced with an MG42/59. The other openings were welded shut. (C. Vermeulen)

A final view of the Sherman turret at Dignano that clearly shows the entrance and the section of tank body that formed the base of the structure. (C. Vermeulen)

drawn up by F/M Montgomery, as chairman of the permanent defence organization of the Western European Union,* with the River Rhine identified as the main defence line. All forces east of the river were to be evacuated in the event of war and were to be deployed along its length. This meant that the Netherlands occupied a crucial position in the defensive plan. However, it was recognized that Dutch forces at this time were too weak to make a material contribution to the defensive strength of the forces arrayed against the Soviet Union. The actions of the retreating German forces and the Allied bombing had left the Netherlands devastated and all the country's resources were invested in rebuilding the infrastructure and not the armed forces. At the same time the few military resources that were available were involved in the war of independence in Indonesia, which had been a Dutch colony before the war.

In spite of the parlous state of the Dutch armed forces, the General Staff, at the beginning of 1949, began to formulate a plan (Plan Leeuw or Lion) to counter the Soviet threat. This coincided with NATO's plan for defending the Rhine, but was also necessary because the old water line† was deemed to be too far west to enable an effective defence of the densely populated conurbations. Those forces that could be scraped together were deployed along the River IJssel, a branch of the Rhine and at the ends of the Afsluitdijk.‡ Before the war this had been heavily fortified and these defences were now modernized and new defences added, including for the first time emplaced tank turrets, which were necessary because all the original anti-tank shelters now mounted only machine guns.

After the war the victorious allies demobilized and left a large amount of equipment in Europe. The Canadians in particular, who liberated much of the Netherlands, left a number of tanks, mostly Rams and Shermans. Many of these were obsolete or were in a poor state of repair and because the Dutch army had neither the money, the expertise, nor the men to operate the tanks even if they were repaired it was decided to use them in a static role. At the eastern end of the Afsluitdijk (at Kornwerderzand) four Sherman Firefly turrets with 17-pounder main armament were employed and a further three emplaced at Den Oever. A number of tank turrets¶ were also installed to defend the IJsselbridges. Many of these had their main armament removed and replaced with machine guns.

This expedient was fine in the short term, but it was recognized that at least five divisions would be needed to defend a line running along the River IJssel. This was considered too expensive and a more cost effective solution was sought. In 1949 studies were begun into the possibility of making the IJssel river into an obstacle of strategic importance. This research led to the idea, eventually accepted in 1951, of using huge caisson-like barriers to dam the River Waal at Nijmegen and the River Rhine at Arnhem so diverting the water into the IJssel to form large inundations from 2–8km (1–5 miles) wide depending on the season. This was estimated to cost 100 million florins – a fraction of the cost of a standing army.

The barriers consisted of large floating steel constructions that could be manoeuvred into place when an attack by the Warsaw Pact was considered imminent and sunk in the river using stones or concrete. This could be achieved in a matter of hours and further shoring up work completed soon after. However, it took some days or even weeks (depending on the season) for sufficient water to amass and at that time it was calculated that the Soviets could reach the IJssel within days of the outbreak of war. As such it was imperative that these strategic points were defended from both air and ground attack. Therefore, each of the three locations§ was provided with perimeter defences that included numerous anti-aircraft defences but also emplaced tank turrets.

At Nijmegen, five Sherman Firefly tank turrets with their original 17-pounder main armament were installed along with a further twenty-nine Sherman turrets mounting machine guns. At Arnhem, twenty-one Sherman tank turrets were emplaced, all fitted with machine guns, and finally at Deventer, a further

*The precursor to NATO.
† The old water line had been established in the seventeenth century and was designed to protect the province of Holland.
‡ An artificial dike built in the 1930s that linked Friesland and Groningen with the Netherlands proper.
¶ Perhaps as many as twenty-five.
§ A further barrier was added on the River Ijssel, north of Deventer (Olst) so as to raise the water level sufficiently to ensure it flowed through the polders east of the river.

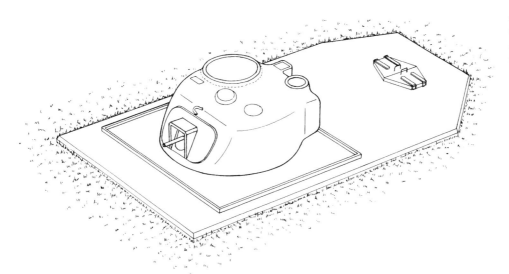

Sherman turret armed with an MG on a concrete shelter, The Netherlands.

six Sherman firefly turrets were employed along with twenty-three Ram turrets mounting machine guns.[32]

The tanks were installed by the *Speciale Werken von Rijkswaterstaat* (Special Works Service of the Department for the Maintenance of Dikes, Roads, Bridges and Canals), in close cooperation with the Ministry of War. Employees of the Department were also recruited to put the dams in place in times of danger and were given extra pay for doing so.[33]

After a certain amount of trial and error it was found that the best way of installing the turret was to move a tank into the prepared position and then remove the tracks and most of the road wheels.[*][34] The majority of the tank's fittings were removed save for the traversing mechanism and the periscopes.

The turrets tended to be positioned in a circle around the caissons with anti-tank and machine gun turrets supporting each other. Machine gun turrets were also used to give protection to the 40cm Bofors guns.

Ram

The machine gun turrets, by far the most numerous, were standard Ram (Cruiser Tank Mk II) or Sherman turrets, which had had their main armament removed and replaced with an MG. On the Sherman the original opening where the main gun had been located was enlarged to approximately 275mm (10in) to allow a small field of fire for the weapon. The

turrets mounted four different weapons: the water-cooled Vickers or Browning machine gun; the air-cooled Browning, or the light Bren machine gun. Each turret was fitted with a special gun carriage to mount the weapon.

Being concreted into position meant that the crew's emergency escape hatch in the hull floor was no longer usable so a new exit was provided in the rear above where the engine had once been.[†] The space left by the removal of the engine served as living quarters for the crew, but with no engine the turret had to be rotated by hand. The only other additions were a small heater and a telephone connection. Surprisingly no artificial ventilation was provided.

The positions were constructed on concrete rafts (supported where necessary by six concrete piles). The base was protected by 30cm- (12in) thick reinforced concrete walls and 3m (10ft) of earth ramparts. Where it was not possible to use earth ramparts, the walls were increased to 60cm (24in).[‡][35]

---

*An attempt to remove them all in trials led to the tank shifting on its mount and damaging the reinforcing rods.
†Exceptionally, where turrets were installed on a dike, a horizontal escape hatch was used.
‡This necessitated increasing the amount of raw materials thus: 58m³ (190ft³) of concrete; 3,175kg (6,959lb)of reinforcing rods and 1,010kg (2,226lb) of metal.

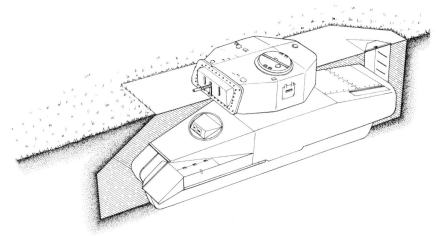

Ram armed with an MG encased in concrete, the Netherlands.

A Ram tank turret located near Olst on the road to Deventer. The main armament was removed and replaced with a machine gun. (Johan Meijer)

A Sherman turret that is till in situ *near Doesburg. The specially widened embrasure for the MG is clearly visible at the front. For safety reasons all the openings have been sealed. (Johan Meijer)*

Sherman Firefly

After the war the Netherlands acquired fifty-seven Sherman Fireflies and eleven of these were installed as fixed fortifications. The turrets retained their main and coaxial armament but, like the machine gun turrets, the original tank engine was removed. In this case the engine was replaced with a Coventry-Victor-Dornhoff 2.5Kw generator, which provided power for heat, light and ventilation – one vent in the turret and one in the hull. The turret still had to be rotated by hand, but generally the turret was only required to cover a narrow front and so power traverse was not essential. The concrete shelter was mounted on six piles and had 60cm (24in) thick walls to withstand the heavy recoil of the main armament.*

Staghound

The Dutch, in common with a number of nations, also used armoured car turrets for airfield protection. Here again the entire hull, stripped of the majority of its parts, was buried in the ground and encased in reinforced concrete.[36] Many of the turrets were exhumed in the 1980s, but several of these turrets still remain, although their future is in doubt.

---

*The turrets in the IJssellinie were heavily influenced by the experience gained in constructing the positions to protect the Afsluitdijk. The engine of the tank in the original positions was replaced by a generator and a battery pack, which drove the traverse gear. Unfortunately the heat generated by the generator caused the battery to emit noxious fumes and may have contributed to an incident in 1959 when the crew of a turret was killed when firing the gun.

Ram

Turret statistics:
Armour (thickness/angle):

Gun mantlet	Front	Side	Rear	Roof
–	76mm	76mm	64mm	25mm

Weapon statistics:
Armament: 1 × MG (various)
             Traverse: 360°

Bunker statistics:

Earth excavation	Concrete	Formed steel	Round steel
–	35m³	1,010kg	1,721kg

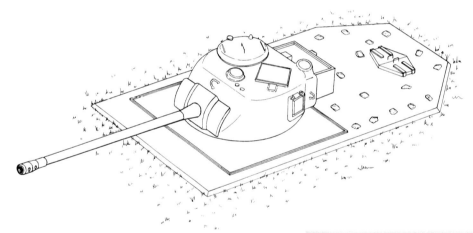

Sherman Firefly mounted on a concrete shelter, The Netherlands.

Sherman Firefly

Turret statistics:
See Italy above

Bunker statistics:

Earth excavation	Concrete	Formed steel	Round steel
–	61m³	1,000kg	3,716kg

A Sherman Firefly turret, which was installed near Olst on the road to Deventer. The access hatch to the crew's compartment is visible at the rear. (Johan Meijer)

Staghound

Turret statistics:
Armour (thickness/angle):

Gun mantlet	Front	Side	Rear	Roof
44mm	25mm	32mm	32mm	13mm

Weapon statistics:
Armament: 1 × 37mm M6
                1 × 0.30 Browning
Traverse: 360°
Elevation: +40° to −7°

Postscript

With the partial restoration of the German Army, NATO changed its strategy in Western Europe to that of a 'forward defence strategy' with the River Weser and River Elbe providing defensive positions for NATO forces. As a result, the IJssellinie became largely redundant and in 1964 it was proposed that the line be dismantled. By 1968 most of the work had been completed and today relatively few of the tank turrets remain:[37]

Nijmegen: 3 MG tank turrets.
                1 AT turret.
Arnhem: 6 MG turrets.
Olst: 4 MG turrets.
                1 AT turret (with a fake barrel).

NORWAY

At the end of the Second World War Norway inherited approximately thirty-two *Panzer* III (5cm and 7.5cm) and *Sturmgeschütz* III Ausf G tanks and assault guns. These were left behind when the German forces, which had occupied the country, departed after the cessation of hostilities. These were given the designation KW-III and were in use from the end of the war until 1960. When they were finally withdrawn from service a number of the turrets were mounted on concrete emplacements. At least one of the *Panzer* III turrets was used to protect Fornebu airport, Oslo (now closed and redeveloped).[38]

Under the Marshall Aid plan, Norway also purchased 124 American M24 Chaffee light tanks along with a number of M8 Greyhound and M20 armoured cars. To prolong their usefulness, around seventy Chaffees were given a mid-life update which saw them fitted with a new engine and a 90mm main gun. The new tank was designated the NM-116 and was not withdrawn from service until 1970. A number of the unmodified turrets (together seemingly with turrets from the M8 armoured cars) were used as fixed fortifications and were manned by Home Guard units.

SOVIET UNION

In the years after the ending of the Second World War the Soviet Union's military thinking was concerned more with offensive rather than defensive strategies. However, with the emergence of China as a major power and the growing tension between the two great communist states the emphasis changed. The border between the two countries stretched for some 7,000km and thinking at the time suggested that one division could defend a 10km-(6-mile) front. The mathematics of this was frightening for the Kremlin. Even a more conservative assumption that one division could hold a 15km-(9-mile) front still meant that the Soviets would need to maintain an army of more than 450 divisions. The solution to this problem was a return to the use of fortifications, including concrete bunkers mounting tank turrets.

The tradition of using turrets in this fashion had

been established in the 1930s with the construction of the Stalin and Molotov Lines and this idea was revisited and was helped in no small part by the military's policy of mothballing rather than scrapping old tanks.* In the 1970s and 1980s a large number of *Tankovaya Ognievaya Totshka* (TOT), or tank firing posts, were constructed. Obsolete T34/85, IS2, IS3, IS4, T10, T44, T54 and T55 tanks with their engines removed were buried in the ground so that only their turrets were visible. The hull was then concreted in place and was linked to a shelter at the rear with access to the tank via the tank's emergency hatch. Alternatively, turrets were mounted on specially designed bunkers which included special compartments for the crew, an ammunition store capable of storing several hundred shells, a diesel engine and air filters.† These tended to be fitted with turrets from T54 and T55 turrets.[39]

The turrets mounted on both these positions were largely unmodified save for the addition of a radar fire control system and appliqué armour. They were generally located about 3km (1½ miles) back from the border, and because it was impossible to install these positions all along the frontier, they were concentrated at strategically important locations with particular concentrations in front of major Far-Eastern cities.[40] They were built so that they were mutually supporting and were reinforced with other defences including concrete bunkers and even turrets from old warships. One Soviet city that was protected with emplaced tank turrets was Vladivostock. In the 1970s, in the Vladivostock Defensive Region, the

One of the reinforced concrete bunkers on the border with China that were built alongside the emplaced turrets to deter a possible attack by Chinese forces. (Sergei Netrebenko)

Soviet Navy installed turrets near the Vladivostock–Khabarovsk highway with nine IS2 turrets emplaced near the village of Uglovoje. Turrets from T34-85, IS2 and IS3 tanks were also used to protect the Kuril Islands near Vladivostock.[41]

It is unclear how many of these TOTs were constructed along the Chinese border, but it certainly ran to hundreds maybe even thousands. What is clear is that they provided a potent deterrent with one commentator noting that, 'The whole forms an excellent firing point, with powerful (often 122mm) tank gun, two machine guns, an excellent optical system, reliable defence against a nuclear blast and an underground cable connecting it with the command post. With these resources, two or three soldiers can defend several kilometres of frontier.'[42]

T44

The turret was based on that of the T34/85, but dispensed with the collar at the base. The first prototype was completed in 1944 and some 150–200 were completed before production ceased in 1947 in favour of the more modern T54.[43] A number of turrets were later released for use in a static role along the border with China.

An early T54 turret mounted on a concrete shelter protecting a section of the border with Communist China. (Sergei Netrebenko)

---

*The Soviet military believed that in wartime an old tank was better than no tank at all!

† It is possible that these shelters were identical to those used in the Karelian UR – *see below*.

IS2

The first prototype was produced in 1943. The turret was very small and restricted the amount of ammunition that could be stowed and slowed the rate of fire.[44] In spite of these shortcomings a number of IS2s were retained and were later buried in the ground along the Chinese border, sometimes strengthened with a concrete surround.

IS3

A prototype was completed in November 1944. It differed from the IS2 in that it had a hemispherical turret. Before the end of the war in Europe 350 IS3s were produced.[45] With the development of more

A T44 turret mounted on a concrete shelter with octagonal base plate. This example was installed on the Soviet border with China. The barrel appears to have been sealed. (Sergei Netrebenko)

An IS2 turret emplaced on the Soviet border with China. The position was protected by reinforced concrete, which can be seen in the foreground. (Sergei Netrebenko)

A rear view of the same IS2 turret which shows that the whole tank was simply buried in the ground and surrounded by reinforced concrete. In the left foreground the engine louvres and barrel rest are visible. The rear machine gun appears to have been removed and the gap sealed with a steel plug. The turrets cast number is clearly visible on the rear bustle. (Sergei Netrebenko)

T44				
Turret statistics: Armour (thickness/angle):				
Gun mantlet	Front	Side	Rear	Roof
–	120mm	75mm	75mm	20mm

Weapon statistics:
Armament: 1 × 85mm D-5T
                      1 × DTM machine gun
Traverse: 360°

		IS2			

Turret statistics:
Armour (thickness/angle):

Gun mantlet	Front	Side	Rear	Roof
–	160mm	100mm	90mm	30mm

Weapon statistics:
Armament: 1 × 122mm D-25T
2 × 7.62mm DT machine gun
Traverse: 360°
Elevation: +20° to −3°

modern tanks a number of the turrets were mounted on concrete shelters, but in addition a unique position for the IS3 was developed and tested at the Scientific Research Institute of Engineering Technical Equipment of the Red Army near Moscow.* An hydraulic system allowed the tank turret to be raised above the ground to fire and then lowered out of sight when not in use.[46]

T10

The IS10 as it was originally known was the last of the IS series of tanks and after Stalin's death it was renamed the T10. Production began in the mid-1950s and it was finally taken out of service in 1993.

An IS3 tank turret installed on the border with China. Interestingly the concrete on this example has been shaped to afford the turret more protection. The small gap may have been cut to allow rain and snow melt to drain away. (E. Hitriak)

However, in spite of this lengthy period of time it was not considered particularly satisfactory, partly because of the slow rate of fire, which was the result of using two-part ammunition. The turret was, though, very well protected and the main armament was capable of penetrating 450mm of armour at a range of 2,000m, which meant that it was ideally suited for use as a static fortification.

Finland

Though far less menacing, a similar solution to that adopted along the border with China was used along the border with Finland. In the Karelian *ukreplinnyje rajony* (UR) a specially designed bunker was built to mount the IS4 turret. These were constructed to the rear of the front line (1–3km (½–1½ miles) back) and tended to be built near main roads so as to be able to cover the likeliest routes of attack.

The position mounting the turret was essentially divided into two distinct sections. The main fighting compartment and an auxiliary section. The main entrance at the rear led into a dog-leg corridor which bisected the auxiliary section. On the left, and the larger of the two rooms, was the quarters for an infantry section, whose job it was to protect the turret from infantry attack. Opposite was a store for their weapons, uniforms and equipment. At the end of the corridor was the main fighting compartment below the turret. This could accommodate fifty rounds of ammunition stored in racks secured to the walls. A

*Later called the Special Test Site for URs.

IS3

Turret statistics:
Armour (thickness/angle):

Gun mantlet	Front	Side	Rear	Roof
110mm–220mm				20mm

Weapon statistics:
Armament: 1 × 122mm D-25T
                         1 × 7.62mm DT machine gun
Traverse: 360°
Elevation: +19° to −2°

A Soviet T10 Tankovaya Ognievaya Totshka (TOT) located on the border with China. The tank, minus its running gear, was buried in the ground and some thin metal sheeting applied. The photograph shows the crew on exercise in the 1970s.
(S. Zaloga)

T10

Turret statistics:
Armour (thickness/angle):

Gun mantlet	Front	Side	Rear	Roof
100mm–250mm				–

Weapon statistics:
Armament: 1 × 122mm D-25TA
                         1 × 12.7mm DShKM machine gun
Traverse: 360°

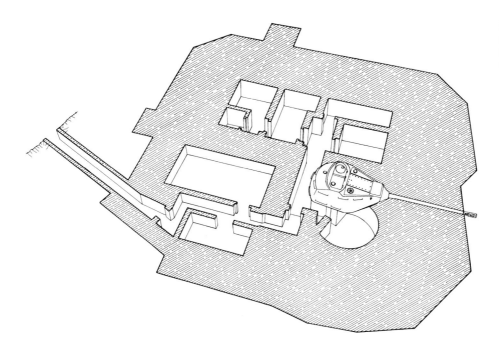

Soviet IS4 turret mounted on a concrete bunker in the Karelian UR.

metal ladder led from here, through an armoured ceiling, to the turret. Below the fighting compartment was a chamber to take spent shell cases.

From the fighting compartment the corridor continued to a hallway, which served as a home for the batteries that provided power to the turret systems. Leading off this hallway were three doors leading to the ammunition store, the crew's quarters and a machine room. The ammunition store, which was located next to the turret, could accommodate one hundred rounds on metal racks. Next to this was the crew's quarters, which was fitted with two beds, a table, chairs and a sink as well as sanitary facilities. Adjacent to this was a room housing a small diesel engine, which powered an AC generator, and a fuel tank. The room was also home to a small stove. A door led from here to another room housing the main ventilation and air filtration systems that protected the crew from NBC attack. A separate compartment in this room housed the various filters. Flues led from here to the outside and were fitted in such a way that they did not appear above the surface.

The walls of the main shelter were 4m thick and the ceiling 2m thick and were impervious to all but the heaviest shells. However, this contrasted with the auxiliary section where the walls and ceiling were noticeably thinner; the outer wall was only 2m thick and the ceiling 1.5m. The difference in the thickness can be attributed to the positioning of the auxiliary rooms at the rear of the shelter which was less exposed to armour piercing shells that would have a flat trajectory and which were considered to pose the greatest threat to the operation of the position. Moreover, when the shelter was under attack the rooms would be unoccupied because the infantry section would most likely be deployed outside.

Separate to the TOT was a small ammunition store. This was located some 50m from the main position. The main entrance led into a small pressure chamber. Through a second door was the main store where it was possible to store 150–300 rounds for the main armament. In addition to the main entrance there was an unsealed loading hatch (which seemed to undermine the effectiveness of the pressure chamber!).

Because the positions were static, secrecy concerning the construction of the bunker and camouflage of the turret was imperative. The structures were built quickly and were described as civilian construction projects to avoid any awkward questions. When complete the turrets, including the barrel, which rested on a metal support, were covered with metal sheeting and the whole was covered with earth. Entrances to both the TOT and ammunition bunker were similarly concealed. The whole position was surrounded with barbed wire and a small wooden cabin on concrete foundation was built and was manned by security personnel, although it could be that these guards were not actually aware of what they were protecting.

Training for the crew was also conducted in such a way that the position of the turrets was not compromised. A single turret which was identical to all the other positions, and which could double as a fully functioning defensive position, was used to train the crews. On mobilization the crew was given the number of their position and were transported to the location. It was only on arrival that the crew was provided with the information necessary to operate the turret effectively – maps, panoramas with the ranges of key features and so on.

Inspite of all these precautions the TOTs could not escape the fact that unlike a standard tank they lacked mobility and as a consequence they were vulnerable to enemy fire once their position had been pinpointed. But these positions also suffered from other shortcomings despite the fact that they were arguably the most advanced in the history of this type of fortification.

The entrance to the position was protected by a series of doors and gates that were not particularly strong. The entranceway also lacked a machine gun embrasure to protect against infantry assault. There was also no provision for the decontamination of uniforms and equipment following an NBC attack. Inside the shelter there were no blast doors and the internal walls were very thin especially for the ammunition room (40mm) and under the turret (25mm). This exposed the crew to a far greater danger if there was an internal explosion, and to make matters worse there was no emergency exit.[47]

IS4

The IS4 was a further development of the IS2, but it was not a popular tank not least because it was extremely heavy by comparison with its siblings and only 250 were built.[48] However, the thick armour of the IS4 meant that it was ideally suited to the role of fixed fortification and as late as 1984 – forty years after it was developed – a manual was issued with instructions for emplacing the turret.

The IS4 turrets used in the Karelian UR were specially designed for the purpose. Hatches on the roof were dispensed with meaning that access to the turret could only be gained from the bunker. No additional protection was provided against shaped charges because the small target was considered the best protection against such a threat.

An IS4 turret located on the Sino-Soviet border and which protected the vast open plains of the region. The tank has been buried in the ground so that just its turret is visible. Reinforced concrete has been used to provide extra protection. (Sergei Netrebenko)

One of the prototype Gorchak turrets armed with a 30mm grenade launcher, machine gun and a rocket launcher. (W. Parad courtesy of M. Sledzinski)

		IS4		

Turret statistics:
Armour (thickness/angle):

Gun mantlet	Front	Side	Rear	Roof
–	250mm	170mm	–	–

Weapon statistics:

Armament:	1 × 122mm D-25T 1943
	1 × 12.7mm DShKM machine gun
Traverse:	360°
Maximum range:	15,000m
Effective range:	1,100m

Postscript

It is not known exactly how many TOTs were installed in the Karelian UR* but they were withdrawn from service in the late 1990s and the turrets removed. The turrets on the Chinese border have also seemingly been abandoned although many are still in place. However, the idea has not been completely dismissed with because as recently as 1999, Russia introduced the *Gorchak*. This is not strictly speaking a tank turret but it is a continuation of the concept. A prefabricated shelter is buried in the ground and is fitted with a 30mm grenade launcher, a 7.62 or 12.7mm machine gun and a 9M113 *Konkurs* rocket launcher. It is manufactured by the same company that makes the armament modules for the BMP-1 and 2, BTR-70 and eighty armoured car turrets. The *Gorchak* will probably remain as a prototype.[49]

SWEDEN

Despite a long-standing tradition of neutrality dating back to 1814, Sweden was always prepared for war. In 1936, with the storm clouds gathering over Europe, Sweden embarked on a rearmament programme that saw an increase in the numbers of aircraft and anti-aircraft guns and later, the commencement of work on a series of coastal defences to protect her exposed southern flank.† The work on the fortifications was

---

*It is known that at least five of these structures were built on the border with Finland. The location of any other turrets remains a secret.
† Sweden already had a series of coastal defence batteries that had been built since the turn of the century. The weapons were of varying calibres and vintages and were mounted on barbette mounts or in armoured turrets.

carried out in four phases between July 1939 and October 1940 and saw the construction of more than 1,000 bunkers and pillboxes, or 'värn', in what later became known as the Per Albin Line.* Twelve basic designs were developed with most of them designed to accommodate a machine gun, although some were designed for the Bofors 37mm anti-tank gun.

Sweden's preparation for war also included the development of a strong armoured force. In the years leading up to the Second World War the Swedish army showed a great interest in a number of tanks that were designed and manufactured in Czechoslovakia and an order was placed for ninety TNHP-S tanks which were to be delivered in the summer of 1940. However, the German authorities, impressed by the performance of the Czech tanks, cancelled the order and took the tanks themselves. Unperturbed, the Swedes entered into negotiations to manufacture the tank under licence and in December 1940 the Germans agreed. The Czech TNHP-S, now given the designation *Stridsvagn* m/41 SI, was to be manufactured by Scania-Vabis. In June 1941 the Swedish army placed an order for 116 of these tanks. The first tank rolled off the assembly line in December 1942 and the last in August 1943. For all intents and purposes, the Strv m/41 was the same as the Panzer 38(t). However, the tank was fitted with either the 37mm Bofors m/38 L/37 or L40 anti-tank tank gun and two 8mm m/39 machine guns – one in the turret and one in the front glacis plate.

Yet, even before the first of the Strv m/41 SI tanks was delivered, it was clear that the original design was dated by comparison with tanks now being used

The Swedish Strv m/41 was based on the Panzer 38(t). When it was taken out of service a number were used for airfield defence as here. (Svein Wiiger Olsen)

A Swedish Strv m/42 tank turret. It is fitted with a 75mm main gun and twin coaxially mounted machine guns. The turret dated from the Second World War and when used for coastal defence was upgraded with a new electro-optical fire control system. (SPHF)

by the Allied and Axis forces. Unable to design and develop a new tank and unable to buy more modern tanks from the main belligerents, the Swedes decided to order an improved version of the original Czech model. The Strv m/41 SII, as it was christened, had thicker armour, a more powerful engine and a larger fuel tank, but mounted the same weaponry. In June 1942, 122 of these tanks were ordered, although only 104 were delivered between October 1943 and March 1944 when production ceased.[†]

This powerful armoured force, together with the extensive fortifications programme and a flexible policy of political realism meant that, despite a number of alarms (including the Russo-Finnish Winter War and the German invasion of Norway which threatened to embroil Sweden in the conflict), Sweden managed to protect her neutral status. With the war over the government in Stockholm undertook a defence review, which led to the introduction of new more modern tanks and a decision to renovate the Per Albin Line, which now became part of the Swedish coastal defence system.

*Named after the Swedish prime minister at the time (although it was later known as the Scandia Line).
[†] The other eighteen chassis were used for a more powerfully armed self-propelled gun.

With the introduction of newer tanks in the mid 1950s it was decided to gradually phase out the older models including the Strv m/41 (but also the m/38, m/39 and m/40), which totalled some 400 tanks. It was suggested that a number* of the surplus turrets should be used as fortifications along the coast, but their weak armour and poor armament meant they were not ideally suited to this role, so instead it was decided to position them around strategic installations, particularly airfields.† However, the potential for using tank turrets for coastal defence was not dismissed. One of the newer tanks to replace the Strv m/41 was the Strv m/42 which entered service in 1944. It was armed with a 75mm gun and three 8mm machines – two mounted coaxially. In total, 282 tanks of this design were delivered to the Swedish army. It was eventually taken out of service in 1957 but a number of the turrets were retained for use as fixed fortifications and because they mounted the more powerful 75mm gun they were deemed suitable for coastal defence. The turrets were used largely unaltered save for the addition of a new electro-optical fire-control system and remained in use until 1980.[50]

The *Stridsvagn 74*‡ that replaced the Strv m/42 (and the Strv m/41 that was finally withdrawn from service in 1960) entered service in 1958. It was armed with a 75mm main gun and two 8mm M/39 machine guns. Some 225 of these tanks were produced but after more than a decade with the Swedish Army they were withdrawn from front-line units and from the early 1970s the turrets were used for fortifications.¶ Approximately half of the turrets were used to reinforce the southern coastal defences with some being mounted on old bunkers to defend harbours and others on new purpose-built shelters. The remainder were used to protect the east coast (where there was a perceived Soviet threat) and to protect other strategically important sights including a nuclear plant.[51]

At the same time as the Strv 74 entered service, the Swedish Army also took delivery of its first batch of Centurion tanks – the Strv 81 – armed with a 20-pounder (83.4mm) main armament. In the mid-1960s these were modified to mount the more powerful 10.5cm gun and in the process were redesignated the Strv 102. Not all the Centurions were seemingly upgunned and a number of the turrets that retained the

The Stridsvagn 74 turret is gently removed from its mount prior to being scrapped. The turret's protective covers can be seen at either side. The bunker at Simrishamn was originally built in the 1940s but was renovated in the 1960s. (Leif Högberg)

20-pounder gun were used as fixed fortifications. The turrets were either permanently emplaced or were placed in store and in times of emergency were carried on trailers to be mounted on prepared concrete bases.[52]

Postscript

The Swedish government went to great lengths to ensure that these defences remained secret and up until the 1990s it was forbidden to take photographs of the structures. They also tended to be covered by camouflage (sometimes false buildings) or by special covers. However, it is known that as late as 1985, in Scania, the southernmost province of Sweden, (between Helsinborg and Kristianstad) there were 110 bunkers mounting 75mm turrets and thirty-five mounting 37mm guns.[53] In the 1990s the Swedish Government decided to remove the country's coastal defences, including the emplaced tank turrets. The turrets were removed and sent for scrap and the

---

*It is believed that the number of Strv 41 turrets installed is roughly equivalent to those manufactured under licence.
† It is interesting to note that when the Swedish Tank Museum at Axvall wanted to restore their Strv m/41 tank they had to negotiate with the military authorities to get a turret from one of their fixed positions.
‡ The Strv 74 was essentially a rebuilt Strv m/42 with a new turret.
¶ Budget restrictions meant that there was only enough money to install approximately fifteen tank turrets in any one year and as such it is believed that not all the turrets were used.

bunkers demolished or filled with concrete. A number of the turrets are still in place, their stay of execution facilitated by their remote location, which made it too difficult to reach by either crane or boat to remove them. It is hoped that some or all of these will be saved to form part of museums devoted to the study of the Swedish defences.

SWITZERLAND

Switzerland is the world's oldest democracy and has had a long tradition of neutrality. But this peace-loving nation has always been prepared to defend her borders with force if necessary. Initially the fortifications were concentrated around the capitals of the respective cantons, which were independent states at that time, but at the end of the nineteenth century, following the creation of the new state of Italy and the Franco-Prussian war, the focus changed to national defence. Work on the fortifications was started but was limited in scope to the Gotthard Pass and at St Maurice because of the huge expense. Work on other defences was undertaken prior to and during the First World War but these positions tended to be much less sophisticated. After the war economic constraints meant there was no money for new fortifications with only sufficient funds available to maintain the current works.[54]

This situation changed in the 1930s when Switzerland's neutrality was threatened with the growth of

fascism in Italy on her southern border and the election of Hitler's Nazi party in Germany. The situation worsened with the *Anschluss* of 1938 when her near neighbour Austria was absorbed into the Third Reich. Sandwiched between these two political heavyweights, and with significant German- and Italian-speaking communities, Switzerland was in a delicate situation. The government's solution was to construct a series of fortifications. These stretched along her borders, but also included a number of fortresses in what was known as the National Redoubt. The defences consisted of bunkers for machine guns or anti-tank guns and larger forts that mounted a variety of artillery pieces.

After the outbreak of the Second World War, efforts to complete the fortifications were redoubled and included the installation of a number of *Panzer Drehtürme* mounting the 10.5cm 1939 L52 gun. For the time, this was a very modern weapon, with an effective range of 19km (12 miles). The turrets were generally installed in artillery forts together with a number of 7.5cm cannons and 4.7cm anti-tank guns. The turrets were often cleverly disguised; the three turrets at Fort Magletsch, for example, were disguised as small Alpine chalets.

The 10.5cm gun was produced in Switzerland at the Maschinenfabrik Oerlikon in Zurich, although it was designed by the Schneider company of France. The turret was also manufactured in Switzerland, but much of the armour plate was produced in Germany

Table 2 10.5cm *Panzer Drehtürme*

Location	Quantity	Construction period
Fortress Gotthard:		
Fort Foppa Grande	1 Pz T	1939–1940/41
Fort Fuchsegg	4 Pz T	1941–1942/43
Fort Guetsch	3 Pz T	1941–(1942)
Fort San Carlo	2 Pz T	1939–1940/41
Fortress St. Maurice:		
Fort Dailly	2 Pz T	1939–(1940)
Fortress Sargans:		
Fort Furggels	4 Pz T	11/39–06/41
Fort Kastels	3 Pz T	09/39–07/41
Fort Magletsch	3 Pz T	10/39–08/40

One of the Panzer Drehtürme mounting a 10.5 cm gun installed around Sargans in north-east Switzerland. (C. Vermeulen)

and supplies became increasingly erratic, especially following the outbreak of war. In spite of this production work was completed and in the period between the outbreak of the war and 1943, 22 *Panzer Drehtürme* were installed – ten in Fortress Sargans; ten in Fortress Gotthard; and two in Fortress St. Maurice.[55]

In 1995 the Swiss Army decided to decommission many of its World War II era fortifications, which were found to be increasingly costly to maintain. This included the removal of the 10.5cm turrets.*

Centurion

In 1955 the Swiss government agreed to purchase one hundred Mk 5 Centurion tanks from Vickers Ltd of the United Kingdom. These were delivered in the course of the next two years and were given the designation *Panzer* 55. In 1957 a further one hundred Centurions, this time Mk 7s, were procured and given the designation *Panzer* 57. A reorganization of the Swiss armed forces in 1961 identified the need for more tanks and a further one hundred Centurions were bought from South Africa. At the same time a programme was introduced to up-gun half of the Centurions with the L7 105mm gun. These tanks were given the new designation *Panzer* 55/60 or *Panzer* 57/60. This programme was subsequently extended to include all the Centurions so that by 1979 all the tanks had one of these designations depending on which model they were.[56] These formed the

backbone of the small Swiss armoured force until 1986 when they were replaced by the more advanced German Leopard 2. The Centurion tank turrets were not scrapped, however, but were used as fixed fortifications.

Somewhat unusually the turrets were not simply mounted on a concrete bunker but were recessed inside a concrete casemate with a large embrasure. This protected the turret roof from guided munitions specifically designed to strike at the thinner turret top armour. As well as the fighting compartment the casemate also had rooms for the crew, storage of ammunition and for a generator that powered all the systems.

A number of improvements were made to the turret, which by the mid-1980s was beginning to show its age. Additional armour was applied to the front of the turret and a Warmtebild-Zielgerät 90 thermal imager was also fitted which enabled the crew to identify and engage targets at night.

As with so many of these turrets it suffered from a number of shortcomings. While the bunker walls provided added protection they also prevented the turret from revolving a full 360 degrees. Moreover, although presenting a small target, a direct hit or a ricochet off one of the embrasure walls, which tended to funnel enemy fire, could have a devastating effect. Finally, the successful operation of the turret was also hampered by the effects of dust and smoke generated by exhaust from the gun and which could obscure the crew's view. To make matters worse the cost of building and maintaining the turrets in these concrete shelters also proved prohibitive and only twenty-seven were installed, with a further four built at a special centre to train the crews. Because of the small number of turrets installed this facility was rarely used and proved to be an expensive white elephant. To cap it all, it now seems that the turrets, as with so many of their fortifications, have been withdrawn from service.[57]

Staghound

In addition to the Centurion turrets, the Swiss also used turrets from Staghound armoured cars as

---

*With the exception of those turrets that form part of museums all these turrets will be, or have been removed.

A Swiss Centurion tank turret mounted in a concrete embrasure. Clearly visible is the additional frontal armour. To the side is a recess in the concrete wall to accommodate the gun barrel when the turret was not in use.

One of the Staghound armoured car turrets installed in experimental positions near Dailly. The 37mm main gun was replaced by water-cooled machine gun. Additional camouflage has been added to the turret to help it blend in with its surroundings. (C. Vermeulen)

Centurion
Turret statistics: *See* Austria above

Staghound
Turret statistics: *See* The Netherlands above

improvised fixed fortifications. The Staghound was designed by the Americans in 1942 for supply to the British. However, by the end of the war the 37mm main gun was obsolete and the Staghound was withdrawn from service. After the war the Swiss Army bought a number of these surplus armoured cars and installed the turrets on prefabricated concrete stands. The original armament was removed and replaced with a water-cooled MG11 machine gun. The silhouette of the turret was disguised with exterior cladding that resembled a rock and ensured that the turret blended in with the landscape. The concept was not considered to be a great success, however, and only a few were used in this way; three turrets are confirmed as being installed in experimental positions around Dailly (St Maurice).[58]

SYRIA

In common with her powerful neighbour, Israel, Syria also used dug-in tank tanks as a form of defence. Of

the 1,000 or so tanks designated as being in store, a number were actually being used in static defence positions. It is assumed that these were older T54/55 and T62 tanks rather than the more modern T72s in service.[59]

UNITED KINGDOM

After the Second World War the British Army sought to procure a new armoured car. The competition was won by Daimler, which offered the Ferret scout car. More than 4,000 of these were produced between 1952 and 1971 and later versions were fitted with a turret. When the Ferret was eventually withdrawn from service the turrets were used as improvised fortifications to protect military airfields. The turret was fitted to an armoured base that was large enough to accommodate a single crew member who would operate the 7.62mm GPMG.[60] The turret was fitted with spaced armour to provide added protection.

A Ferret armoured car turret used for airfield security. Noteworthy are the lifting lugs on the top of the base, the canted turret ring and the spaced armour on the turret side. (Bernard Lowry)

UNITED STATES

Following the end of hostilities in Europe the American military began to consider post-war security. One option considered was the use of tank turrets mounted on concrete emplacements to provide the nucleus for strong points. In particular their use was considered for the landward defence of harbours and for beach defence.

At that time the Chief of Ordnance noted that some 500 75mm M4 turrets were available at the Baldwin Locomotive Works, Philadelphia for use in this way. It was recommended that they be released for the defence of overseas bases, however, the need for space at the Locomotive Works was pressing and it seems that the turrets were scrapped.[61] Another memorandum at that time recommended the retention of 1,000 M4 turrets, 'in view of the projected need for weapons of this type in preparation of satisfactory post war defense of overseas bases'.[62] However, it seems that the idea did not progress beyond the planning stage.

5 Conclusion

In the political turmoil that overshadowed the later years of the interwar period the nations of continental Europe, almost without exception, feared the very real possibility of another war. This unease manifested itself in the construction of a series of fortifications the like of which Europe had never seen before and would never see again.

Many of these defences were huge in scale with fighting positions served by a subterranean network of tunnels, often with light railways, linking ammunition stores, living and sleeping quarters and even recreation facilities. Alongside these massive concrete structures were smaller positions that included for the first time emplaced tank turrets that melded two arms of the military that were seemingly diametrically opposed: tanks and fortifications.

Tanks, the natural descendant of the cavalry, were designed for speed and mobility. They were designed to provide the armoured fist, the rapier blow. By contrast, fortifications were designed as a shield. They were built to deter the enemy, or if that failed, to slow them sufficiently to enable the main body of the army to be mobilized to meet the threat. Yet despite this apparent dichotomy, emplaced tank turrets provided a potent combination, just as in medieval times the sword and the shield worked in perfect harmony. However, in the early stages of the war the power of this amalgam was not truly realized. Many of the turrets installed by Belgium and France were outflanked as the German *blitzkrieg* bypassed pockets of resistance and thrust deep into the enemy rear, leaving the infantry to mop up.

Nevertheless, the potential of this type of fortification was recognized by the Germans and as the battles of conquest slowly turned into a battle for survival the idea was widely adopted with emplaced turrets used in all theatres of the European campaign. The success of these defences in protecting Hitler's 'Fortress Europe' were somewhat mixed not least because of the fact that the turrets were often poorly armed. The one notable exception was the Panther turret, which took a terrible toll on Allied tanks in Italy and persuaded the high command to avoid this type of defence wherever possible.

With the war over there were vast quantities of surplus tanks available and this, together with the straitened financial circumstances that many governments found themselves in, persuaded a number of countries to adopt the idea as a cost effective way of protecting their borders, airfields and other strategically important installations. Few turrets saw action in this period, but they provided a powerful deterrent and helped ensure that in Europe at least, the Cold War did not degenerate into open conflict.

As the years passed and the communist threat disappeared, so a new security threat emerged: terrorism. This menace could not be countered with fixed fortifications nor indeed with conventional forces full stop. As a consequence, and as countries sought to realize the 'peace dividend', these defences were, and are being, dismantled or scrapped. Almost without exception the turrets have been removed and shelters filled with concrete or demolished. This fate is also true of many of the original turrets, as the demands of modern life gradually see such fortifications ripped out to make way for new developments. Progress cannot be denied, but there has to be a balance and it is to be hoped that some of these fortifications can be saved for future generations. If not, this book will hopefully go some way towards preserving the memory of this oft overlooked but nevertheless interesting arm of modern fortifications.

Source Notes

Introduction

[1] *Denkschrift: uber die russische: Landbefestigung,* published by the German army in 1942.
[2] P. Chamberlain, H. Doyle and T. Jentz, *Encyclopaedia of German Tanks of World War Two,* (Arms and Armour Press, London, 1978).

Chapter 1

[1] Q. Hughes, 'Some Thoughts on the Rotating Gun Platform', *Fort,* Vol. 19 (1991), pp.59–72.
[2] A. Lecomte, 'The Séré de Rivière Fortifications 1873–1914', *Fort,* Vol. 17 (1989), pp.43–56.
[3] H. Jäger, 'The Model Fort of Kaiser Wilhelm II in the Sanssouci Park', *Fort,* Vol. 22 (1994), pp.39–56.
[4] W. Lacoste, *'Die Festung Neubreisach und die Rheinbrückenköpfe im System der deutschen Oberrheinbefestigungen 1871-1916', DAWA Nachrichten,* Sonderheft 29 (1997), pp.37–40
[5] D. Crow and R. Icks, *Encyclopedia of Armoured Cars and Half Tracks (*Barrie and Jenkins Ltd, London, 1976), p.61.

Chapter 2

[1] E. Hitriak, e-mail to author dated 8 June 2004.
[2] S. Zaloga, 'Tank Archeology in Poland', *Journal of Military Ordnance* (March 1999), pp.26–28.
[3] E. Coenen and F. Vernier, *La Position Fortifiee De Liege, Tome 2, Les Abris de la PFL 1* (De Krijger, Erpe), p.41.
[4] J-Y. Mary and A. Hohnadel, *Hommes et Ouvrages de la Ligne Maginot, Tome Deux* (Histoire & Collections, Paris, 2001), p.148.
[5] C. Tavard, *Bellona Military Vehicle Prints Series 24* (Model and Allied Publications Ltd, Hemel Hempstead, 1970), p.11.

Chapter 3 – Part 1

[1] Bundesarchiv, RH11 III/143.
[2] BA, RH11 III/128.
[3] *Ibid.*
[4] Unless otherwise stated the turret details are taken from original German records, principally BA, RH11 III/128. The data on Availability is taken from a report dated 5 May 1944 in T. Jentz, 'Panzerstellung – Part Three', *AFV News,* Vol. 9, No. 5 (September 1974), pp.10–11 and details on locations from a report dated 26 March 1945 in T. Jentz, 'Panzerstellung – Part Four – Type and Location', *AFV News,* Vol. 23, No. 1 (Jan.-Apr. 1988), p.20.
[5] D. Fletcher, Librarian, Bovington Tank Museum letter to author dated 28 November 2000.

[6] B. Perrett, *The Churchill. Armour in Action 4* (Ian Allan Ltd, London,1974), p.14.
[7] T. Jentz, 'Panzerstellung – Part Three', *AFV News,* Vol. 9, No.5 (September 1974), pp.10–11.
[8] BA, RH11 III/143.
[9] P. Chamberlain, H. L. Doyle and T. L. Jentz, *Encyclopedia of German Tanks of World War Two* (Arms and Armour Press, London, 1978), p.213.
[10] S. Zaloga, *The Renault FT Light Tank, Osprey Vanguard 46* (Osprey Publishing Ltd, London, 1988), p.42.
[11] W. Regenberg and H. Scheibert, *Beutepanzer unterm Balkenpanzer, Französische Kampfpanzer, Waffen Arsenal 121* (Podzun-Pallas-Verlag, Friedberg, 1990), p.6.
[12] Report dated 5 May 1944 in T. Jentz, 'Panzerstellung – Part Three', *AFV News,* Vol. 9, No. 5 (September 1974), pp.10–11.
[13] L. Bertelsen, e-mail to author dated 25 February 2004.
[14] W. J. Spielberger, *Beute-Kraftfahrzeuge und Panzer der deutschen Wehrmacht* (Motorbuch Verlag, Stuttgart, 1989), p.147.
[15] P. Chamberlain, H. L. Doyle and T. L. Jentz, *op.cit.,* p.220.
[16] *Ibid.,* p.218.
[17] W. Regenberg and H. Scheibert, *Captured Tanks Under the German Flag* (Schiffer Publishing Ltd, Pennsylvania, 1990), p.26.
[18] W. J. Spielberger, *op.cit.,* p.185.
[19] P. Chamberlain, H. L. Doyle and T. L. Jentz, *op.cit.,* p.215.
[20] W. Fleischer, 'Festungs Panzerturm 38(t)', *KIT,* 3 (1992), pp.76–78.
[21] J. Stahlmann, 'Felmäßigen Anlagen in Stahlbetonbauweise Bauformen', *IBA Informationen,* Sonderheft 9 (1985), pp.3–103.
[22] P. Chamberlain, H. L. Doyle and T. L. Jentz, *op.cit.,* p.226.
[23] Der Oberbefehlshaber Südwest (Oberkommando Heeresgruppe C) Ia Nr.7391/45 dated 13 January 1945.
[24] *Ibid.,* p.228.
[25] P. Chamberlain, H. L. Doyle and T. L. Jentz, *op.cit.,* p.229.
[26] BA, RH11 III 147 K3.
[27] BA, RH11 III 147 K9.
[28] BA, RH11 III 147 K2 and K4.
[29] Der Oberbefehlshaber Südwest (Oberkommando Heeresgruppe C) Ia Nr.7391/45 dated 13 January 1945.
[30] P. Chamberlain, H. L. Doyle and T. L. Jentz, *op.cit.,* p.229.
[31] T. L. Jentz and H. L. Doyle, *Panzer Tracts No.21-1 Stände mit Pz.Kpfw. Türmen* (Panzer Tracts, Boyd MD,

2004), pp.21–44.
32 W. Regenberg and H. Scheibert, *op.cit.*, p.11.
33 J. Milsom, *AFV/Weapons Profiles No 37 Russian BT Series* (Profile Publications Ltd, Windsor, 1971).
34 F. Hahn, *Waffen und Geheimwaffen des deutschen Heeres 1933–45* (Bernard & Graefe Verlag, Koblenz, 1986), p.174.
35 M. Gross, *Der Westwall zwischen Niederrhein und Schnee-Eifel* (Rheinland-Verlag GMBH, Köln, 1989), p.382.
36 Anonymous, 'Bildheft Neuzeitlicher Stellungbau', Merkblatt 57/5,15 September 1942. Reprinted as *German Fieldworks of World War II* (Bellona Publications Limited, Bracknell, 1969).
37 BA, RH11 III/143.
38 W. Regenberg and H. Scheibert, *op.cit.*, p.7.
39 P. Chamberlain, H. L. Doyle and T. L. Jentz, *op.cit.*, p.27.
40 T. L. Jentz and H. L. Doyle, *op.cit.*, p.21–4.
41 BA, RH11 III/143.
42 Anonymous, 'Gepanzerte Kampfstande', *Waffen Revue*, 23 (1976), pp.3,721–3,737.
43 T. L. Jentz and H. L. Doyle, *op.cit.*, p.21–6.
44 BA, RH12-20/45, p.79 and p.83.
45 P. Chamberlain, H. L. Doyle and T. L. Jentz, *op.cit.*, p.34.
46 BA, RH11 III/143.
47 T. L. Jentz and H. L. Doyle, *op.cit.*, p.21–14.
48 BA, RH11 III/143.
49 T. L. Jentz and H. L. Doyle, *op.cit.*, p.21–14.
50 BA, RH11 III/143.
51 T. L. Jentz and H. L. Doyle, *op.cit.*, p.21–17.
52 T. Basarabowicz, 'German Strongpoint Still in Poland', *Tankette*, 28/1 (1993), p.2.
53 M. Gross, *op.cit.*, p.353.
54 T. L. Jentz and H. L. Doyle, *op.cit.*, pp.21–22.
55 BA, RH11 III/143.
56 P. Chamberlain, H. L. Doyle and T. L. Jentz, *op.cit.*, p.67.
57 T. L. Jentz and H. L. Doyle, *op.cit.*, pp.21–32.
58 BA, RH11 III/149 dated 10 February 1945.
59 W. Fleischer, 'Festungs Panzerturm 38(t)', *KIT*, 3 (1992), pp.76–78.
60 T. L. Jentz and H. L. Doyle, *Panzer Tracts No.6 Schwere Panzerkampfwagen* (Panzer Tracts, Boyd MD), p.6-2.
61 BA, RH11 III/143.
62 M. Gross, *op.cit.*, p.353.
63 BA, RH11 III/143.
64 T. L. Jentz and H. L. Doyle, *Panzer Tracts No. 6 Schwere Panzerkampfwagen* (Panzer Tracts, Boyd MD), p.6-8.
65 T. L. Jentz and H. L. Doyle, *Panzer Tracts No.21–1 Stände mit Pz.Kpfw. Türmen* (Panzer Tracts, Boyd MD, 2004), pp.21–35.
66 BA, RH11 III/143.
67 T. L. Jentz and H. L. Doyle, *Panzer Tracts No.21–1 Stände mit Pz.Kpfw. Türmen* (Panzer Tracts, Boyd MD, 2004), p.21–29.
68 W. Fleischer, 'Festungs Panzerturm 38(t)', *KIT*, 3 (1992), p.76–78.
69 V. Francev and C. K. Kliment, *Praga LT vz.38* (MBI, Prague, Czechsolovakia, 1997), p.33.

70 T. L. Jentz and H. L. Doyle, *Panzer Tracts No.21–1 Stände mit Pz.Kpfw. Türmen* (Panzer Tracts, Boyd MD, 2004), p.21–29.
71 BA, RH11 III/143.
72 W. Fleischer, *Feldbefestigungen des deutschen Heeres 1939–1945* (Podzun-Pallas, 1998), p.57.
73 W. Fleischer, 'Festungs Panzerturm 38(t)', *KIT*, 3 (1992), pp.76–78.
74 Anonymous, 'Gepanzerte Kampfstande' *Waffen Revue*, 23 (1976),pp.3,721-3,737.
75 T. L. Jentz and H. L. Doyle, *Panzer Tracts No.21–1 Stände mit Pz.Kpfw. Türmen* (Panzer Tracts, Boyd MD, 2004), p.21–28.
76 *Ibid.*, p.21–28.
77 T. L. Jentz and H. L. Doyle, *Panzer Tracts No.21–1 Stände mit Pz.Kpfw. Türmen* (Panzer Tracts, Boyd MD, 2004), p.21–28.
78 T. Gander and P. Chamberlain, *Small Arms, Artillery and Special Weapons of the Third Reich* (MacDonald and Jane's, London, 1978), p.277.
79 BA, RH11 III/144.
80 BA, RH11 III/144.
81 BA, RH11 III/128 from original document dated Nov. 1944.
82 Anonymous, 'Gepanzerte Kampfstande' *Waffen Revue*, 23 (1976), pp.3,721–3,737.
83 D. Bettinger and M. Büren, *Der Westwall Vol.1* (Biblio Verlag, Osnabrück, 1990), p.564.
84 BA, RH11 III/149 K2.
85 BA, RH11 III/149.
86 P. Chamberlain, H. L. Doyle and T. L. Jentz, *op.cit.*, p.202.
87 J. Stahlmann, 'Felmäßigen Anlagen in Stahlbetonbauweise Bauformen', *IBA Informationen*, Sonderheft 9 (1985), p.102.
88 W. Fleischer, 'Die Bergung einer 75mm KwK 51 L/24 aus der Festung Frankfurt/Oder', *IBA Informationen*, Heft 18 (1991), pp.25–33.
89 P. Chamberlain, H. L. Doyle and T. L. Jentz, *op.cit.*, p.192.
90 Report dated 5 May 1944 in T. Jentz, 'Panzerstellung – Part Three', *AFV News*, Vol. 9, No. 5 (September 1974), pp.10–11.
91 Report dated 26 March 1945 in T. Jentz, 'Panzerstellung – Part Four – Type and Location', *AFV News*, Vol. 23 No.1 (Jan.-Apr. 1988), p.20.
92 W. Fleischer, 'Die Bergung einer 75mm KwK 51 L/24 aus der Festung Frankfurt/Oder', *IBA Informationen*, Heft 18 (1991), pp.25–33.

Chapter 3 – Part 2
1 T. Davenport, *Festung Alderney – The German Defences of Alderney* (Barnes Publishing Limited, 2003).
2 R. Heaume, 'Panzers in Guernsey', *Channel Islands Occupation Review* (1979), pp.38–42.
3 Much of the information for this section was taken from L. Bertelsen, 'Ringstände in Dänemark – Die Bauformen 58c-69 (201-260)', *IBA Informationen*, Heft 39 (2003), pp.3-16 and subsequent communication with the author.
4 A. Johansen, e-mail to author dated 1 October 2000.

[5] A. Chazette, *Atlantikwall Südwall – Sur les Traces du Temps* (Les Editions Histoire et Fortifications, Paris), p.296.

[6] Imperial War Museum, M114/264(G).

[7] J. E. Kaufmann and H. W. Kaufmann, *Fortress Third Reich – German Fortifications and Defence Systems in World War II* (Greenhill Books, London, 2003), p.328.

[8] J. Miniewicza et al., 'Niemieckie Fortyfikacje Doliny Rudawy', *Fortyfikacja*, Tom III (1995), pp.119–136.

[9] J. Miniewicz and B. Perzyk, *Miedzyrzecki Rejon Umocniony 1934-1945* (MEGI, Warsaw, 1993), p.70.

[10] R. Riccio, *Italian Tanks and Fighting Vehicles of World War 2* (Pique Publications, Watford, 1975), p.16.

[11] P. Chamberlain, H. L. Doyle and T. L. Jentz, *Encyclopedia of German Tanks of World War Two* (Arms and Armour Press, London, 1978) p.229.

[12] Bundesarchiv, RH20-10/170b.

[13] Note from *Armee Oberkommando Der Chef des Generalstabes* to *OB Sudwest Gen d. Pi.* On 3 September 1944. See BA, RH20-10/170a.

[14] W. Jackson, *The Mediterranean and Middle East, Vol.VI, Victory in the Mediterranean, Part II, June to October 1944* (HMSO, London, 1987), p.104.

[15] M. Sledzinski, e-mail to author dated 16 July 2003.

[16] W. Jackson, *The Battle for North Africa 1940–43* (Mason Charter, New York, 1975), p.121.

[17] *Ibid.*, p.130.

[18] *Ibid.*, p.200.

[19] BA, RH12-20/45, p.84.

[20] BA, RH12-20/45, p.83 and p.89.

[21] D. Bettinger and M. Büren, *Der Westwall Vol. 1* (Biblio Verlag, Osnabrück, 1990), p.551 and p.564.

[22] BA, RH11 III/159 p.9.

[23] BA, RH12 20/45 p.79 and p.89.

[24] M. Gross, *Der Westwall zwischen Niederrhein und Schnee-Eifel* (Rheinland-Verlag GMBH, Köln, 1989), p.353.

[25] J. E. Kaufmann and H.W. Kaufmann, *Fortress Third Reich – German Fortifications and Defence Systems in World War II* (Greenhill Books, London, 2003), p.273.

[26] G. L. Rottman, *Japanese Pacific Island Defenses 1941–45 – Fortress 1* (Osprey Publishing, Oxford, 2003), p.56.

[27] G. L. Rottman, *The Marshall Islands 1944 – Campaign 146* (Osprey Publishing, Oxford, 2004), p.35 and p.76.

[28] W. Fleischer, 'Die Bergung einer 75mm KwK 51 L/24 aus der Festung Frankfurt/Oder', *IBA Informationen*, Heft 18 (1991), pp.25–33.

[29] D. Bettinger and M. Büren, *Der Westwall Vol. 2* (Biblio Verlag, Osnabrück, 1990), p.213.

[30] BA, RH11 III/159, p.164.

[31] D. Bettinger and M. Büren, *Der Westwall Vol. 1* (Biblio Verlag, Osnabrück, 1990), p.580.

[32] BA, RH11 III/189 K5, p.132.

[33] P. Chamberlain, H. L. Doyle and T. L. Jentz, *op.cit.*, p.113.

[34] P. Malmassari, *Les Trains Blindés 1826–1989* (Editions Heimdal, Bayeux Cedex, 1989), p.54.

[35] W. Sawodny, *German Armoured Trains in World War II Volume II* (Schiffer Publishing Ltd, Pennsylvania, 1990), p.24.

[36] R. Hadler, 'Floating German Armour, or, River Monitors During WW2', *Tankette*, 31/1 (1996), p.5.

Chapter 3 – Part 3

[1] Canadian National Archives, RG24 Vol. 10755 Technical Intelligence Summary No. 30.

[2] Bundesarchiv, RH11III/150.

[3] D. Bettinger and M. Büren, *Der Westwall Vol. 2* (Biblio Verlag, Osnabrück, 1990), p.219.

[4] CNA, RG24 Vol. 10755 Technical Intelligence Summary No. 30.

[5] *Ibid.*

[6] BA, RH12-20/44 p.174.

[7] CNA, RG24 Vol. 10755 Technical Intelligence Summary No. 30.

[8] T. L. Jentz and H. L. Doyle, *Panzer Tracts No.21–2 Pantherturm I und II* (Panther Turrets on Steel, Concrete and Wood Stands (Panzer Tracts, Boyd MD, 2005), p.21–54.

[9] CNA, RG24 Vol. 10755 Technical Intelligence Summary No. 30.

[10] BA, RH11 III/150 Drawing WA Pruf Fest IV No 827.

[11] BA, RH12-20/44.

[12] BA, RH12 20/45, p.128.

[13] BA, RH11 III/150.

[14] BA, RH12-20/44, p.265–268.

[15] BA, RH12-20/44, p.174.

[16] *Ibid.*

[17] BA, RH11 III/105, p.66.

[18] T. L. Jentz and H. L. Doyle, *Panzer Tracts No.21-2 Pantherturm I und II* (Panther Turrets on Steel, Concrete and Wood Stands (Panzer Tracts, Boyd MD, 2005), p.21–64.

[19] BA, RH12-20/44, p.200.

[20] BA, RH 12-20/44, p.198.

[21] C. Molony, *The Mediterranean and Middle East, Vol.VI, Victory in the Mediterranean, Part I, 1st April to 4th June 1944* (HMSO, London, 1986), p.185.

[22] *Ibid.*, p.124

[23] J-Y. Nasse, *Green Devils! – German Paratroopers 1939–1945* (Histoire & Collections, Paris, 1997), p.112.

[24] CNA, RG24 Vol. 6933, The Italian Campaign, 4 January 1944-4 June 1944, p.83.

[25] BA, RH20-14/48.

[26] Letter from OKH Group C dated 19 December 1944.

[27] G. Tessin, *Verbände und Truppen der deutschen Wehrmacht und Waffen SS im Zweiten Weltkrieg 1939–1945* (Biblio Verlag, Osnabrück, 1976), p.331.

[28] G. F. Nafziger, *The German Order of Battle: Panzers and Artillery in World War II* (Greenhill Books, 1999), p.353.

[29] BA, RH20-14/48.

[30] BA, RH11 III/159, p.147.

[31] Report dated 26 March 1945 in T. Jentz, 'Panzerstellung – Part Four – Type and Location', *AFV News*, Vol. 23 No.1 (Jan.-Apr. 1988), p.20.

[32] BA, RH20-10/170b.

[33] BA, RH20-10/170a.

[34] D. Guglielmi, *Panzer in Italy* (Publimodel, Taranto, 2001), p.211.

[35] Maj L. Smith (ex RTR) letter to author dated 24 January 1991.

[36] Maj L. Smith (ex RTR) letter to author dated 24 January 1991 and E. Thomas (ex 12 RTR) letter to author dated 19 Nov 1992.

[37] D. Amicarella, 'Anti-tank emplacements on the hills above Pistoia' *Storia & Battaglie*, 10 (September 2001).

[38] BA, RH20-14/48, p.43

[39] Der Oberbefehlshaber Südwest (Oberkommando Heeresgruppe C) Ia Nr.7391/45 dated 13 January 1945.

[40] BA, RH12-20/44.

[41] AOK 1 War Diary dated 5 July 1944.

[42] BA, RH12-20/45, pp.87–127 and BA, RH11 III/159.

[43] BA, RH11 III/159, p.172

[44] BA, RH12-20/45, p.48 and BA, RH11 III/205.

[45] BA, RH12-20/44, p.265 and RH12-20/45 p.141.

[46] BA, RH12-20/44, p.181.

[47] BA, RH12-20/45, p.9.

[48] BA, RH12-20/45, p.127.

[49] BA, RH11 III/159, p.147.

[50] T. L. Jentz and H. L. Doyle, *Panzer Tracts No.21–2 Pantherturm I und II* (Panther Turrets on Steel, Concrete and Wood Stands (Panzer Tracts, Boyd MD, 2005), p.21–82.

[51] BA, RH12-20/45, pp.79–89.

[52] BA, RH12-20/45, p.84.

[53] M. Gross, *Der Westwall zwischen Niederrhein und Schnee-Eifel* (Rheinland-Verlag GMBH, Köln, 1989), p.354.

[54] T. L. Jentz and H. L. Doyle, *Panzer Tracts No.21–2 Pantherturm I und II* (Panther Turrets on Steel, Concrete and Wood Stands (Panzer Tracts, Boyd MD, 2005), p.21–80.

[55] BA, RH11 III/159, p.169.

[56] F. Hahn, *Waffen und Geheimwaffen des deutschen Heeres 1933–45* (Bernard & Graefe Verlag, Koblenz, 1986), p.174.

[57] CNA, RG24, Vol. 1920, Operations of the 1st Canadian Armoured Brigade in Italy May 1944 to February 1945.

[58] J. Ellis, *Cassino. The Hollow Victory: The Battle For Rome January–June 1944* (Andre Deutsch, London, 1984), p.388.

[59] Col W. N. Nicholson, *The Suffolk Regiment 1928–1946* (The East Anglian Magazine Ltd, Ipswich), p.278.

[60] Anonymous, *North Irish Horse Battle Report North Africa – Italy 1943–1945* (W. & G. Baird, Belfast, 1946), p.35.

[61] Col W. N. Nicholson, *op.cit.*, p.279.

[62] Maj W. H. Hare (C Squadron 51 RTR) telecon with author 31 January 1991.

[63] CNA, RG24, Vol. 1920, Operations of the 1st Canadian Armoured Brigade in Italy May 1944 to February 1945.

[64] G. Nicholson, *The Canadians in Italy, Vol. II, Official History of the Canadian Army in the Second World War* (Queen's Printer, Ottawa, 1956), p.396.

[65] W. D. Dawson, *18 Battalion and Armoured Regiment* (War History Branch, Department of Internal Affairs, Wellington, New Zealand, 1961), p.544.

[66] *Ibid.*, pp.545–548.

[67] J. Plowman, *Rampant Dragons – New Zealanders in Armour in World War II* (Kiwi Armour, Christchurch, New Zealand, 2002), pp.177–179.

[68] New Zealand National Archives, WAII 1 401.28/3 Campaign Narrative compiled by AG Protheroe War History Branch, pp.29–57 and WA II 1 48/1/57 Appx 9, War Diary, 18th NZ Armoured Regiment.

[69] R. Kay, *Italy Volume II From Cassino to Trieste* (Historical Publications Branch, Department of Internal Affairs, Wellington, New Zealand, 1967), p.232.

[70] *Ibid.*, p.232.

Chapter 4

[1] R. M. Urrisk, *Die Bewaffnung des österreichischen Bundesheeres 1918–1990* (H Weishaupt Verlag, Graz, 1990), p.131.

[2] H. Jäger, 'Kampfpanzer und Befestigungen Achtzig Jahre einer Symbiose', *Fortifikation*, 10 (1996), pp.24–30.

[3] R. Urrisk, e-mail to author dated 7 May 2004.

[4] The International Institute for Strategic Studies, *The Military Balance* (Oxford University Press, London, 1988/89).

[5] P. Blume, 'The T34–85 in Austrian Army Service', *The Tankograd Gazette*, No. 11 (January 2001), pp.04-07.

[6] The International Institute for Strategic Studies, *The Military Balance* (Oxford University Press, London, 1990/91).

[7] C. Vermeulen, e-mail to author dated 22 April 2003.

[8] The International Institute for Strategic Studies, *The Military Balance* (Oxford University Press, London, 1997/98).

[9] The International Institute for Strategic Studies, *The Military Balance* (Oxford University Press, London, 1991/92 and 2000/01).

[10] M. Sledzinski, e-mail to author dated 24 Sept 2003.

[11] The International Institute for Strategic Studies, *The Military Balance* (Oxford University Press, London, 1988/89).

[12] The International Institute for Strategic Studies, *The Military Balance* (Oxford University Press, London, 1990/91).

[13] M. Dubánek, 'Ceskoslovensky zkusebni object s vezi z tanku PzKpfw IV', *Novodobe Fortifikace*, No. 9 (2002), pp.49–54.

[14] M. Dubánek, 'Pevnostni object KZ-3 pro vez tanku T-34', *Novodobe Fortifikace*, No. 8 (2001), pp.55–60.

[15] The International Institute for Strategic Studies, *The Military Balance* (Oxford University Press, London, 1988/89).

[16] C. Foss, *Jane's Armour and Artillery* (Jane's Information Group, Coulsdon, Surrey, 2000/01).

[17] The International Institute for Strategic Studies, *The Military Balance* (Oxford University Press, London, 2001/02).

[18] D. Seguin, 'Panzerstellung – Part Two', *AFV News*, Vol. 9, No. 1 (January 1974), pp.4–5.

[19] S. Zaloga, 'Char Léger 1935R (Renault 35) R-35', *AFV News*, Vol. 7, No. 4 (July 1972), pp.6–8.

[20] Y. Delefosse, 'Quand le Panzer devient Stellung', *Fortifications & Patrimoine*, No.8 (1998), pp.2–8.

[21] D. O'Hara, e-mail to author dated 30 November 2000.

[22] T. Tsiplakos, letter to author dated 16 December 1992.

[23] M. Truttmann, e-mail to author dated 21 July 2004.

[24] T. Gannon, *Israeli Sherman – Tracing the history of the Sherman tank in Israeli service* (Darlington Productions Inc., Darlington, USA, 2001), pp.115–128.

[25] *Ibid.*, p.126.

[26] Svein Wiiger Olsen, letter to author dated 10 May 2000.

[27] C. Clerici, G. Muran and S. Poli, 'Le Fortificazioni di Frontiera Italiana de Secondo Dopoguerra', *Notizie Ai Soc i– Gruppo di Studio Delle Fortificazioni Moderne*, (Jan–Feb 1995), pp.13–22.

[28] M. Milanese and E. Celotti, 'La Fortezza va in Pensione', *Panorama Difesa*, pp.59–63.

[29] C. Vermeulen, e-mail to author dated 22 April 2003.

[30] C. Clerici, G. Muran and S. Poli, 'Le Fortificazioni di Frontiera Italiana de Secondo Dopoguerra', *Notizie Ai Soci – Gruppo di Studio Delle Fortificazioni Moderne*, (Jan.–Feb. 1995), pp.13–22.

[31] M. Milanese and E. Celotti, 'La Fortezza va in Pensione', *Panorama Difesa*, pp.59–63.

[32] P. van Kerkum Brig. Gen. (rtd), letter to author dated 22 July 1997.

[33] J. Beekmans and C. Schilt *Drijvende stuwen voor de landsverdediging – Een geschiedenis van de IJssellinie* (Uitgeverij Walburg Pers i.s.m. Stichting Menno van Coehoorn, Utrecht, 1997), p.146.

[34] C. Vermeulen, e-mail to author dated 27 April 2003.

[35] *Ibid.*

[36] *Ibid.*

[37] *Ibid.*

[38] Svein Wiiger Olsen, E-mail to author dated 21 October 2001.

[39] V. Kalinin, e-mail to author dated 1 May 2003.

[40] Jane's, *International Defence Review,* Vol. 13 (1980) No.1.

[41] V. Kalinin, e-mail to author dated 1 May 2003.

[42] V. Suvorov, *Inside the Soviet Army* (Hamish Hamilton Ltd, London, 1982), p.78.

[43] S. J. Zaloga and J. Grandsen, *Soviet Tanks and Combat Vehicles of World War Two* (Arms and Armour Press, London, 1989), p.184.

[44] *Ibid.*, p.175.

[45] *Ibid.*, p.176.

[46] E. Hitriak, e-mail to author dated 4 June 2004.

[47] B. Perzyk, 'Karelski Rejon Umocniony – fortyfikacje nieznane', *Nowa Technika Wojskowa*, (May 2002), pp.27–33.

[48] S. J. Zaloga and J. Grandsen, *op.cit.,* p.176.

[49] Fuglewicz, 'Uniwersalne stanowisko ogniowe Gorczak', *Nowa Technika Wojskowa*, (October 2000), pp.23–26.

[50] Jane's, *International Defence Review,* Vol. 13 (1980) No. 1.

[51] T. Roth (Head of Research Dept Armémuseum Stockholm), e-mail to author dated 10 September 2001.

[52] C. Foss, *Jane's Armour and Artillery* (Jane's Information Group, Coulsdon, Surrey, 1994/95), p.749.

[53] T. Roth (Head of Research Dept Armémuseum Stockholm), e-mail to author dated 10 September 2001.

[54] G. Reiss, 'Fortifications in Switzerland from 1860 to 1945', *Fort*, Vol. 21 (1993), pp.19-54.

[55] O. Schwitter, *Swiss Revolving Armoured Turrets (PzT 10,5cm 1939 L 52)* (Internet site, 2003).

[56] S. Dunstan, *Modern Combat Vehicles 2 – Centurion* (Ian Allan Ltd, Surrey, 1980), p.119.

[57] C. Vermeulen, e-mail to author dated 27 April 2003.

[58] *Ibid.*

[59] The International Institute for Strategic Studies, *The Military Balance* (Oxford University Press, London, 1986/87-2001/02).

[60] B. Lowry (FSG), letter to M. Pinsent (FSG) dated 9 January 1998.

[61] File 470.4 14 May 1945 courtesy of B. Smith, e-mail to author dated 6 November 2000.

[62] Memorandum from director, Planning Divisions ASF to Assistant Chief of Staff G4 and General Staff dated 15 May 1945, courtesy of B. Smith, e-mail to author dated 6 November 2000.

Glossary of Terms and Abbreviations

Abbreviation	Full Term	English Translation
AOK	Armee Oberkommando	Army HQ Staff
	Artillerie Schlepper	Artillery tractor
	Artillerie Werkstatt die Kommandantur	Garrison HQ workshop
APX	Ateliers de Puteaux	
AMX	Atelier d'Issy-les-Moulineaux	
	Aufbau	Superstructure
Ausf	Ausführung	Model, mark or design
ACGD	Automitrailleuse de Combat de Grande Découverte	
AMC	Auto-Mitrailleuses de Combat	Armoured Combat Car
	Bauform	Construction design
	Baufortschrittsplan	Building progress plan
	Behelfsmäßig	Improvised, makeshift
	Beobachtungsspiegel	Periscope
	Betonsockel	Concrete body
	Beutepanzer	'Booty tank' or captured tank
	Boyevoe Krasnoye Znamya	Fighting Red Banner
	Bugpanzerdach	Superstructure roof
CFE Treaty		Conventional Armed Forces in Europe Treaty
Chef d.St.d.H	Chef des Generalstabs des Heeres	Chief of General Staff Army
ChefHRüst. U. BdE	Chef Heeresrüstung und Befehlshaber des Ersatzheeres	Chief of Military Armaments and Commander of the Reserve Army
CE	Circulaire élargie	Widened turret ring
	Comités de l'Artillerie et du Génie	Artillery and Engineering Committee
CORF	Commission d'Organization des Régions Fortifées	Commission for the Organization of the Fortified Regions
	Corps de Cavalerie	Cavalry Corps
DT	Degtarov	
	Doppelschartenstand	Double loophole shelter
	Drehhaube	Rotating hood
	Drehturm	Rotating turret
	Eisenbahn Panzerzug	Armoured Train
Fgst	Fahrgestell	Chassis
	Fahrpanzer	Grüson turret
	Fahrschulefahrzeug	Driver training vehicle
	Fahrzeug	Vehicle
	Fallschirmjäger	German paratrooper
	Feste	Fortification, castle
	Festung	Fortress
	Festungs PaK Verband	Fortification anti-tank gun unit
Fest Pi Kdr	Festungspionierkommandeur	Fortification engineer commander
Fest Pi Stab	Festungspionierstab	Fortification engineer staff
F Pz DT	Festungspanzerdrehturm	Fortification armoured rotating turret
	Fieldwork	A non-permanent fortification, generally constructed from earth and timber, although sometimes reinforced with concrete
F Stand	Flankierungsstand	Flanking gun position

	Flugplatz	Landing ground, airfield
FRC	Fonderie Royale de Canons	Belgium Royal Gun Foundry
	Führerbefehl	Führer Order
	Fundament	Base or baseplate
Gen d Pi u Fest	General der Pioniere und Festung	General in Charge of Engineering Works and Fortifications
Gen.Insp.d.Pz.Tr	General-Inspekteur der Panzertruppen	Inspector General Armoured Troops
Gep	Gepanzert	Armoured
	Gerät	Equipment
Gesch	Geschütz	Gun
	Geschützwagen	Gun carriage
GPMG		General Purpose Machine Gun
	Grundplatte	Baseplate
	Hängelafette	Swinging mount
	Haute Commission des Places Fortes	High Commission on Fortresses
	Heeresgruppe	Army Group
H. Kfz	Heeres Kraftfahrzeug	Army MT vehicle
	Heeres-Zeugamt	Army Stores Depot
Heimat Fest Pi Park	Heimat Festungspionierpark	Home Fortifications Engineering Depot
	Heuschrecke	Grasshopper
	Holzsockel	Wooden body or stand
	Holzunterstand	Wooden shelter
	Hülsengrube,	Open pit for spent shell cases
HVSS		Horizontal Volute Spring Suspension
IDF		Israel Defence Forces
	Igel	'Hedgehog' pattern of defence
Insp.d.L.West	Inspekteur für die Landesbefestigung West	Inspector of Fortifications West
In Fest	Inspektion der Festungen	Fortress Inspectorate
IS	Iosef Stalin	Joseph Stalin
	Jäger	Hunter
Kal	Kaliber	Calibre
Kpfw; Kw	Kampfwagen	Tank, armoured vehicle
KwK	Kampfwagenkanone	Tank gun
K	Kanone	Cannon
KV	Klimenti Voroshilov (Marshal)	Soviet Heavy Tank series
	Kommandant	Commander
Kfz	Kraftfahrzeug	Motor vehicle
	Kreuzbettung	Four-legged stand
Kg ZF/KZF	Kugelzielfehrnrohr	Ball-mounted telescope
KVA	Küsten Verteidigung Abschnitt	Coast defence sectors
	Ladeschütze	Loader
Laf	Lafette	Gun carriage
L	Lauf (Kaliberlange)	Length of barrel in calibres
Le	Leichte/leicht	Light
MS	Malyi Soprovozhdieniya	Small Soviet infantry support tank
MG	Maschinengewehr	Machine gun
MGZF	Maschinengewehr Zielfehrnrohr	Machine-gun telescope
	Mitrailleuse	Machine gun
Mun	Munition	Ammunition
	Munitionsschlepper	Munitions carrier
	Nahverteidigungswaffe	Close defence weapon
	Narkomat	People's Commissariat of Defence
NATO		North Atlantic Treaty Organization
NBC		Nuclear, Biological and Chemical
Ob. Südwest	Der Oberbefehlshaber Südwest	Commander in Chief South West
Ob.West	Der Oberbefehlshaber West	Commander in Chief West
OKH	Oberkommando des Heeres	Army GHQ
OKW	Oberkommando der Wehrmacht	Supreme Command of Armed Forces

	Oberteil	Upper chamber
OT	Organization Todt	Paramilitary organization employed in the construction of major state and party building programmes.
	Ostbefestigung	Specially designed Panther turret
	Ostwallturm	Specially designed Panther turret
	Ouvrages	French 'work' in Maginot Line
Pz	Panzer	Armour, tank
PaK	Panzerabwehrkanone	Anti-tank gun
	Panzerdraisinen	Armoured trolley
	Panzer Drehturm	Armoured rotating turret
Pz Gr; Pzgr	Panzergranate	Solid shot; armour piercing shell
Pz Jäger Abt	Panzer Jäger Abteilung	Anti-tank unit
PzKpfw	Panzerkampfwagen	Tank, armoured fighting vehicle
	Panzerspähwagen	Armoured car
	Panzerturm Kompanie	Tank turret company
	Pionier	German term for engineers
	Regelbau	Standard design
	Regiment Etranger de Cavalerie	Foreign Legion Cavalry Regiment
	Richtshütze	Gunner
	Ringstand	Open observation post, similar to a tobruk shelter
RKKA	Robochiy Krestyanskaya Krasnaya Armiya	The Workers' and Peasants' Red Army
RAC		Royal Armoured Corps
RTR		Royal Tank Regiment
	Schnelleinbau	Rapid installation
	Schützenpanzerwagen	Armoured troop carrying vehicle
S	Schwere	Heavy
s.Pz.Abt	Schwer Panzerabteilung	Heavy Tank Battalion
	Schwerslastengerätepark	Heavy Equipment Depot
	Sockellafette	Tank gun fitted on pivot mount
	Sogplatte	Suction plate
	Sonder	Special purpose
SK	Sonder Konstruktion	Special construction
Sdkfz	Sonderkraftfahrzeug	Armoured vehicle
	Spähwagen	Armoured car
	Speciale Werken von Rijkswaterstaat	Special Works Service of the Department for the Maintenance of Dikes, Roads, Bridges and Canals
	Sperrtruppe	Barricade force
Sprgr/Spgr	Sprenggranate	High-explosive shell
SS.Pz.Abt	SS Panzerabteilung	SS Tank Battalion
	Stahlbeton	Reinforced concrete
	Stellung	Position, line
	Stahluntersatz	Steel shelter
Strv	Stridsvagn	
	Sturmgeschütz	Assault gun
	Sturmtruppen	Storm troops
	Stützpunkt	Strong point – German term for a position designed for all-round defence which tended to include a series of emplacements.
TOT	Tankovaya Ognievaya Totshka	Soviet emplaced tank turrets
	Tobruk	Small concrete structure with ring-shaped opening at the top primarily designed to accommodate a machine gun.
	Tourelle démontable	Rotating armoured hood for MG
TZF	Turmzielfernrohr	Tank telescope site
	Uberteil	Lower chamber

UR	Ukreplinnyje rajony	Soviet fortified areas
VTMV	Velitelství tankomechanizovaného vojska	Command of the Mechanized Armoured Corps
VK	Versuchskonstruktion	Experimental construction
VVSS		Vertical Volute Spring Suspension
VZV		Czech Engineering Corps
	Waffenamt	Ordnance Board of War Ministry
Wa Prüf Fest	Waffenamt Prüf Festung	Fortification Design Office
	Wehrkreis	Military District
	Widerstandsnest	Resistance nest – the smallest type of German defensive position.

Sources and Bibliography

Archival Sources

Bundesarchiv (Freiburg)

RH11 III/105
RH11 III/128
RH11 III/143
RH11 III/144
RH11 III/147
RH11 III/149
RH11 III/150
RH11 III/159
RH11 III/205

RH12-20/44
RH12-20/45

RH20-10/170a
RH20-10/170b

RH20-14/48

Canadian National Archives (Ottawa)

RG24, Vol. 1920, Operations of 1 Canadian Armoured Brigade in Italy, May 1944–February 1945.
RG24, Vol. 6933, The Italian Campaign, 4 January 1944–4 June 1944.
RG24, Vol. 10755, Technical Intelligence Summary No. 30.
RG24, Vol. 10883, The Enemy on the Adolf Hitler Line.
RG24, Vol. 10888, Report on the Hitler Line Defences by GS 1 Canadian Infantry Division June 1944.
RG24, Vol. 13729, 1 Canadian Division Intelligence Summary No. 78.

RG24, Vol. 14238, 11th Canadian Armoured Regiment (Ontario Regiment), May 1944.
RG24, Vol. 20513, The Senger Riegel Maj Gen Erich Rothe.

Imperial War Museum (London)

M114/264(G).

Report on damage to Churchill tanks during the breaking of the Hitler Line between Pontecorvo and Aquino between 20 May and 23 May 1944 by Capt S. A. McAuliffe.

New Zealand Archives

WAII 1 401.28/3, Campaign Narrative compiled by A.G.

Protheroe War History Branch.
WA II 1 48/1/57, War Diary 18th NZ Armoured Regiment.

Public Records Office (London)

Canadian forces

WO 204/8202, 1 Canadian Division in the Liri Valley 15–28 May 1944.
WO 204/8205, Operations in the Liri Valley (1 Canadian Division).
WO 204/8207, 5 Canadian Armoured Division: Reports on Operations.

Polish forces

WO 204/8221, Operations of 2 Polish Corps against Monte Cassino.
WO 204/8226, Operations of 2 Polish Corps against Piedimonte.

Miscellaneous

CAB 106/733, Leese Papers (to October 1944).
WO 204/8209, Report on the Hitler Line Defences by GS 1 Canadian Division.
WO 216/168, Leese to ACIGS.
WO 291/1315, Operational Research Section The Defences of a portion of the Hitler Line.

War Diaries

WO 170/498, 78th Infantry G., January–May 1944.
WO 170/591, 25th Tank Brigade Battle Report.
WO 170/829, 17th/21st Lancers, January–December 1944.
WO 170/836, Derbyshire Yeomanry, January–June 1944.
WO 170/846, North Irish Horse, January–December 1944.
WO 170/865, 51st Royal Tank Regiment, January–December 1944.
WO 170/867, 142nd Royal Armoured Corps, January–June 1944.

Bibliography

Anonymous, 'Bildheft Neuzeitlicher Stellungbau', Merkblatt 57/5, 15 September 1942 Reprinted as German Fieldworks of World War II (Bellona Publications Limited, Bracknell, 1969).
Anonymous, *North Irish Horse Battle Report: North Africa*

– *Italy 1943–45* (W. and G. Baird Ltd, Belfast, 1946).

Badsey, S. and Bean, T., *Omaha Beach* (Sutton Publishing, Stroud, Gloucestershire, 2004).

Badsey, S., *Utah Beach* (Sutton Publishing, Stroud, Gloucestershire, 2004).

Beekmans, J. and Schilt, C., *Drijvende stuwen voor de landsverdediging – Een geschiedenis van de IJssellinie* (Uitgeverij Walburg Pers i.s.m. Stichting Menno van Coehoorn, Utrecht, 1997).

Bernage, G., *Gold, Juno, Sword* (Editions Heimdal, Bayeux Cedex, 2003).

Bernage, G., *Omaha Beach* (Editions Heimdal, Bayeux Cedex, 2002).

Bernage, G. and Francois, D., *Utah Beach* (Editions Heimdal, Bayeux Cedex, 2004).

Bettinger, D. and. Büren, M., *Der Westwall* (Biblio Verlag, Osnabrück, 1990).

Chamberlain, P., Doyle, H. L. and Jentz, T. L., *Encyclopedia of German Tanks of World War Two* (Arms and Armour Press, London, 1978).

Chazette, A., Destouches, A. and Paich B., *Album Memorial – Atlantikwall Le Mur de L'Atlantique en France 1940–1944* (Editions Heimdal, Bayeux Cedex, 1995).

Chazette, A., *Atlantikwall Südwall – Sur les Traces du Temps* (Les Editions Histoire et Fortifications, Paris).

Coenen E. and Vernier, F., *La Position Fortifiee De Liege, Tome 2, Les Abris de la PFL 1* (De Krijger, Erpe).

Crow, D. and Icks, R., *Encyclopedia of Armoured Cars and Half Tracks* (Barrie & Jenkins Ltd, London, 1976).

Dancocks, D., *The D-Day Dodgers: The Canadians in Italy 1943–1945* (McClelland and Stewart, Toronto, 1991).

Davenport, T., *Festung Alderney – The German Defences of Alderney* (Barnes Publishing Limited, 2003).

Dawson, W. D., *18 Battalion and Armoured Regiment* (War History Branch, Department of Internal Affairs, Wellington, New Zealand, 1961).

Doyle, H. L. and Jentz, T., *Panther Variants 1942-1945, Osprey New Vanguard Series 22* (Reed International Books Ltd, London, 1997).

Dunstan, S., *Modern Combat Vehicles 2 – Centurion* (Ian Allan Ltd, Surrey, 1980).

Ellis, J., *Cassino. The Hollow Victory: The Battle For Rome January – June 1944* (Andre Deutsch, London, 1984).

Fisher, E., *Cassino to the Alps* (Centre for Military History, Washington, 1977).

Fleischer, W., *Feldbefestigungen des deutschen Heeres 1939–1945* (Podzun-Pallas, 1998).

Fletcher, D., *Mr Churchill's Tank, The British Infantry Tank Mark IV* (Schiffer Publishing Ltd, Atglen, Pennsylvania, 1999).

Forty, G., *German Tanks of World War II 'In Action'* (Blandford Press, London, 1988).

Foss, C., *Jane's Armour and Artillery* (Jane's Information Group, Coulsdon, Surrey, 1994/95–2001/02 inclusive).

Francev, V. and Kliment, C. K., *Praga LT vz.38* (MBI, Prague, Czechsolovakia, 1997).

Francev, V. and Kliment C. K., *Skoda LT vz.35* (MBI, Prague, Czechsolovakia, 1995).

Frost, C. Sydney, *Once a Patricia* (Vanwell Publishing Limited, St. Catharines, Ontario, 1988).

Gander, T. and Chamberlain, P., *Small Arms, Artillery and Special Weapons of the Third Reich* (MacDonald and Jane's, London, 1978).

Gannon, T., *Israeli Sherman – Tracing the History of the Sherman tank in Israeli service* (Darlington Productions Inc., Darlington, USA, 2001).

Gavey, E., *A Guide to German Fortifications on Guernsey* (Guernsey Armouries, Guernsey, 2001).

Ginns, M., *Jersey's German Bunkers – Archive Book No. 9* (CIOS, Jersey, 1999).

Gross, M., *Der Westwall zwischen Niederrhein und Schnee-Eifel* (Rheinland-Verlag GMBH, Köln, 1989).

Guglielmi, D., *Panzer in Italy* (Publimodel, Taranto, 2001).

Hahn, F., *Waffen und Geheimwaffen des deutschen Heeres 1933–45* (Bernard & Graefe Verlag, Koblenz, 1986).

Horne, A., *To Lose a Battle France 1940* (Macmillan & Co. Ltd, London, 1969).

The International Institute for Strategic Studies, *The Military Balance* (Oxford University Press, London, 1986/87–2001/02 inclusive).

Jackson, W., *The Battle for Italy* (Harper & Row, New York, 1967).

Jackson, W., *The Battle for North Africa 1940–43* (Mason Charter, New York, 1975).

Jackson, W., *The Battle for Rome* (Batsford, London, 1969).

Jackson, W., *The Mediterranean and Middle East, Vol. VI, Victory in the Mediterranean, Part II, June to October 1944* (HMSO, London, 1987).

Jentz, T. L. and Doyle, H. L., *Panzer Tracts No. 21–1 Stände mit Pz.Kpfw. Türmen* (Panzer Tracts, Boyd MD, 2004).

Jentz, T. L. and Doyle, H. L., *Panzer Tracts No. 21–2 Pantherturm I und II (Panther Turrets on Steel, Concrete and Wood Stands* (Panzer Tracts, Boyd MD, 2005).

Kaufmann, J. E. and Jurga, R.M., *Fortress Europe – European Fortifications in World War II* (Combined Publishing, Pennsylvania, 1999).

Kaufmann, J. E. and Kaufmann, H.W, *Fortress Third Reich – German Fortifications and Defence Systems in World War II* (Greenhill Books, London, 2003).

Kay, R., *Italy Volume II From Cassino to Trieste* (Historical Publications Branch, Department of Internal Affairs, Wellington, New Zealand, 1967).

Kliment, C. K. and Doyle, H. L., *Czechoslovak Armoured Fighting Vehicles 1918–1945* (Bellona Publications, Watford, 1973).

Kliment, C. K. and Francev, V., *Czechoslovak Armored Fighting Vehicles 1918–1948* (Schiffer Publishing Ltd, Atglen, Pennsylvania, 1997).

MacDonald, C. B., *United States Army in World War II The European Theater of Operations The Siegfried Line Campaign* (Center of Military History, United States Army, Washington, 1984).

Malmassari, P., *Les Trains Blindés 1826–1989* (Editions

Heimdal, Bayeux Cedex, 1989).

Mary, J-Y. and Hohnadel, A., *Hommes et Ouvrages de la Ligne Maginot, Tome Deux* (Histoire & Collections, Paris, 2001).

Milsom, J., *AFV/Weapons Profiles No. 37 Russian BT Series* (Profile Publications Ltd, Windsor, 1971).

Miniewicz, J. and Perzyk, B., *Miedzyrzecki Rejon Umocniony 1934–1945* (MEGI, Warsaw, 1993).

Molony, C., *The Mediterranean and Middle East, Vol. VI, Victory in the Mediterranean, Part I, 1st April to 4th June 1944* (HMSO, London, 1986).

Nafziger, G. F., *The German Order of Battle: Panzers and Artillery in World War II* (Greenhill Books, 1999)

Nasse, J-Y., *Green Devils! – German Paratroopers 1939–1945* (Histoire & Collections, Paris, 1997).

Nicholson, Lt Col G. W. L., *Official History of the Canadian Army in the Second World War, Volume II, The Canadians in Italy 1943–1945* (Department of National Defence, Ottawa, 1957).

Nicholson, Col W. N., *The Suffolk Regiment 1928–1946* (The East Anglian Magazine Ltd, Ipswich).

Orgill, D., *The Gothic Line, The Autumn Campaign in Italy, 1944* (Pan Books Ltd, London, 1967).

Partridge, C., *Hitler's Atlantic Wall* (D.I. Publications, Guernsey, Channel Islands, 1976).

Perrett, B., *The Churchill. Armour in Action 4* (Ian Allan Ltd, London, 1974).

Plowman, J., *Rampant Dragons – New Zealanders in Armour in World War II* (Kiwi Armour, Christchurch, New Zealand, 2002).

Ray C., *Algiers to Austria: A History of the 78th Division in the Second World War* (Eyre and Spottiswoode, London, 1952).

Regenberg, W. and Scheibert, H., *Beutepanzer unterm Balkenpanzer, Französische Kampfpanzer, Waffen Arsenal 121* (Podzun-Pallas-Verlag, Friedberg, 1990).

Regenberg, W. and Scheibert, H., *Captured tanks Under the German Flag* (Schiffer Publishing Ltd, Pennsylvania, 1990).

Riccio, R., *Italian Tanks and Fighting Vehicles of World War 2* (Pique Publications, Watford, 1975).

Rolf, R. and Saal, P., *Fortress Europe* (Airlife Publishing Ltd, Shrewsbury, England, 1988).

Rottman, G. L., *Japanese Pacific Island Defenses 1941–45 – Fortress 1* (Osprey Publishing, Oxford, 2003).

Rottman, G. L., *The Marshall Islands 1944 – Campaign 146* (Osprey Publishing, Oxford, 2004).

Saunders, A., *Hitler's Atlantic Wall* (Sutton Publishing, Stroud, Gloucestershire, 2001).

Sawodny, W., *Die Panzerzüge des Deutschen Reiches 1904–1945* (EK Verlag, Freiburg, 1996).

Sawodny, W., *German Armoured Trains in World War II* (Schiffer Publishing Ltd, Pennsylvania, 1989).

Sawodny, W., *German Armoured Trains in World War II Volume II* (Schiffer Publishing Ltd, Pennsylvania, 1990).

Seck, D., *Unternehmen Westwall* (Bucherverlag Saarbrücker Zeitung, Saarbrücken, 1980).

Short, N., *Hitler's Siegfried Line* (Sutton Publishing, Stroud, Gloucestershire, 2002).

Spielberger, W. J., *Beute-Kraftfahrzeuge und Panzer der deutschen Wehrmacht* (Motorbuch Verlag, Stuttgart, 1989).

Stacey, Col C. P., *The Canadian Army 1939–1945, An Official Historical Summary* (Department of National Defence, Ottawa, 1948).

Starr, C., *From Salerno to the Alps: a History of the Fifth Army 1943–1945* (Infantry Journal Press, Washington, 1948).

Stevens, G. R., *Princess Patricia's Canadian Light Infantry 1919–1957 Volume Three* (Historical Committee of the PPCLI, Alberta, Canada).

Suvorov, V., *Inside the Soviet Army* (Hamish Hamilton Ltd, London, 1982).

Tavard, C., *Bellona Military Vehicle Prints Series 24* (Model & Allied Publications Ltd, Hemel Hempstead, 1970).

Taylor, F., *Dresden – Tuesday 13 February 1945* (Bloomsbury Publishing plc, London, 2004).

Tessin, G., *Verbände und Truppen der deutschen Wehrmacht und Waffen SS im Zweiten Weltkrieg 1939–1945* (Biblio Verlag, Osnabrück, 1976).

Trojca, W., *PzKpfw. V Panther Vol. 6* (A. J. Press, Gdansk, Poland, 2003).

Truttmann, P., *La Muraille de France ou la Ligne Maginot* (Thionville, 1985).

Urrisk, R. M., *Die Bewaffnung des österreichischen Bundesheeres 1918–1990* (H. Weishaupt Verlag, Graz, 1990).

Willems, W. and Koschik, H., *Der Westwall Vom Denkmalwert des Unerfreulichen* (Rheinland-Verlag GmbH, Köln, 1998).

Williams, J., *Princess Patricia's Canadian Light Infantry* (Leo Cooper, London, 1985).

Zaloga, S. J., *IS2 Heavy Tank 1944–1973, Osprey New Vanguard Series 7* (Osprey Publishing Ltd, London, 1994).

Zaloga, S. J., *The Renault FT Light Tank, Osprey Vanguard 46* (Osprey Publishing Ltd, London, 1988).

Zaloga, S. J. and Grandsen, J., *Soviet Tanks and Combat Vehicles of World War Two* (Arms and Armour Press, London, 1989).

Other Publications

Amicarella, D. 'Anti-tank emplacements on the hills above Pistoia' *Storia & Battaglie*, 10 (September 2001).

Andersen, J. 'Der F-Stand – ein 'dänischer' Atlantikwallbunker', *IBA Informationen*, Heft 37 (2001), pp.82-91.

Anonymous, 'Gepanzerte Kampfstande', *Waffen Revue*, 23 (1976), pp.3,721–3,737.

Basarabowicz, T. 'German Strongpoint Still in Poland', *Tankette*, 28/1 (1993), p.2.

Bertelsen, L. 'Ringstände in Dänemark – Die Bauformen 58c–69 (201–260)', *IBA Informationen*, Heft 39 (2003), pp.3-16.

Blume, P. 'The T34-85 in Austrian Army Service', *The*

Tankograd Gazette, No. 11 (January 2001), pp.04–07.

Clerici, C. and Vajna de Pava, E. 'Coastal Defences of Genoa During the Second World War', *Fort*, Vol. 23 (1995), pp.111-126

Clerici, C., Muran, G. and Poli, S. 'Le Fortificazioni di Frontiera Italiana de Secondo Dopoguerra', *Notizie Ai Soci – Gruppo di Studio Delle Fortificazioni Moderne*, (Jan–Feb 1995), pp.13–22.

Danilow, I. 'Radzieckie Rejony Umocnione – Historia I Terazniejszosc', *Forteca*, No. 1 (1997), pp.61–63.

Delefosse, Y. 'Quand le Panzer devient Stellung', *Fortifications & Patrimoine*, No.8 (1998), p.2–8

Dubánek, M. 'Ceskoslovensky zkusebni object s vezi z tanku PzKpfw IV', *Novodobe Fortifikace*, No. 9 (2002), pp.49–54.

Dubánek M. 'Pevnostni object KZ-3 pro vez tanku T-34', *Novodobe Fortifikace*, No. 8 (2001), pp.55–60.

Fleischer, W. 'Die Bergung einer 75mm KwK 51 L/24 aus der Festung Frankfurt/Oder', *IBA Informationen*, Heft 18 (1991), pp.25–33.

Fleischer, W. 'Festungs Panzerturm 38(t)', *KIT*, 3 (1992), pp.76–78.

Fuglewicz, S. 'Uniwersalne stanowisko ogniowe Gorczak', *Nowa Technika Wojskowa*, (October 2000), pp.23–26.

Grentzinger, G. 'Die Steinbrüche von Amanweiler, die Horimont-Stellung und das I-Werk Fèves – Teil 3 (Schluss)', *IBA Informationen*, Heft 35 (2000), p.15–18

Guglielmi, D. 'Linee fortificate tedesche in Italia 1943–1945', *Storia & Battaglie* pp.21–32.

Hadler, R. 'Floating German Armour, or, River Monitors During WW2' *Tankette*, 31/1 (1996), p.5.

Heaume, R. 'Panzers in Guernsey', *Channel Islands Occupation Review*, (1979), pp.38–42.

Hughes, Q. 'Some Thoughts on the Rotating Gun Platform', *Fort*, Vol. 19 (1991), pp.59–72.

Jäger, H. 'Kampfpanzer und Befestigungen Achtzig Jahre einer Symbiose', *Fortifikation*, 10 (1996), pp.24–30.

Jäger, H. 'The Model Fort of Kaiser Wilhelm II in the Sanssouci Park', *Fort*, Vol. 22 (1994), pp.39–56.

Jane's, *International Defence Review*, Vol. 13 (1980) No.1.

Jentz, T. 'Panzerstellung – Part Three', *AFV News*, Vol. 9, No. 5 (September 1974), pp.10–11.

Jentz, T. 'Panzerstellung – Part Four – Type and Location', *AFV News*, Vol. 23, No.1 (Jan–Apr 1988), p.20.

Lacoste, W. 'Die Festung Neubreisach und die Rheinbrückenköpfe im System der deutschen Oberrheinbefestigungen 1871-1916', *DAWA Nachrichten*, Sonderheft 29 (1997), pp.37–40.

Lecomte, A. 'The Séré de Rivière Fortifications 1873–1914', *Fort*, Vol. 17 (1989), pp.43–56.

Lippmann, H. 'Die 5cm KwK im Atlantikwall', *DAWA Nachrichten*, Sonderband 5 (2003).

Milanese, M. and Celotti, E. 'La Fortezza va in Pensione', *Panorama Difesa*, pp.59–63.

Miniewicza, J. *et al.* 'Niemieckie Fortyfikacje Doliny Rudawy', *Fortyfikacja*, Tom III (1995), pp.119–136.

Miniewicza, J. 'Obiekty Zelbetowe Niemieckiej Fortyfikacji Polowej z Lat 1938–1945', *Konserwatorska Teka Zamojska*, (1988), pp.44–60.

Perzyk, B. 'Karelski Rejon Umocniony–fortyfikacje nieznane', *Nowa Technika Wojskowa*, (May 2002), pp.27–33.

Reiss, G. 'Fortifications in Switzerland from 1860 to 1945', *Fort*, Vol. 21 (1993), pp.19–54.

de Reijer, E. 'Dijkverzwaring bedrijgt de IJsellinie', *Vesting*, No.1 (1995), pp.16–23.

Seguin, D. 'Panzerstellung', *AFV News*, Vol. 8, No. 4 (July 1973), pp.6-7

Seguin, D. 'Panzerstellung – Part Two', *AFV News*, Vol. 9 No. 1 (January 1974), pp.4–5.

Short, N. 'Duplication, Innovation, Desperation. The German Use of Tank Turrets as Fixed Fortifications', *Osprey Military Journal*, Vol. 3, Issue 3 (2001), pp.46–55.

Stahlmann, J. 'Felmäßigen Anlagen in Stahlbetonbauweise Bauformen', *IBA Informationen*, Sonderheft 9 (1985), pp.3–103.

Tarleton, R. 'What Really Happened to the Stalin Line? Part I', *The Journal of Soviet Military Studies*, Vol. 5, No. 2 (June 1992), pp.187–219.

Tarleton, R. 'What Really Happened to the Stalin Line? Part II', *The Journal of Slavic Military Studies*, Vol. 6, No. 1 (March 1993), pp.21–61.

Vollert, J. 'T-18 Pillbox', *The Tankograd Gazette*, No. 13 (July 2001), p.39.

Zaloga, S. 'Char Léger 1935R (Renault 35) R-35', *AFV News*, Vol. 7 No. 4 (July 1972), pp.6–8.

Zaloga, S. 'Tank Archeology in Poland', *Journal of Military Ordnance*, (March 1999), pp.26–28.

Internet

Schwitter, O., Sw*iss Revolving Armoured Turrets (PzT 10,5cm 1939 L 52)*, 2003.

INDEX

References in italics refer to footnotes.
References in bold refer to illustrations.